The Ultimate Heresy

. . . the Doctrine of Biblical Inerrancy

The Ultimate Heresy

. . . the Doctrine of Biblical Inerrancy

by

Rodger L. Cragun

To Myra & Brett
God bless and
keep walking in
the light
Rodger

cover design by Bill Cragun

edited by Thomas V. Koehler

Boreal Light

Two Harbors, Minnesota

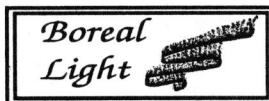

Boreal
Light

Boreal Light, Two Harbors 55616

Printed in the United States of America

Library of Congress Catalog Card Number: 96-60495

Permissions

Bruner, (1987) Word, Inc., Dallas, Texas. All rights reserved. Used with permission.

The Midrash Rabba, edited by Freedman & Simon, London, The Soncino Press Ltd., 1983, (pp. 63, 76, 77, 91, 119 in *The Ultimate Heresy*)

New Testament Commentary: Exposition of the Pastoral Epistles, William Hendricksen (1957) by permission of Baker Publising, Grand Rapids, MI. Used with permission.

The Old Testament Pseudepigraph (1985), James Charlesworth, ed., translation by O.S. Wintermute, by permission of Bantam Doubleday Dell.

The Revised Standard Version of the Bible, copyright by Division of Christian Education of the National Council of the Churches of Christ in the United States of America (1952), New York. Used with permission.

The Scroll of the War of the Sons of Light against the Sons of Darkness (1962), Yigael Yadin, ed., by permission of Oxford University Press.

The Babylonian Talmud, edited by I. Epstein, London, The Soncino Press Ltd., 1935-48, (pp. 79, 80, 82, 84 in *The Ultimate Heresy*)

Taken from: *Bible Dictionary* by Merrill Unger. Copyright 1966, Moody Bible Institute of Chicago. Moody Press. Used by permission.

The Ultimate Heresy

is

dedicated to the Glory of God

and

the Healing of the Church

with special

Thanksgiving

for Christ's Servant's

Markus Barth (1915-1994)

My Cousin and his Wife, Harry and Laura Robie

My Parents, Horace and Sylvia Cragun

My Wife, Penny Cragun

Table of Contents

⚜

Errata

fourth line in Preface should read, "...one of the most committed Christians I have ever met..."

Table of Contents errors, p. x

Chapter VIII starts on p. 125

Chapter IX starts on p. 145

Chapter X starts on p. 160

Boreal Light, P.O. box 152
Two Harbors, MN 55616-0152

Principal Abbreviations

Dictionaries

AG   W. F. Arndt and F. W. Gingrich A Greek-English Lexicon of the New Testament and Other Early Christian Literature. A translation and adaptation of Walter Bauer's Griechisch-deutsches Wörterbuch (1952 ed.). Chicago: The University of Chicago Press, 19(?).

BDB   *A Hebrew and English Lexicon*, based on Edward Robinson's translation of William Gesenius' Handwörterbuck über das Alte Testament, Francis Brown, S. R. Driver, & Charles A. Briggs, eds., Oxford: Claredon Press, 1978.

IDB   *The Interpreters Dictionary to the Bible*, 4 vols., George Buttrick, ed. Nashville: Abingdon Press, 1962.

LOx   Oxford Latin Dictionary, 8 vols. Oxford: Oxford University Press, 1968-1982.

LS   H. G. Liddell & Robert Scott, A Greek-English Lexicon (1843), 2 vols., 9th ed., 1953 reprint, revised and edited by H. S. Jones et. al. . Oxford: Clarendon Press

TDNT   Gerhard Kittle, ed.,*Theological Dictionary to the New Testament*, 10 vols., Geoffry Bromiley, general translator and editor. Grand Rapids, MI: Wm. Eerdmans Publishing Company, 1964-1976.

Bibles

JB   *The Jerusalem Bible.* New York: Doubleday, 1966.

KJ   The King James Version or Authorized Version of 1611

LXX   *The Septuagint,* ed . E. Ralhfs. Stuttgart: Württembergische Biblelgesellschaft, 1935, reprint,1965.

MT   (Masoretic Text) Biblica Hebraica, edited by Rudolf Kittel, 3rd. ed. Stut

Nestle Novum Testamentum Graece, 25th ed., edited by E. Nestle and K. Aland

NEB   The New English Bible with the Apocrypha. Oxford University Press and Cambridge University Press, 1970

RSV   TheRevised Standard Version

TEV   The Good News Bible: The Bible in Today's English Version, The
Catholic Study Edition. Nashville: Thomas Nelson,Publishers

Intertestmental:

Charlesworth James H. Charlesworth, ed.,*The Old Testament
Pseudepigrapha*, 2 Volumes Garden City, NJ: Doubleday & Company,
Inc., 1985. Biblical Commentaries

Biblical Commentaries:

AB   William Foxwell Albright and David Noel Freedman, *The Anchor
Bible*, 59 Volumes. Garden City, NY: Doubleday & Company, Inc.
1964-1995.

BBC   *Broadmann Bible Commentary*, 12 Volumes. Nashville: Broadmann
Publishing

IB   George Arthur Buttrick, ed. *The Interpreters Bible*, 12 vols.
Nashville: Abingdon Press, 1951-1957.

ICC(year) S. R. Driver, A. Plummer, and C. A. Briggs, eds., *The
International Critical Commentary*, Edinburgh: T&T Clark, 1895-
1995

Str.-Biller. Hermann L. Strack and Paul Billerbeck, *Kommentar zum Neuen
Testamentum aus Midrash*, Munchen: CH Beck'sche Verlags
Buchlung: Öskar Beck, 1922-1961.

Theological:

Dogmatics Karl Barth, *Church Dogmatics,* 13 Volumes. General Trans. G.
W. Bromily . New York: Charles Scribner and Sons, 1936 .

Luther's Works Jaroslav Pelikan and Helmut Lehmen, general editors, , 55
Volumes. Volumes 1-30, St. Louis, MO: Concordia Publishing House;
Volumes 31-55, Philadelphia, PA: Fortress (Muhlenberg) Press,
1958-1968. (Luther's Works)

Zwingli E. C. Furcha, Translator and Editor, *Huldrych Zwingli Writing*, 2
Volumes. Allison Park, PA: Pickwick Press, 1984.

Institutes John T. McNiell and Ford Lewis Battles, ed and trans. Calvin:
Institutes of the Christian Religion, Two Volumes. Philadelphia, PA:
Westminster Press, 1960.

Calvin's Commentaries T. F. Torrence and D. W. Torrence, Editors, *Calvin's*

New Testament Commentaries, 10 Volumes. Grand Rapids, MI:
William B. Eerdmans, 1959.

Historical:

AN   Alexander Roberts and James Donaldson, *The Ante-Nicene Christian
Library*, 24 Volumes

ANET   James B. Pritchard, ed., *Ancient Near Eastern Texts,* 3 vols Princeton,
NJ: Princeton University Press, 1969

CF   Joseph Deferrari, ed.The Church Fathers, Washington, D. C.: The
Catholic University of America Press.

De Vita Moses   C. D. Yonge, Ed. and Trans., *The Work of Philo Judaeus ,* in
3 Vol. London: Henry S Bohr, 1855.

GB   Robert Hutchinson and Mortimer Adler, Editors, *The Great Books of
the Western World* (54 Volumes). Chicago, IL: Encyclopædia of
Britannica, 1952.

Leith   John Leith, ed., Creeds of the Churches. Garden City, NY: Anchor
Books, Doubleday & Company, Inc., 1963.

Migne   J. P. Migne, editorem, *Patrologiæ Cursus Completus*, Montrouge,
Paris: Seu Petit, 1857-1928.

NF (1st series)   Philip Schaff, *A Select Library of the Nicene and Post-Nicene
Fathers of the Christian Church* (1st Series) 25 Volumes. New York:
Christian Literature Company, 1892.

NF (2nd series)   Philip Schaff and Henry Wace, *A Select Library of the
Nicene and Post-Nicene Fathers of the Christian Church* (2nd Series)
14 Volumes. New York: Christian Literature Company, 1890–1900.

Schaff, Creeds   Philip Schaff, *Creeds of the Christian Church*. Grand Rapids,
Michigan: Baker Publishing House, 1990.

Schaff, History   *History of the Christian Church ,* 8 Volumes   New York:
Charles Scribner's Sons, 1910

Preface

This work could be said to be in formulation for over thirty years. It began after I committed my life to the Lord Jesus Christ as a young college student and was attending a Sunday School class taught by one of the most committed Christians I have met ever met, Louise Orr. Ms Orr introduced me to the writings of Karl Barth (1886–1969). For me, Barth was sheer inspiration. He was the greatest theologian of the twentieth century. I went to Pittsburgh Theological Seminary because his son, Markus, was Professor of New Testament and because Robert Clyde Johnson, a Barthian Theologian, and Tusculum professor taught theology there. There I was greatly influenced by Markus Barth who was not only a very committed Christian, but a great scholar. Having found in Markus and Karl Barth the dedication and love of the Lord Jesus Christ that I would expect in all Christians, it was to my surprise and chagrin that conservatives and fundamentalists reacted so vehemently against the Barths and their teaching. It was as if these conservatives and fundamentalists did not believe that the Barths were Christian. Because I knew the Barths to be deeply dedicated Christians and that the way they read the Bible was the way the Bible read to me. I questioned whether the conservatives and fundamentalists could actually read the Bible. After having worked with Markus Barth on his Anchor Bible Commentary to the Ephesians and having been tutored in Barth's scholarly methodology, I launched my investigation to see why there was such a discrepancy between these persons who I knew to be Christian and others who *claimed* to be Christian.

The most logical place to begin the study was, of course, with the foremost doctrine of conservatives and fundamentalists, that the Bible is the inerrant word of God. Having intensely studied the Scriptures in seminary, I did not remember any verse that said the Bible or the Scriptures were the word of God, much less the *inerrant* word of God. Conceding that I may have missed something along the way, I went back and restudied the Bible but came up with the same results. There were no statements in the Bible that said it was the word of God. From where, then, did the doctrine originate? The answer began to unfold while I was doing research at the Regenstein Library of the University of Chicago in 1975. I discovered an ancient lexicon of the Church Fathers by Caspari. In this lexicon was every reference to the word of God in the Church Fathers. The earliest date that Caspari had recorded for the idea that the Bible proclaimed itself as the word of God was around 370 C.E. This gave me the locus of the doctrine. Then came the arduous study of how and why the doctrine developed.

Along the way I had the help of many professors, friends, and associates. The work, of course, owes its inception to the impact that Karl Barth had upon my thinking and the hours that I spent in preparation for — and in attending — Markus Barth's seminars. The long hours and days that I spent poring over Markus' manuscript for his Anchor Bible Commentary on

Ephesians, checking Biblical quotes, translations of the fathers and rabbis served as the training ground for my own work. In the initial phases of my project, particularly the first three chapters, I had invaluable help from the critical insights of my good friend and colleague Harold Rainey, as well as stenographic assistance from his wife Lois. Early stages of typing were also done by my secretary in Danville, Nancy Rarey. The first four Chapters were edited by Russ Eanes in Elkhart. Many others have also contributed. Mike Clevet and Mary Helgesen, friends in Duluth, served as excellent initial editors. Of the whole work, the finished product resides with the intelligent and insightful direction of Thomas Koehler, the editor of Boreal Light Press. Friends Cathy Peterson and Jay and Mary B. Newcomb have helped out along the way by loaning their computers. The title, *The Ultimate Heresy* was suggested to me by Professor Dale Brown, of Bethany Theological Seminary. Others who have been extremely helpful are Professors William Orr, James Walther, Dietrich Ritschl, Neil Paylor, and John Howard Yoder, of Notre Dame; Dale Brown, and Dr. Alice Chang.

After all of the work done by these fine people, any errors which remain in this book are solely my own. It is my fondest hope that this book will herald the reawakening of Christianity as it was first practiced.

Rodger L. Cragun
Duluth, Minnesota
1996

Introduction

In a few years the Twenty-first century will be upon us. The struggles that we face as human beings and as Christians may be immense and unimaginable. From where we are in the twentieth century there are indications that there may be major climate changes and cataclysmic cultural upheavals. Whether there are or not, the question must be raised: What will be the witness of Christianity in the next century? Will the witness be meaningful or will the world look at us as being filled with pious nonsense that provides no hope or value in the world?

There have been many theologians and preachers who have attempted to modernize the Church by advocating that Christians think abstractly and philosophically. Paul Tillich attempted to focus Christians on God as the ground of their ultimate *Being* and that their task as Christians was to become *new beings* connected to one another and the ground of their being. Teilhard de Chardin advocated that Christians should see the world as evolving towards the Omega point, of humanity's scientific, societal and spiritual fulfillment. Rudolf Bultmann saw the task of theology was to demythologize the stories of Christianity and allow humanity to see the depth of their meaning. Schubert Ogden asserted that as humankind was in process of development, so God also in relationship was in process of development.

While I cannot claim to be expert in or even understand all the insights that these men have offered, I can claim that the impact of their theologies has been negligible on most of Christianity. Their thinking is abstract and esoteric and it may remain so forever since it is mainly comprehended by philosophers, theologians and scientists .

Conservatives have long rejected the tendency of these theologians, and those like them, to make Christianity and particularly the resurrection of Jesus Christ, a philosophical abstraction rather than a concrete historical reality. As correctly as conservatives have perceived the deprecation of historical Christianity by these theologians, I believe it is time for conservatives, fundamentalists, and indeed most Christians to realize that it is not just these liberals whose view of Christianity has been distorted through philosophical thought. This work is one of three in which I intend to expose the reality that most of Christianity has not been based in "biblical thought," but has been entrapped in a philosophical thought shroud for most of history.

I assert that as the Church moves into the twenty-first century, she must shred this philosophical shroud and reaffirm more precisely and clearly her Lord Jesus Christ and His teachings.[1] Whereas most of the major world religions, such as Islam, Judaism, Buddhism, and Hinduism, have had to modify or re-interpret their roots to meet the demands of modern society, the

---

[1]There have been others in this century who have attempted this task. This was the point for Protestants of the massive work of Karl Barth, *The Church Dogmatics*, Twelve Volumes (Edinburgh: T. & T. Clark, 1936–1974). Likewise, this was the point for Roman Catholics and all Christians of Hans Kung's inspiring work, *On Being Christian* (Garden City, NY: Doubleday & Company, Inc., 1976).

same conditions compel Christians to reclaim the teachings of their Lord Jesus Christ.

Such language would send shivers up the spines of liberals and they would close their minds. In conservative circles it would be hailed as a *back to the Bible* movement. While I would advocate a Christianity that is faithful to a biblical witness, it will be clear by the conclusion of this book that most people who today claim to be fundamentalists or literalists are neither fundamental nor literal. They are wrapped just as tightly in a shroud of philosophy as the liberal theologians whom they would denounce. Because the shroud covers their minds, they can not read the Bible which they proclaim.

While there are a great many areas of Christian theology which have been shaped more by philosophy than by the Scriptures, this work can only deal with one. This one, however, is so deeply entrenched in the belief system of most Christians that challenging it has meant that denominations and families have been wrenched apart. Furthermore there has been more written on this subject than any other single subject in literary history. The subject should not surprise anyone. It is the doctrine that the Bible is the inerrant word of God, commonly called *biblical inerrancy*.

A resident of the United States would practically have to be a life-long hermit not to have been affected in some way by this doctrine. From the pilgrims who landed on the shores of this country, to the Koresh Compound in Waco, Texas; from the Scopes trial in Tennessee, to the perennial issue of prayer in school; from slavery, prohibition, fear of communism, and abortion, to any form of gay rights, whether it be from adamant support of, or reaction to the doctrine of inerrancy, this doctrine has played a major role in the psyche (*geist*) of the American people.

Despite the fact that this doctrine has had a strong impact on almost every Protestant denomination, and that it is still strong within large segments of the Christian population, this work will show that the doctrine is the worst heresy that has ever afflicted the Church, and it is an evil from which the Church must repent. In the history of humankind the doctrine has been instrumental in producing countless wars, murders, excommunications, and schisms in the Church. Citing a few verses of the Bible, and calling them "the very word of God," nations have waged war against other nations; Christians have justified slavery; burned accused witches; murdered alleged heretics; annihilated entire native populations in newly-discovered lands, and forced others, after nearly obliterating them, to accept western ways which have nothing whatsoever to do with the teachings of Jesus Christ. Women have been oppressed and suppressed with the aid and comfort of a few verses of the Bible. Great wealth has been amassed at the expense of native populations and natural resources. Even several contemporary television evangelists have justified decadent life-styles by citing a few verses.

While having stated all this I want it to be clear that I am not saying that every person who espouses inerrancy is a heretic. There have been countless numbers of pious and devout followers of the Lord Jesus Christ who have accepted inerrancy as valid and who have been faithful to the Lord. It is the *doctrine* that the Bible is the inerrant word of God that is the heresy. Many people who subscribe to the heresy have their hearts rooted deeply in the spirit and love of Christ Jesus, and that spirit and love is what controls their lives, not the doctrine or dogma.

Those who rigidly hold and assert the doctrine of inerrancy are found on the other side of the perspective, however. For them the doctrine is all controlling. These are the people who split Churches and create grief in other human lives. These are the people who wage war because the Bible told them so. *These* are the heretics.[2]

It would come as a great surprise to these people as well as to most other people that the roots of the doctrine of inerrancy are not found in the Bible, but rather in the Greek philosophers.[3] The argument for inerrancy is essentially based on Aristotelian logic and proceeds in the following fashion:

1. God is perfect.
2. What God thinks is perfect.
3. From that which God thinks he reveals to people.
4. What he reveals to people must therefore be perfect.

This then, is the classic argument offered for inerrancy: Since the Bible is, *not contains*, revelation from God, the Bible therefore must be perfect. Perfect means without any human weakness, that is, it is without errors. Since the Bible is perfect revelation from God, to take exception to material found within it or to find errors in it, is to disagree with God and to impugn God's abilities.

---

[2]The conservative Christian reader may protest here saying that the basis of Fundamentalism and conservative Christianity is the incarnation and resurrection of our Lord Jesus Christ. The reality is Fundamentalist and most Conservative theologians and preachers argue that having Christ is contingent on having an inerrant Scripture. A statement from B. B. Warfield, Professor of Theology at the Theological Seminary 1887–1920, who is described as the "greatest defender" of inerrancy, is sufficient to summarize everything written before and after him. Warfield wrote:

> Let it suffice to say that to a plenarily (every word) inspired Bible, humbly trusted as such, we actually, and as a matter of fact, owe all that has blessed our lives with hopes of an immortality of bliss, and with present fruition of the love of God in Christ. This is not an exaggeration...It is actually to the Bible that you and I owe it that we have a Christ-a Christ to love, to trust, and to follow, a Christ without us the ground of our salvation, a Christ within us the hope of Glory. () parenthesis are mine.

Warfield does speculate that it might be possible for God to have spoken through some other form, but according to Warfield, God did not, and therefore, it is a moot point. The plenary inspired Scriptures are our means to Christ. B. B. Warfield, *The Inspiration and Authority of the Bible* (Philadelphia: The Presbyterian and Reformed Publishing Company, 1948), 126–127. Henceforth, Warfield, *Inspiration.*

In almost every polemic that conservative theologians have raised against biblical criticism since the end of the nineteenth century has linked the acceptance of inerrancy with the acceptance of Christ. See Heinrich Heppe, *Reformed Dogmatics,* revised and edited by Ernest Bizer, trans. by G.T. Thompson (Grand Rapids, Michigan: Baker Book House, 1978), 22–41. Henceforth, Heppe, *Dogmatics*; Charles Hodge, *Systematic Theology* (Grand Rapids, MI: Eerdmans Publishing, 1958), I, p.1 ff.; Francis Schaeffer, *The God who is there,* (Downers Grove, IL: Inter-Varsity Press, 1968), p. 13 ff.; Schaeffer, *How Shall we then Live?* (Old Tapan, NJ: Fleming Revell Company, 1976), pp. 79–119; 144–166; 205–227; J. J. Packer, *Fundamentalism,* (Grand Rapids: Eerdmans, 1978) p. 1 ff.; Carl F. H. Henry, *God who Speaks and Shows,* Vol. I: *God, Revelation and Authority* (Waco, Texas: Word Books, Publishers, 1976), p 1 ff. Henceforth, Henry, *Revelation.*

[3]This is to state that the framework for the doctrine as it has been developed in the Church is within Aristotelian thought. In the ninth chapter of this work the evidence will be shown that the actual concept of inerrancy is derived from the Greek Philosophy of Heraclitus, Plato and Plutonius.

This reasoning has been unquestionable dogma in the Church for hundreds of years. Even raising the possibility that the logic was flawed would raise the wrath of the theologians and bombastic preachers, resulting in countless persecutions and even excommunication. However, belief in this doctrine is certainly not a requirement for many who call themselves Christian today. In the twentieth century it became possible for a Christian to accept errors in the Bible and still be considered a believer. So-called "mainline" denominations such as the Episcopalians, the Church of England, the United Methodist, United Presbyterian and Reformed Church of America, the Lutheran Church (ELCA), and the American Baptist Convention began to accept the rational examination of the Bible to perceive differences in authorship, style, etc.

Within these "mainline" churches there are those who steadfastly maintain inerrancy, and who look upon Biblical critics as Godless liberals. They are convinced that those who find errors in the Scripture cannot be Christian, and that such people are deeply in need of salvation. *The liberals*, in turn, have adopted a condescending attitude toward those who accept inerrancy, maintaining that such views are mindless religion. They read the Bible critically and find in it errors, yet maintain their faith, still believing themselves to be devout Christians. Thus, there is a great split among believers today. The debate often reaches a fever pitch.

There may be those who might object to my advocating that inerrancy is heresy, much less the *worst* heresy. They might argue that, while they themselves do not subscribe to inerrancy, they would consider fundamentalists and conservatives to be misguided or having suspended their reasoning power for sake of their faith, but not heretics. I will contend that the Church must come to grips with the fact that she has for much of her history been in the grips of heresy much worse than the Arianism she rejected early in her history. Two major ecumenical councils met, at Nicaea (325) and Constantinople (381), and three confessions were drawn up to refute Arianism. The problem that the *orthodox* Church had with Arianism was that it denied the equality of the persons of the Trinity. It claimed that Jesus was a lesser being than God the Father who "begat" Him. [4]

But, inerrancy eclipses Arianism as the Church's worst heresy in two ways. First, while Arianists may have erred in their understanding of the Trinity, this did not detract from their devoutness of belief in the teachings of Christ. They confessed that Jesus was Lord and assiduously tried to follow his teachings. Nowhere in the Bible is there a requirement that a believer must understand or accept the doctrine of the Trinity to be saved, only that "if you confess with your lips that Jesus is Lord and believe in your heart that God raised him from the Dead you will be saved." (Romans 10:9) In fact, other Christians, including two early bishops of Rome (Popes), were not trinitarians, claiming that God was one and one only, that Jesus was God and God, Jesus.[5]

---

[4] The heresy was named after Arius, a priest from Alexandria (c. 250–336 A. D.). The reader must remember, also, that most of what is known about Arius is reported by Arius' detractors and must be held with suspicion. One thing is certain; his teachings were very attractive to many early Christians. There were a great many Bishops who likewise accepted his teachings. For more details on the Arian controversy see F. J. Foakes Jackson, *The History of the Christian Church from the Earliest of times to 461 A. D.* (Cambridge: Deighton, Bell & Company, LTD., 1951), 297–432. Henceforth, Jackson, *History*.

Arians were considered dangerous, in part, *because* of their devoutness. They gained such credibility by their lives of faith that the question of "heresy" was not settled by the Church until nearly 45 years after Arius' death. Those who advocate the doctrine of inerrancy, on the other hand, have used the doctrine to justify or excuse all kinds of atrocities which would be completely rejected by the Lord Jesus. By applying this doctrine to specific verses, church people have defended every abuse which the Church has perpetrated since the days of Constantine, and have split the Church into thousands of pieces.

The wars, the persecutions, the oppressions, and the excommunications which Christians have participated in and promoted would never have been blessed or condoned by Jesus. Something — the power of the world, Satan, evil, egotism, what ever one would like to call it — corrupted the church, and the vehicle through which this corruption came was none other than the doctrine that the Bible is the inerrant word of God.

This leads to the second reason why the inerrancy doctrine is worse yet than Arianism. It has elevated the Bible itself to equality with God. In short it has led the Church into idolatry. The Bible has become something to be worshipped. The doctrine claims that the Bible is exactly what God says and thinks in all time and throughout eternity. Extrapolating on the statement in the New Testament that "Jesus is the Word," inerrancy equates scripture with God, expanding the Triune God to a Quartet: Father, Son, Holy Spirit, and The Word, the Bible.

This is no joke! This is a fair and true description of what the Bible has become, particularly in Protestant fundamentalist, conservative and orthodox circles.[6] Whereas fundamentalists have accused Roman Catholics of enshrining the crucifix, statues of the saints, etc., in Protestant churches, often a huge, unheld, unread Bible flanked by two candles and sometimes a cross becomes the focus of worship. In almost every conservative hymnal, there are hymns which offer worship to the Bible as hymns normally honor God. One particularly blatant example is a nineteenth century hymn composed by John Burton:

> Holy Bible, Book Divine
> precious treasure thou art mine,
> Mine to tell me whence I came,
> Mine to teach me what I am.

---

[5]There were large numbers of people, who, in the early Church had misunderstandings of what the Trinity and incarnation were all about, but still professed that Jesus was Lord. Two of the early Bishops of Rome, Zephrinius (198–211) and Callistus (211–217) were followers of Montanius who did not believe in a Trinitarian formula. They believed that God was one. Jesus was God and God was Jesus. There were other Christians like Origen and Tertullian, who believed in the Lord Jesus with all their hearts, whose "orthodoxy" later generations questioned. In the early years of the Church there were great struggles in grasping the greatest mystery of all, the incarnation, and there would naturally be misunderstandings.

[6]The terms conservative and liberal are essentially irrelevant. On some issues people can be considered conservative, and on other issues they can be considered liberal. In this work (religious) conservative means a person who considers the Bible the inerrant word of God but who does not necessarily take everything literally. Likewise, a fundamentalist is a person who considers the Bible to be the inerrant word of God and also believes that he or she takes it literally. The term orthodox Protestant usually refers to a person who accepts a creedal position of a church as derived from the inerrant Scriptures.

Mine to chide me when I rove,
Mine to show a Saviour's love,
Mine to guide and guard:
Mine to punish and reward.

...O Thou Holy Book Divine,
Precious Treasure Thou art mine.[7]

God the Father, God the Son, and God the Holy Spirit are not even addressed in this hymn! The intimate "Thou" refers not to God in the Trinitarian form at all, but to God the Bible. The Bible has been personified, indeed deified, by the hymn. It is the Bible which teaches, punishes and rewards, guides and guards the singer, and is worshipped in return.

Most of the church's Protestant reformers would likely have been repulsed by such idolatry, particularly Zwingli, John Calvin, and the Anabaptists. These reformers would not tolerate even a barren cross like those found in the front of many churches, an enshrined Bible, or a hymn sung to the Bible. The reformers are not, however, absolved of guilt. While they may not have offered enthroned scriptures to their congregations for worship, this book will show that it was indeed their teachings which gave form and substance to the idolatry of worshipping the Bible; that they were responsible for the canonization of Bible idolatry.

In 1977, James Barr, Oxford University Professor of Holy Scripture, in his book, *Fundamentalism*, moved beyond the traditional liberal view of fundamentalists as being pious, well-meaning, but unenlightened folks. He argued that fundamentalists pervert scripture to their own ends and deify their interpretation. Rather than originating from spiritual strength, he argued that fundamentalism develops out of psychological and sociological sickness.[8]

This book will insist that the Church in the twenty-first century must move beyond tolerating fundamentalism or even considering adherents psychologically and sociologically maladjusted. The Church must declare that the doctrine that the Bible is the inerrant word of God can no longer be accepted as a part of Christianity, and that it is a contradiction and denial of the Lord Jesus Christ. Presently, most readers will think this is a most radical position. By the end of this book, however, it will be clear that declaring inerrancy to be heresy is not radical at all, but the valid conclusion of sound study of the Bible and Church history. If there is anything radical about this book, it is the call to the Church to take seriously the Lordship of Jesus, whom the Scriptures declare to be the Word of God. It is a call to Christians to stop finding a verse here or there in Scripture to do away with the teachings of Jesus.[9] When Jesus states, "Love your enemy," and then shows how on the

---

[7]John W. Peterson and Norman Johnson, eds., Hymns of Praise (Grand Rapids, MI: Zondervan Corp., 1979), 124.

[8]James Barr, *Fundamentalism* (Philadelphia: Westminster Press, 1978), p.1 ff.

[9]This is the essence of a tract written by Eberhard Arnold, founder of the Bruderhof, entitled, *The Living Word*, Volume V of *The Innerland* (Rifton, NY: Plough Publishing House, 1975), pp. 441–425. This, Arnold correctly sees also as the distillation of Anabaptist thought.

cross, the Church shows its unfaithfulness by finding a verse in Scripture permitting the killing of the enemy. Loving one's enemy, loving one's neighbor, and living simply as Jesus lived and taught is the message that needs to be heard in America, Bosnia, Lebanon, Iraq, Iran, Korea, Israel, Syria, and throughout the whole world.

The methodology of this book will differ from almost every work that has been previously written attacking inerrancy. This work will not attack the doctrine by showing that there are errors and inconsistencies in the Bible. Rather, this work will show that the doctrine itself has no biblical basis; that the doctrine owes its existence to the intertwining of Greek philosophy with biblical texts and thus is a perversion of the Bible; that the doctrine cannot be found in the earliest antiquities of the Church; that the doctrine grew out of, and is fostered by, a spiritually weak Church; that the doctrine is the sword of evil which is cutting asunder the church; and, finally and most importantly, that the doctrine is idolatry from which the Church must repent.

In short, the doctrine that the Bible is the inerrant word of God is the ultimate heresy!

Chapter I

What Is At Stake?

The Results of Dogmatism: Devastation and Death

In the history of the world, religion cannot be described as a factor unifying diverse peoples. It has not brought humanity closer together in dependence upon God, whom each different group of people views through different glasses, but nevertheless in whom they all believe. Far from it! Religion has been one of the most divisive factors in the world. Some of the bloodiest of humanity's conflicts have been religious.

These conflicts may have had other economic and social factors as well, but their focal point has been religion. Such has been the case with the Christian crusades to liberate Palestine; the Turkish campaigns to convert the known world; the bloody struggle between Muslims and Hindus; and the pogroms carried out against the Jews in Europe. The list could go on and on.

In almost every case, the religions involved in these struggles led each side to believe that it, and it alone, had the "truth." All other views were wrong and evil. Therefore, the people holding these false views were converted, condemned, or eliminated. While these intolerant attitudes may find their roots in psychological and sociological traits, their inception is found in each group's concept of revelation.

For instance, the Hindu religion makes the following claim about its scripture:

> The Supreme Isvara is the source of Veda. He breathes forth all knowledge effortlessly—like human breathing. The Supreme Isvara is omniscient. The Veda is said to be apaurusseya, independent of human origin. The Purva Memamsa [the Supreme Philosopher] teaches the transmission of the eternal Veda through a succession of teachers and pupils who are not its authors. The Veda is said to be independent. Even as the World is beginningless so are the Vedas. [ ]Brackets mine.[1]

This attitude of religious Hindus towards their scriptures is what has kept Christianity from having more of an impact in India. It has also prevented India from modernizing and making changes that are essential to meet the economic, social, and physical health needs of its people. It has also led Hindus into persecuting Moslems and driving them from their midst to form the state of Pakistan. In recent years it has also led to the destruction of sacred and ancient mosques of Indian Moslems, re-igniting ancient passions.

The purported production of Buddhist Scripture was different from that of the Hindu, but, nevertheless, the concept of the end product of the inspiration is identical to that of the Hindu. While the Vedas were "breathed forth" by

---

[1]S. Rad Hakrishnan, *The Brahma Sutra* (New York: Harper Bros., 1960), p. 240

the Supreme Isvara, the Buddhist scriptures, the Vinaya-pitaka, the Sutta-pitaka, and the Abhidh ammapitaka are set forth by a human who, in the eyes of most Buddhists, became a god.

In traditional Buddhist thought, Bohisattva, son of Buddhodaana, of the wealthy king of Sakya, somewhere in the Himalayan Mountains in the sixth century B.C.E., sought the answers to birth, death, aging, and sickness. In his search, according to Buddhist beliefs, he abstained from all pleasures of earthly life, particularly those of his father's castle. Finally, through this ascetic life, it is claimed Bohisattva overcame all struggles and became perfect so that, under the "Bodhi tree," he became one with the universe; he became perfect knowledge.

It should be realized that the term Buddha was originally applied to those in Hindu society's highest caste, the Brahman, and only to those in that caste who reached the intellectual status of philosopher or rishis. Before Bohisattva, Buddhists believe, all other Buddhas had somehow compromised themselves with earthly pleasures. Consequently, their knowledge was imperfect. Since Bohisattva was not compromised with earthly pleasures, Buddhists believe that his knowledge was perfect. The writings he produced and the notes his disciples took from him were perfect knowledge.[2]

In the Hare Krisna movement, a recent development of Hinduism, there is found the same emphasis on perfect Scriptures, as in Hinduism and Buddhism. Not only are the Vedas most perfect, but Krisna's Swami A.C. Bhaktiveda Prabhupada claims that his commentary on the Vedas, Srimad Bhagavatan, reveals God "most perfectly."[3]

Of all the religions that make claims of perfection about their Scriptures, Islam makes the ultimate claim of perfection. Islam's Scripture, the Koran, has no human words in it. Other Scriptures may contain human narrative, responses, and even historical realities, but Islam teaches that the entire Koran was given to Mohammed while he was in a trance. The first person voice is always used in the text because it is not Mohammed who speaks but Allah, himself.[4] Today many struggles and wars are being fomented by Muslims who desire to have the Koran instituted as the law of their nations.

"The Truth," the Possession of Other Christian Sects

At least two sects that have found their roots in Christianity, Christian Science and the Church of the Latter-Day Saints, or the Mormon Church, consider their founding works along with the Bible to be divinely revealed truth. On September 26, 1827, Joseph Smith was reportedly given golden

---

[2]Asvaghosha Bodhisattva, "The Life of Buddha," trans. Samuel Beal, *in Sacred Books of the East,* edited Epipahanius Wilson, Volume 41, *The World's Greatest Literature,* ed. Justin McCarthy Timothy, et al. (New York and London: The Co-operative Publication Society, 1901), pp. 295–457. See also Heinz Bechert and Richard Gombrich, eds. *The World of Buddhism* (New York Facts on File Publications, 1984) specifically, "Buddha: His Teachings and Sanghi" Etienne Lanontte, pp 41–60.

[3]A.C. Bhaktivedanta Swami Prabhupada, *Srimad Bhagavatan* (Los Angeles: The Bhaktivedanta Book Trust, 1975), Canto I, preface p. x.

[4]Mohammed Marmaduke Pickthall, ed. and trans., *The Meaning of the Glorious Koran* (New York: Mentor Books, 1963), pp. ix–455.

tablets by the Angel Moroni. Mormons believe that these tablets contained divine revelation by Jesus and the prophets to the lost tribes of Israel who had migrated to the North American continent.[5] The Book of Mormon claims that its words were written by God the Father and are to be considered the very word of God and "the word of the Lamb," meaning Jesus.[6]

In *Science and Health*, Mary Baker Eddy stated that in 1866 she discovered "the Christ Science or divine laws of life, Truth, and love," and called it, "Christian Science." "God has been graciously preparing me during many years for the reception of this final revelation of the absolute Principle of scientific mental healing," she wrote.[7] While for Eddy the Bible contained the outline or witness to the truth, Christian Science practitioners considered its teachings to be the "Truth" — always spelled with a capital T. Her revelation was the ultimate and final revelation.[8] Mary Baker Eddy claimed that this revelation was "prefigured" or prophesied in chapter 10 of the book of Revelation. In this passage, John has a vision of a mighty angel who was clothed with a cloud; his face was like the sun with a rainbow around it; his feet, like pillars of fire, were found on land and sea. In his hand was a book. In this book, according to Mary Baker Eddy, was the revelation which was given to her. But the book alone was not the whole revelation. The angel was, indeed, part of the complete revelation. According to Eddy, when a person looks into the "face" of the message of Christian Science, "you perceive the very face of God."[9]

The Religion of the Incarnation

It must be underscored that Christianity differs from all other world religions in one significant way: it is much more than a revealed religion, it is the religion of the incarnation. That is to say, we Christians believe that God did not just reveal himself to this or that prophet but, rather, God took the form of a human and lived exactly as people lived. Christians killing Christians and non-Christians does not result from the doctrine of the incarnation or, for that matter, from the doctrine of the resurrection or ascension of our Lord Jesus Christ, but from not having a relationship with their powerful and risen Lord. In place of this relationship, they substituted the authority of an idolatrous view of revelation. This idolatrous view of revelation is similar to the type of revelation that is expressed in Hinduism, Buddhism, Islam, Mormonism and Christian Science. For Christians the idolatrous view of revelation finds its expression in the doctrine that the Bible is the inerrant word of God. This book will show that the doctrine of biblical inerrancy finds no support in

---

[5]Joseph Smith, *The Book of Mormon* (Salt Lake City, Utah: The Church of Latter-day Saints, 1980), pp. 2–582.

[6]Smith, 449–451, 16–19, 92–98, passim.

[7]Mary Baker Eddy, *Science and Health* (Boston: The Trustees of the Will of Mary Baker Eddy, 1934), p. 107. Henceforth, Eddy.

[8]Eddy, vi–700.

[9]Eddy, 558–9.

the Bible; it did not exist in the earliest Church; in fact, it is a total contradiction of Jesus' teaching.

Very Late Confessional Statement of Inerrancy

Every major doctrine which the Church has deemed essential to the Christian faith has been spelled out in a creed. For example, the doctrines of the Trinity and incarnation were spelled out in the creeds drawn up at the Church councils of Nicaea, and Calcedonia, but never has there been a universal Church Council to decree that the Bible is the inerrant word of God. The earliest (1536) formulation of this doctrine in creedal form is found in the First Helvetic Confession drawn up by a committee delegated by magistrates of the Reformed Church Swiss cantons of Zurich, Bern, Basel, Schaffhausen, St. Gall, Mühlhausen, and Biel, and the German city of Strassburg. Heinrich Bullinger (1504–1575), and Oswald Myconius (1488–1552), were leading Swiss delegates with Martin Bucer (1491–1551) and Wolfgang Capito (1478–1541) from Strassburg. The Confession was an attempt by Bucer and Capito to bridge the gap between the Lutheran and the Reformed churches. (Schaff, History, VIII, pp. 204–221) Of the Scripture, the confession stated, "The Holy divine, biblical Scripture, which is the Word of God inspired by the Holy Spirit and delivered to the world by the prophets and apostles, is the most ancient, most perfect and loftiest teaching and alone deals with everything that serves the true knowledge, love and honor of a Godly, honest and blessed life ."[10]

One hundred and ten years later, the Westminster Confession was to formulate a statement of the doctrine of inerrancy that would serve as the standard for much of the Protestant religion for the next three hundred years. Drawn up in Westminster Abbey in London, the confession was the by-product of the struggle between King Charles I, a strong supporter of the Church of England, and the Calvinists of Scotland (See Chapter 10, pp. 230 ff.). The Calvinists in control of Parliament accepted the Westminster Confession as the criterion of 'true faith and practice'. Its very first statement deals with Scripture:

> Although the light of nature and the works of creation and providence do so far manifest the goodness, wisdom, and power of God as to leave men inexcusable, yet they are not sufficient to give that knowledge of God and of his will which is necessary unto salvation; therefore it pleased the Lord, at sundry times, and in divers manners to reveal himself, and to declare his will unto the Church; and afterwards, for the better preserving and propagating of the truth, and for the more establishment and comfort of the Church against the corruption of the flesh, and the malice of Satan and of the world, to commit the same wholly to writing; which maketh Holy Scripture to be most necessary, those former ways of God's revealing his will unto his people being now ceased.
> Under the name of Holy Scripture, of the Word of God written,

---

[10]Rogers and McKim, The Authority and Interpretation of the Bible (San Francisco: 1979.), p. 483, henceforth Rogers and McKim.

4

are now contained all the books of the Old and New Testament...
[the confession then lists all the books of the "Protestant" Canon.]... All which are given by God to be the rule of faith and life.
The authority of the Holy Scripture, for which it ought to be
believed and obeyed, dependeth not upon the testimony of any
man or church, but wholly upon God (who is truth itself), the
author thereof; and therefore it is to be received because it is
the Word of God. (Schaff, Confessions, III)

There is no point to be made from knowing that some of the other
Protestant Churches have not included a confessional statement on inerrancy.
Almost every Protestant church would subscribe to the Westminster statement.
The Lutherans do not have any similar statement in their creedal formulations,[11] but everything Luther wrote, and almost everything that Lutheran
theologians have written down to recent ages confirm that Lutherans have
likewise maintained the same view as the Reformed Church.[12] Martin Chemnitz
(1522–1588), the most important Lutheran theologian immediately following
Luther's death, made it crystal clear that the Lutheran and Reformed views
of Scripture were identical. Chemnitz wrote:

What we have until now adduced from the very words of Scripture
are the most reliable testimonies on which the pious heart can
safely rest. For they set before us the judgement of the Holy
Spirit concerning the Scripture. For, as the ancients say, that
concerning God, nothing should be believed unless God, HIM-
SELF, reveals and testifies it. (de Deo nihil credendum esse,
nisi ipso Deo revelante et testificante) Thus, we should also
believe that about Scripture, what the Scripture says about —
yes what its Author, the Holy Spirit, judges and pronounces
about His work. But also all the consensus of the Ancient Church
concerning the perfection, and sufficiency of the Scripture. For
we love and venerate the testimonies of the ancient and pure
Church whose consent we are both aided and confirmed in this
that faith must rest on the Word of God, not human authority.[13]

No Challenge to Inerrancy in the 16th through 18th Centuries

B. B. Warfield, the famous Princeton theologian (1886–1921), and Harold
Lindsell, editor of the conservative and prestigious *Christianity Today*, claim
that the absence for sixteen centuries of a creedal statement on biblical inerrancy
was due to universal acceptance of the doctrine in the Church.[14] Lindsell and
Warfield did not know church history very well. The statements on inerrancy

---

[11]After the Augsburg Confession had been adopted, the Lutheran fathers, in 1580,
affixed a title to it which stated that the Confession was *"Firmly Founded on the Word of
God as the only Norm,"* Theodore G. Tappert, ed., The Book of Concord (Philadelphia:
Fortress Press, 1959), pp. 1–4.

[12]Edwin Schlink, *The Theology of the Lutheran Confessions*, trans. by Paul F. Koehneke
and Herbert Bowman (Philadelphia: Muhlenberg Press, 1963), pp. v–36.

[13]Martin Chemnitz, *The Examination of the Council of Trent*, trans., Fredrick Hassold
(Springfield, Illinois: Concordia, 1963), p. 118.

in these confessions were not defenses of the doctrine in the face of challenge. There existed no need at the time of the drafting of these confessions for a defense of this doctrine. Though there had been many challenges to biblical inerrancy earlier in church history,[15] at the time that both the Westminster and Second Helvetic Confessions were written, the doctrine was widely accepted.

Even the Roman Catholic Church, arch-enemy of every Protestant church at the time, accepted the Bible as the inerrant word of God. In fact, the fourth session of the Council of Trent (April, 1546) formulated a statement that is as emphatic as the Second Helvetic and Westminster confessions. The Council stated:

> The sacred and holy, œcumenical, and general Synod of Trent – lawfully assembled in the Holy Ghost, the same three legates of the Apostolic See presiding therein – keeping in view, that errors being removed, the purity itself of the Gospel be preserved in the Church: which (Gospel), before promised through the prophets in the holy Scriptures, our Lord Jesus Christ, the Son of God, first promulgated with His own mouth, and then commanded and preached by His Apostles to every creature, as the fountain of all both saving truth and moral discipline; and seeing clearly that this truth and discipline are contained in the written books, and written traditions which received by the Apostles themselves, the Holy Ghost dictating, have come down even unto us, transmitted as it were from hand to hand: [the Synod] following the examples of the orthodox Fathers, receives and venerates with an equal affection of piety and reverence, all the books both of the Old and of the New Testament–seeing that the one God is the author of both.[16]

Neither did a challenge to inerrancy come from the scientific discoveries of Copernicus (1473–1543) and Galileo (1564–1642), which occurred before and during the Reformation. Neither Copernicus nor Galileo saw himself as being outside the faith, nor did the Church accuse Copernicus or Galileo of attacking the Bible. These scientists attacked the archaic view of the solar system held during the Middle Ages. The attack on biblical inerrancy from the scientific community did not come until the nineteenth century with Charles Darwin.

Even the Deists of the seventeenth and eighteenth centuries were not really attacking the Bible but the faith in general. While they believed in a God, their God was not identical with the God of the Bible. They believed that God had set the world up to work according to scientific principles and that God did not work directly in the world. When Thomas Jefferson, the American Patriot and Deist, excised the Bible, he simply removed all elements of the

---

[14]Harold Lindsell, *The Battle for the Bible* (Grand Rapids, Michigan: Zondervan Publishing House, 1976), pp. 41–42; Warfield, *Revelation*, p. 52 ff.

[15]See Chapter X.

[16]J. T. Schroeder, trans. and ed. *The Canons and Decrees of the Council of Trent* (London: B. Herder Book Co. Ltd., 1941), p. 17.

supernatural from the text. He could hardly be described as attacking the Bible. He was attacking the Christian faith in general.

The Challenge to Inerrancy, Biblical Criticism

The earliest apparent challenge to the doctrine of inerrancy was in the nineteenth century. This challenge came through the introduction of literary criticism into biblical studies. While there were earlier attempts at biblical criticism, it was primarily through the works of Ferdinand Christian Baur (1772–1862), founder of the Tübingen School of Theology, that biblical criticism came of age. Through the critical method and Hegelian philosophy, Baur discovered that there were inconsistencies, contradictions and even errors in the text of Scripture, specifically found in the differences of Acts and the Pauline epistles.[17] Later Julius Wellhausen (1844–1918) attacked the assumption that Moses wrote the Pentateuch. In his *Prolegama History of Israel* (1878), Wellhausen suggested that there were three different strains of thought in the first five books of the Bible. These strains were to be known as the Yahwist, Priestly, and the Elohist.[18] This was thought to be such an attack on the doctrine of inerrancy that two proponents of Wellhausen, Robertson Smith of Scotland, and Charles Briggs of America, were convicted of heresy.

The reason biblical criticism was more threatening to orthodoxy than was Deism was the simple matter that the biblical critics were believers and not skeptics, like the Deists. In the eyes of most theologians of the nineteenth and early twentieth centuries, biblical critics were attacking the very word of God. Theologian Heinrich Heppe, one of the most able defenders of the Reformed Faith in the nineteenth century, took great pains to document how Protestant theologians of the past would not tolerate even the idea that there might be errors within the text of the Bible.[19] Heppe put it succinctly: "Since the authority of Holy Scripture coincides with the authority of God, it is essentially absolute."[20]

Heppe, however, did open the door for a change in direction of conservative thought. He asserted that the mechanical view of inspiration was not an accurate understanding of inspiration of the Bible. The mechanical view of the inspiration of Scripture had been the predominant view of inspiration that prevailed in the church from about the fourth to the nineteenth century C.E. This view of inspiration claimed basically that the writers of the Scriptures, "the prophets and the apostles," were passive recipients of what God wanted to communicate, only incidental to the process of writing Scripture. The church fathers had referred often to the fact that God spoke Scripture. It was apparent in the Confessions quoted above that God was thought to be the "Author" of

---

[17]Ferdinand Christian Baur, *Paul, The Apostle of Jesus Christ,* trans. by E. Zeller, 2nd ed. (Edinburgh: A. C. Black, 1873), Volumes I and II, p. 1 ff. Particularly Volume II, p. 115 ff.

[18]Julius Wellhausen, *Prolegamma History of Israel,* trans. by J. Sutherland and Allan Menzies (Edinburgh: Charles & Allan Black, 1885), pp. 1–164.

[19]Heppe, 22–41.

[20]Heppe, 26. Rogers and McKim suggest that the change came in Archibald Alexander (1772–1851), and that indeed may be so, but Heppe was in the same time frame. Rogers and McKim, pp. 266–273.

Scripture. Heppe believed that the inspiration of the Bible was much more dynamic. He believed that the apostles and prophets were not simply passive, that God used their individuality, but at the same time protected them from making mistakes.[21] Princeton theologian B.B. Warfield, (1851–1921) picked up this concept and called it "concursive inspiration."[22] In this view of inspiration, the authors of Scripture are not viewed as sublimating their personalities and intelligences. Instead, through "special and direct activity of the Holy Spirit," the authors were "urged to write," given the "thoughts and words to write," so that what they wrote was preserved from all error and thus was indeed the "written word of God."[23] Warfield described this theory as the Holy Spirit working "confluently" with the human personality so that the end product was raised above anything that could be considered human, and was the very word of God.[24] For Warfield and Heppe to consider that there might be mistakes or inconsistencies within Scriptures was to impugn the very word of God. Questioning the accuracy of Scripture was questioning the accuracy of God.

Karl Barth's Theology, Christ-Centered Faith, and Criticism

The threat to the Bible that biblical criticism posed, and that Warfield, Heppe, and other reformed theologians fought against during the nineteenth and early part of the twentieth centuries was confined to a few universities, liberal seminaries, and a few churches. It could not be described as pervasive. The matter changed however in the twentieth century primarily through the work of one person: Karl Barth (1886–1968). Barth rejected the idea that the Bible was in itself the Word of God. Barth wrote:

> In the Bible we are invariably concerned with human attempts to repeat and reproduce in human thoughts and expressions, this Word of God in definite situations, e.g. in respect to the complications of Israel's political position midway between Egypt and Babylon, or of errors and confusion in the Christian Church at Corinth between C.E. 50–60. In one case Deux Dixit, in the other Paulus Dixit. These are two different things and precisely because, where the Word of God is an event, it is not two different things but becomes one... (Dogmatics, I , 1, p.127, by permission of publisher)

While many people find Barth impenetrable, he is far from being so. One must realize that Barth took great pains to make absolutely clear what he was and was not writing. Consequently, Barth spent a great deal of time in historical, theological and biblical analysis. He did not use code words or key phrases that had esoteric meanings so that only a select group of his inner disciples knew, or thought they knew what he meant (Dogmatics, I, 1, pp.

---

[21]Heppe, 16.

[22]Warfield, *Revelation*, p. 26 ff.

[23]Heppe, 16.

[24]Warfield, *Revelation*, 26–27.

1–47). He developed and redeveloped themes throughout his eleven volumes of dogmatics. It is not surprising then, to find one of Barth's most eloquent statements on the event of the word of God in Volume I, Part 2, several hundred pages from where he originally developed the idea. Here Barth stated:

> In the statement that "the Bible is the word of God," we cannot suddenly mean a lesser, less potent, less ineffable and majestic Word of God, that which has occupied us in the doctrine of the Trinity and in the doctrine of Christ and of the Holy Spirit. There is only one Word of God and that is the eternal Word of the Father which for our reconciliation became flesh like us and has now returned to be present in His Church by the Holy Spirit. In Holy Scripture, too, in the human word of His witnesses, it is a matter of this Word and its presence. That means that in this equation it is a matter of the miracle of the divine majesty in its condescension and mercy. If we take this equation on our lips, it can only be as an appeal to the promise in virtue of which this miracle was real Jesus Christ and will again be real in the word of His witnesses. In this equation we have to do with the free grace and the gracious freedom of God. That the Bible is the Word of God cannot mean that with the other attributes the Bible has the attribute of being the Word of God. To say that would be to violate the Word of God which is God Himself—to violate the freedom and sovereignty of God... The statement that the Bible is the Word of God cannot therefore say that the Word of God is tied to the Bible. On the contrary, what it must say is that the Bible is tied to the Word of God... The Bible is not the Word of God on earth in the same way as Jesus Christ, very God and very man, is that Word in heaven. (Dogmatics, Vol I, pt 2, pp. 512–513, by permission of publisher)

For many Christians, Barth's thinking was a liberating experience. They no longer had to subscribe to a mindless religion. They could admit what their minds knew all the time, biblically, that in the Bible there were inconsistencies, errors, cultural relevancies and even contradictions. Yet, in making that admission, they knew that they were not challenging the central doctrines of Christianity: the providence of God, the incarnation, the resurrection etc. Furthermore, for many Christians the faith moved from dogmatic abstractions to concrete life experiences.

However, for many conservative Christians, the intrusion of Barth's thinking and acceptance of biblical criticism into their midst has been highly threatening. The conservative Reformed theologian Cornelius Van Til edited a book the title of which is descriptive of the antagonism that many conservatives have felt towards Barth. The book is entitled *Christianity and Barthianism*, as if there were no relationship between the two. In this book, Van Til compiled the views of Barth by such theologians as G.C. Berkouer, Klaas Runia, and Klaas Schilder as well as his own and others' views. Basically they accused Barth of having a subjective view of Scriptures, and thus having a subjective view of Christ, so that Christ is "no Christ."[25] This is about the worst accusation

---

[25]Cornelius Van Til, *Christianity and Barthianism* (Philadelphia, PA: The Presbyterian

that could be levelled against a Christian theologian. Francis Schaefer, founder of the famous L'Abri Fellowship in Switzerland, likewise asserts that to accept Karl Barth's interpretation, or for that matter any view that does not maintain an authoritative inerrant Scripture, is to end in the philosophical nihilism of the world.[26]

The Painful and Costly Struggle over Biblical Criticism

In the twenty-six years that this book has been in process (1970–95), almost every major denomination has had major confrontations over the issue of biblical inerrancy. The Missouri Synod Lutheran Church split over the issue. At the center of the controversy in the Missouri Synod were J.A.O. Preuss, president of the synod and leader of the conservative elements in the Synod, and John H. Tietjen, the president of Concordia Seminary in St. Louis. Preuss and the conservatives made the focal point of the dispute the question of whether professors in the seminary would be allowed to teach biblical criticism. Tietjen believed, for the integrity of the institution, the professors had the right to do so. He saw no conflict between teaching criticism and the Lutheran standards. After a lengthy struggle, Preuss suspended Tietjen on January 24, 1974 and placed an administrative board in charge of the seminary. This precipitated a huge walk-out of students and professors. These protesting faculty and students formed Seminex or Concordia Seminary in Exile. From the formation of Seminex and the numerous Churches that supported Tietjen, a new denomination called the Association of Evangelical Lutherans emerged.[27]

The more liberal United Presbyterian Church has suffered long over the issue of authority of the Bible. The conflict came to a head when the denomination attempted to express its faith in a modern confession. In the confession's first draft was the following statement: "The one sufficient revelation of God is Jesus Christ, the Word of God incarnate, to whom the Holy Spirit bears witness in many ways. The Church has received the Old and New Testament as the normative Witness to this revelation and has recognized them as Holy Scripture." If this statement, which was written by Markus Barth, Karl Barth's son, would have been accepted, the United Presbyterian Church would have split apart. The negative response can be understood when it is realized that the Presbyterians accepted the Westminster Confession, quoted on page 6, as containing "the system of doctrine taught in Holy Scripture."[28] The pastors of the denomination had to state in their ordination vows that they believed

---

and Reformed Publishing Company, 1965), p. 1 ff. See also Norman Geisler, *Biblical Errancy* (Grand Rapids, MI: Zondervan Publishing House, Inc., 1981), particularly p. 231 f. It is interesting to note that since 1965 Berkouer became a strong supporter of Barth. Another Conservative to endorse Barth was Bernard Ramm, *After Fundamentalism* (San Francisco: Harper & Row Publishers, 1983), pp. 1 ff. See Donald McKim: *How Karl Barth Changed Me* (Grand Rapids, MI: Wm. B. Eerdmans & Co., 1986) p. 1ff.

[26]Francis Schaeffer, *The God Who is there* (Downers Grove, Il, Intervarsity Press, 1968), pp. 13–175.

[27]Fredrick W. Danker, *No Room in the Brotherhood* (St. Louis, Missouri: Clayton Publishing House, 1978). In 1988, the Association of Evangelical Lutherans (A.E.L.C.) merged with the American Lutheran Church (A.L.C.) and the Lutheran Church in America (L.C.A.) to form Evangelical Lutheran Church in America (E.L.C.A.).

that "the Scriptures of the Old and New Testament to be the Word of God, the only infallible rule of faith and practice." With such a hostile reaction, the authors of the Confession of 1967 changed the phrase "normative witness" to read "the word of God written," thus preventing the United Presbyterian Church from being torn apart at its seams.[29]

The conflict over the authority of Scripture continued unabated in the United Presbyterian Church for the next twenty years. This conflict presented itself over the issues of the ordination of "avowed practicing homosexuals" and the ordination of women as elders within the Session, the ruling body of the church. When, in 1987, the United Presbyterian Church and the Presbyterian Church in the U.S. reunited, there was an escape clause that allowed churches to withdraw from the parent organization and take their property with them.

On the opposite end of the spectrum from Presbyterians are Southern Baptists. They are not only the largest of the United States' Protestant denominations, but they are one of the most conservative churches. For many years, they have been involved in an ongoing struggle over the inerrancy of Scripture. In June of 1979, the annual convention of Southern Baptists elected as its President Adrian Rogers, a proponent of absolute inerrancy. He was elected on the pledge that he would purge all the denomination's seminaries of professors who did not subscribe to the 1963 statement on the inerrancy of Scriptures. This statement said Scripture had "God for its author, salvation for its end, and contained truth, without any mixture of error." The convention of 1979 clarified the southern Baptist belief that it was "the original autograph" or the first writing of the manuscript that was totally without errors. The convention conceded the present manuscripts included corrections and additions. These corrections and errors were due to scribal or copyist mistakes rather than any deficiency in the original text. This compromise made it possible for professors who could read Greek and Hebrew to stay in the Southern Baptist Convention, but it was little consolation for those scholars who accepted even a modicum of the biblical critical method.[30] Things have worsened since the 1979 convention. In the 1988 convention the "moderates" attempted to elect Richard Jackson, but he was defeated by Jerry Vines, a fundamentalist. Julia Duin, a reporter for Christianity Today, described the election this way:

> Theologically the candidates were indistinguishable. Both are inerrantists; people who believe the Bible is without error. However, conservatives believe the Bible is without error in matters of science, history, faith and revelation. Moderates believe that the Bible must be understood in context of its historical setting and limited world views.[31]

---

[28]*The Book of Common Worship* (Philadelphia, PA: Office of the General Assembly of the United Presbyterian Church in the United States of America, 1946), p. 227.

[29]*The Constitution of the United Presbyterian Church in the United States of America*: Part I, *Book of Confessions* (Philadelphia: The Office of the General Assembly of the United Presbyterian Church in the United States of America, 1967), p. 27.

[30]See Duane A Garrett and Richard R. Melick, eds, *Authority and Interpretation* (Grand Rapids, MI: Baker Book House, 1987), p. 1 ff.

Harold Lindsell, the former editor of *Christianity Today*, believes that the invasion of biblical criticism into the Southern Baptist seminaries, and, in his opinion, almost every denominational seminary, is a major threat to Christianity. He considered it such a threat that he entitled his book addressing the issue, *The Battle for the Bible*.[32] Most alarming, in Lindsell's view, is that even among conservative evangelicals the doctrine of biblical inerrancy is being undermined. He believes that the undermining of this doctrine will have disastrous effects; that it will totally undercut the churches' mission and evangelism within the world.[33] In fact, he asserts, the espousal of biblical criticism will lead many evangelicals to deny Christ as he believes that has brought many liberals to already deny Christ.[34]

J.J. Packer, in his book, *'Fundamentalism' and the Word of God*, states that the attack on the Bible as the inerrant word of God is "the most fundamental problem the Christian Church has ever faced."[35] Packer believes that any rejection of the Bible as the inerrant word of God is not only rejection of the authority of the Bible, but is in the end "disobedience to Christ, himself."[36] Another great conservative scholar, Carl F.H. Henry, in his systematic theology, *God, Revelation and Authority*, argues that, in this day when there seems to be no certainties in society, the Church must maintain the authoritative position of Scripture or lose the battle to the world.[37]

Over three hundred conservative scholars and theologians gathered in Chicago in October of 1978 because of their concern for the erosion of inerrancy. This conference drafted the first real contemporary statement on the inerrancy of Scripture since the formulations in the Westminster and First Helvetic confessions. The statement asserted that, "Holy Scripture, being God's own Word, written by men and superintended by His Spirit . . . " so that the Holy Spirit was its "divine author." Since the Holy Scripture is "wholly and verbally God-given" it is "without error or fault in all its teaching" and its authority is "inescapably impaired if this total divine inerrancy is limited in any way." [38]

There is a fantastic alarm among conservative scholars and preachers that the doctrine of inerrancy is being eroded. It is simply impossible to keep up with all the articles and books being written in defense of the doctrine. But it would appear from all the evidence in the American church that if the

---

[31]Julia Duin, "Conservatives Rule Southern Baptists," *Christianity Today*, July 15,1988: vol. 32, no. 10, p. 33.

[32]Lindsell, 17–212.

[33] Lindsell, 17–27.

[34] Lindsell, 43–44.

[35]Packer, 42.

[36]Packer, 21.

[37]Henry, *God who Speaks and Shows, Vol. I*: 17–69.

[38]John Tinder, "Pro-inerrancy Forces Draft their Platform," *Christianity Today*, November 17, 1978, pp. 36–37.

doctrine is under attack, that attack is hardly more than a whisper of wind. In 1987, George Gallup conducted an opinion poll in which he asked people their opinion of the Bible. The poll gave three statements from which to choose. These statements were:

1. The Bible is the actual word of God and is to be taken as the literal word.
2. The Bible is the inspired word of God, but not everything is to be taken literally.
3. The Bible is an ancient book of fables, legends, history and moral precepts recorded by men.[39]

While extreme fundamentalists would subscribe to the first statement, most persons accepting inerrancy would subscribe to the second statement. The third statement would naturally be a position that would be acceptable to those persons who accept the biblical critical method. According to Gallup, thirty-two per cent of Americans subscribe to the Bible as the actual Word of God to be taken literally; forty nine percent, the inspired word of God; and a scant thirteen percent accepting the Bible as containing fables and legends. The rest did not accept any of the three categories or had no opinion. Accordingly, then, eighty one percent of Americans accept the Bible as the word of God.[40]

The enormous amount of conservative religious literature that has poured off the presses would all tend to support the Gallup poll, and so would the large number of evangelists who saturate the media of television and radio. When one considers the impact that all these evangelists and preachers have had on the American public for at least the last twenty years, plus that of the great number and variety of conservative churches, it is no wonder Gallup found that eighty-three percent of Americans accept the Bible as the Word of God.

It would be difficult to pinpoint any erosion of the doctrine of inerrancy. It would seem that the huge amount of material produced and the vehemence of emotion in the defense of inerrancy is indicative of serious problems in conservative Christianity, rather than showing that huge numbers of Christians are being led astray by the "false teaching of biblical criticism." It is easier to bash the "Godless liberals" than to face the inherent problems within conservatism.[41]

In spite of the success stories told by the huge increases in numbers of fundamentalist Christians, and their political clout,[42] conservatives and fundamentalists are very insecure. In *Today's Gospel: Authentic or Synthetic?*,

---

[39]*The Gallup Poll* (Princeton, N. J.: The Gallup Opinion Index, 1987), pp. 23–24. Each of Gallup's three categories do not do justice to the great variety of shades of thought within the various views of inspiration of and attitudes towards Scripture.

[40]The same poll was conducted in 1976 at which time 33% held a fundamentalist position, 48 % a conservative position with 11% holding a liberal position. Religion in America (Princeton, New Jersey: Gallup Research, 1976)

[41]James Barr, *Fundamentalism*, p. 11 ff.

[42]Dean M. Kelley, *Why the Conservative Churches are Growing* (New York: Harper & Row, 1972), p. 3 ff.

the conservative and evangelical Elmer Chantry analyzed the situation well. Chantry stated,

> Evangelicals know that all is not well in their churches and missions. Behind the façade of glowing missionary reports and massive statistics, there is a profound awareness that the church has little power of evangelism.[43]

Harshly, but realistically, he went on to state:

> When the excitement of the latest campaign has subsided, when the choir sings no more thrilling choruses, when large crowds no longer gather, when the emotional hope of the evangelists' invitation has moved to another city, what do we have that is real and lasting? When every house in mission village has been visited, what has been done? The honest heart answers, "Very little." There has been a great deal of noise and dramatic excitement, but God has not come down with his frightful power and converting grace. [44]

This description of contemporary Christianity is in stark contrast to the description of the Church in the New Testament. Here is not found a record of ineffectual power. Here is the history of God coming "down with his frightful power and converting grace." When the disciples proclaimed the gospel message, they proclaimed it in power. Lives were changed. Such an impact did they have on the world, that they were accused of "turning the world upside down. (Acts 17:6)"

God's mighty work within the church did not stop with the New Testament church. The history of the great and wonderful transforming power of God goes on unabated into the second, third, and fourth centuries. Early Christians had their problems. The New Testament and the early church fathers' writings reveal that the Christians of the first few centuries were plagued with divisions and with people who had their own self-interest at heart. Yet, with all their shortcomings, Christians were different from the society within which they lived. They were so different that the Roman society considered them a threat and persecuted them.

---

[43]Walter J. Chantry, *Today's Gospel: Authentic or Synthetic?* (London: Banner of Truth Trust Press, 1972), p. 9.

[44]Chantry, 13.

Chapter II

"Thus Says The Lord God"

One in the Lord, One with Each Other

Remember Jesus' great and glorious prayer for the Church as it was recorded in John:

> I do not pray for these only [meaning the disciples who followed Jesus while he was on earth], but also for those who believe in me through their word; that they may all be one; even as thou, Father, art in me and I in thee, that they may be in us, so the world may believe that thou hast sent me. The glory which thou has given me I have given them, that they may become perfectly one, so that the world may know that thou hast sent me . . . (John 17:20–23, RSV [ ] Brackets mine)

This is one of the strongest statements about the divinity of Christ in the Scriptures, but is not just a statement about Jesus. It is a statement about the church, and evangelism within the world. It is clear that the Father and Son are perfectly one. It is also clear that for the world to understand that fact, the world must perceive a Church that is one also. Even though the Church has formulated eloquent statements on the divinity of Christ as it has in the Nicene and Calcedon Creeds, according to Jesus as long as there are divisions in the Church, these Creeds will be totally ineffective in the world. Furthermore, the Church can plot great evangelistic programs to convert the world to Christ Jesus; these programs, again, will not be effective until there is unity. If the Church is interested in organizing an evangelistic program, the Church must not first look at how to make the message palatable to the unbelievers, but first seek unity among believers.

Many evangelicals claim that such unity already exists, a spiritual unity – an invisible unity between all true believers. Many evangelicals are suspicious of any attempt to bring about unification of Churches. Such programs as the Consultation on Church Union between Episcopal, Presbyterian, Methodist, United Church of Christ, and other churches, have been all but scuttled because conservatives within each of these churches have considered such a union the work of the anti-Christ.[1]

Karl Barth correctly and most emphatically branded such thinking by conservatives on Church unity as a modern day form of *Docetism* (Dogmatics, Vol. IV, pt. 1, pp. 653–658). Docetism was an early heresy within the church. Docetists believed that God was Spirit, and if Jesus was by nature God, he must likewise have been Spirit. The fact that he appeared in the body was mere illusion, and thus because he was Spirit he could not really have died. Barth refuted such spiritualizing tendencies of conservatives by pointing out

---

[1]Thanks to Laurie Skiba for the inclusion of this thought within the book.

that Christ chose twelve very visible disciples and that after the resurrection they multiplied by the thousands – not as invisible, but as the Church most visible. Barth stated eloquently, "Where the Holy Spirit is at work, the step to visibility is unavoidable . . ." (Dogmatics, IV, I, pp. 650–672).

According to Jesus' statement in John 17, the function of Christian unity is not so that God can recognize "the true believers." Unity among Christians is so that the world may know that the Father had sent Jesus. By "the world," it is apparent that Jesus means the persons who do not yet believe in Jesus, and because of the "oneness" among Christians they come to believe. This oneness, then, has to be observable by the nonbelieving or the not-now-believing world. It would thus follow that the persons who are to observe this unity would not be able to judge the unity from a doctrinal position, because no one had "yet" taught them what "true doctrine" was. Furthermore, according to Jesus this oneness, this unity, is not some far-off reality, such as when he returns and establishes his final reign. This oneness which Jesus prayed for was to be among his disciples with whom he associated and among those who believed because of the word of the disciples. It can be safely assumed that the oneness which Jesus prayed for ought to be a reality in the Church today!

I am afraid, however, that if the world is to see this oneness it will have to have a great endowment of fantasy. Any person with a thread of objectivity can plainly perceive the Christian Church as so fragmented and divided as to make Jesus' prayer seem a joke. The World Christian Encyclopedia reports that there are 2050 divisions in the Christian Church.[2] If the oneness in the Church reveals the oneness between the Father and the Son, then God really has problems.[3]

The Reformation and the Destruction of the Church

The basis for the massive splintering of the church came about during the reformation, and it is that exact time in which the doctrine that the Bible is the inerrant word of God becomes firmly established and canonized within the churches. It is very evident from the literature of the reformation that it is this precise doctrine that is the instrument through which the divisions are brought into existence.

When Luther nailed his ninety-five theses to the Wittenburg Cathedral

---

[2]David B. Barrett, ed., *World Christian Encyclopedia* (Oxford, New York, and Nairobi: Oxford University Press, 1980), p. 780.

[3]A text, which many Christians have used to justify the divisions within the Church, has been Matthew 10:34–36. Here Jesus stated, "Do not think that I have come to bring peace on earth; I have not come to bring peace but a sword. For I have come to set a man against his father, and a daughter against her mother and a man's foes will be those of his own household." (RSV) This text has been used to justify a huge amount of perfidy in the Church. While Mann and Albright are right that the Aramaic meaning of the original text may be obscured [*Matthew, (AB)* v. 26, in loc.], it is very clear from the context that the followers of Christ are not purveyors of the sword. It is also apparent from the context that Jesus did not mean that he came to set Christian brother and sister against each other. Verses 32 and 33 indicate that Jesus has in mind Christians proclaiming him as Lord. The sword, of which Jesus speaks in vs. 34, was the fact that when a person accepted Jesus as Lord and proclaimed Him as Lord, he/she might find him/her self rejected by his/her very own parents, brothers, or sisters. The sword here is not the Spirit of the Lord as it is in Ephesians 6:17, but rather the hostility of the pagans or Jews to the Christian faith.

door, he had no intention of splitting the Church. He desired to expose abuses in the Church. He believed that Rome's sale of indulgences to raise money to continue the building of St. Peter's Cathedral was completely against God's will. Luther did not consider himself a prophet. He thought that if the matter of the selling of indulgences was openly discussed, the Church hierarchy and the Pope would rectify the situation. Luther's heart was broken, and he became embittered. He was thrown out of the Church. On June 25, 1520, Pope Leo X excommunicated Luther. Thus, it was the Pope who created the Protestant Church and not Luther. Luther found himself in a position like that of the early Christians who were thrown out of Judaism.

Unlike the early Church which remained a comparatively monolithic structure for fourteen centuries, the Protestant Church shattered apart within a few years after Luther's excommunication. The splinters into which the Protestant Church shattered were not factions of loving brothers and sisters separated by geography, but antagonistic, hostile and even warring factions. The Bride of Christ was in total disarray. The Protestant Church was not one reforming Church, but was to become well over two thousand factions going their separate, individualistic ways.

To absolve Luther of the responsibility for the further fragmentation of the Church by stating that the teacher cannot be blamed for the disciples' errors is to ignore the fact that the seeds for the destruction of the church were, indeed, within Luther's thought and person. To maintain his authority and control within the church, he perpetuated and maintained the idolatrous view of the Scriptures. The other reformers did likewise.

After Luther's excommunication, the next two splits in the Church came over the issues of communion and baptism. It is not the intent of this book to argue on any side of these issues. The whole point is to show how the doctrine of the Bible being the inerrant word of God is an unholy sword severing the Church from its source of power. The way all sides use the Scriptures in disputes over communion and baptism are simply case studies in how further splits came about in the Church.

The first division of Protestantism after Luther was excommunicated from the Roman Church came over the issue of Communion.[4] The division occurred between those who followed Martin Luther and those who followed the Swiss reformer Huldrych Zwingli (1484–1531). Zwingli, also a priest, had come to the reformation from a different direction than Luther, but he had read and liked much of what Luther had written. In 1519, he was elected "the peoples' priest" in Zurich. After a great deal of biblical preaching and popular acceptance of Zwingli, the Zurich city council declared themselves outside the Bishop's authority and thus outside the Holy Roman Empire.

Zwingli's views on Communion had been greatly influenced by a Dutch lawyer and biblical scholar, Cornelius Hoen. In 1523 Zwingli read a tract on the Lord's Supper written by Hoen. Hoen stipulated that when Jesus said of the bread, "This is my body," he meant, "This signifies my body." Likewise of the cup, Hoen advocated that Jesus meant, "This signifies the blood of the covenant which is poured out for many."[5] This interpretation appealed to the

---

[4]This can be debated. Technically the Anabaptists were separating themselves as early as 1523, but as far as the Reformation was concerned the Reformed and Lutheran split was the major split. In comparison the Anabaptist factions were in size and impact minor splits, but spiritually and dynamically they were equally or more important.

humanistic leanings in Zwingli. Zwingli then interpreted Jesus' admonition, "Do this in remembrance of me," as indicating that communion was to be a memorial meal. The wine and bread were symbols through which the Christian remembered the death of Jesus. The Church historian Williston Walker described Zwingli's attitude towards the physical presence, "To Zwingli, Luther's assertion of the physical presence of Christ was an unreasoning remnant of Catholic superstition."[6] Zwingli put it this way in his "Friendly Exegesis, that is, Exposition of the Matter of the Eucharist," addressed to Martin Luther:

> . . .To declare that the flesh of Christ is physically eaten in the supper seems to be the really pestilential thing, through which as it sprouts and spreads the gospel is laid waste. For it would strengthen faith and remit sins, who would not return to the vomit of works? I confess clearly by heaven, that if I was told by the word of the Lord that sins were forgiven through this supper I would partake of it every time my conscience troubled me. Would not faith in works straight way come back? . . .Believe me, the papists have scarcely any hope left unless they can keep live that superstition of the physical eating of Christ's body.[7]

Zwingli's words to say the least are graphic: "pestilential thing . . . sprouts and spreads . . .Vomit of works," but even more, Zwingli goes on to condescendingly lecture Luther,

> For so far as I understand your position, you seem to be wholly ignorant of my arguments. For those which I have brought forward are enough to demolish, begging your pardon, without any trouble, all that you offer to the contrary. If you have examined them and intentionally passed them by, I am afraid that even an ajax could not prevent your enemies from fixing you the name of a deceiver of the people.
> . . .You have seemed to many, not yet having got over your wrath you were feeling towards certain persons, to have treated a difficult subject in the heat of your anger, and not to have shown good and innocent men the consideration that was due to them and worthy of yourself. If this is so, my book will make an appeal from your wrath to calm and favorable judgement. For you are aware how dangerous it is to admit into deliberation anger, petulance, stubbornness, jealousy and the like that boldly and shamelessly gives themselves out for righteousness, courage, firmness and authority.

One can understand from the tone of this message that Luther would

---

[5]Williston Walker, *A History of the Christian Church,* revised by Cyril Richardson, Wilhelm Pauck, and Robert Handy (New York: Charles Scribner's Sons, 1959), p. 324. Henceforth, Walker.

[6]Walker, 324.

[7]E.J. Furch, Huldrych Zwingli: Writing II (Allison Park, PA: Pickwick Press, 1984), pp. 246–247. Henceforth Zwingli

react very negatively to Zwingli's dissertation. Besides the innuendoes which would naturally infuriate most people, Luther felt that Zwingli was moving beyond Faith. For Luther, Jesus' words "this is my body," meant that the bread was indeed Jesus' actual body. Likewise, when Jesus took the cup and said, "This is the blood of the covenant," Luther interpreted this to mean that in communion the wine actually became the blood of Christ. Zwingli's response, that the resurrected Christ was in heaven and that his body could not be everywhere,[8] was a denial of faith in the power of God to do what ever he wished including having his son become incarnate in the virgin Mary, the resurrection etc.. (Luther's Works 34, pp. 49 ff.).

The ensuing debate between Luther and Zwingli was not just a friendly discussion between brothers, but developed into an out-and-out brawl that almost irreparably damaged the fabric of the Church. Luther could hardly be described as being charitable towards Zwingli. In fact, he used some language that is not always fit to translate into English (Luther's Work, Volume 38, pp. 15–80). In one of his retorts Luther says of Zwingli and Zwingli's friend, Oecamlapadius: " . . .We can thoroughly refute all babbling of the seditious Spirits who regard the sacraments, contrary to the word of God [the Bible], as human performances."[9]

And so it went. One side calling the other unfaithful to "God's word." In 1529, Philip of Hesse, one of the German princes, brought Luther and his associate Melancthon and Zwingli and his associate Oecamlapadius, to Marburg, Germany. Philip had hoped that the two reformers would work out their differences, so that the German and Swiss Evangelical Protestant states could present a united force against the papal forces. But the conference was a dismal failure with both sides becoming further entrenched. Luther and Zwingli each saw the other as being unfaithful to God's holy Word, the Bible, and therefore wrong. Luther, finally, in complete and utter exasperation with Zwingli exclaimed his classic statement: "You have a different Spirit than we! (*Ihr habt einen anderen Geist als Wir* !)" Then Luther walked out. Melancthon likewise said to Zwingli and Oecamlapadius: "You do not belong to the Communion of the Christian Church." Both Luther and Melancthon believed that their communion was of the Lord and Zwingli's and Oecamlapadius' communion was of demons. They quoted Paul: "You cannot drink the cup of the Lord and the cup of demons. You cannot partake of the table of the Lord and the table of Demons (I Corinthians 10:21)." (Schaff, VII, 644) Luther and Melancthon said that they would part as friends but they could not part as brothers in the faith. They would pray for Zwingli and Oecamlapadius that God would show them "the truth (Luther's Works, 38, 35;73–81)." But, the espousal of friendship was meaningless. The fabric of the bridal gown of the bride of Christ was ripped that much more.

Here at work were the true fruits of the doctrine that the Bible is the Word of God. A chasm was cut so deeply into the structure of the Church that it has yet, after four hundred and fifty years, to be bridged or healed. The tragedy of it all is magnified when it is realized, as Philip of Hesse did, that there were no reasons for the division and that the reformers had nothing to

---

[8]Zwingli, 250

[9]The Book of Concord, p. 447. [ ] Brackets mine.

gain and everything to lose by it. It was very apparent, at least from the Protestant perspective, that Luther and Zwingli had more in common than they had differences. Both men risked their lives by exposing the perversions in the Roman Church. On the Lordship of Jesus Christ, they were in total agreement. They even both accepted infant baptism which was to become an issue with other Protestants later. There were no serious political or economic issues underlying the division. The blame for animosity between individuals who should have been loving brothers in the faith (John 13:34) can be placed squarely upon the doctrine that the Bible is the inerrant word of God. They each saw the other as "teaching and preaching against the word of God." Therefore, the other side was against God and "the true religion."

Sadly, this evil and idolatry did not die with Luther and Zwingli but was perpetuated and exaggerated by their disciples. Today, because of it, we have had more than sixty-two Lutheran divisions and one hundred twenty-five in the Reformed church.[10] While some of these resulted because of political, linguistic, and geographical barriers, most were from a direct struggle to be faithful to the 'pure word of God'. In an appropriately titled book, *We Condemn*, Hans Werner Gensichen quotes Luther: "When a point of disunity in doctrine is reached, then there must be a separation, and it will become apparent who the true Christians are – namely those who have God's Word, pure and straight."[11] It is clear that such thinking was behind the division between Luther and Zwingli. Such thinking has divided almost every Lutheran group since that time, or at least kept groups apart.

In this day of increasing cooperation between Christians of various denominations, two major mergers of five denominations, and increasing dialogues between previously very hostile groups, Luther's thinking seems almost humorous. Most contemporary Christians do not think in terms of the "true Christians," or that they are the possessors of God's word "pure and straight." For over four hundred years, however, the type of exclusivity portrayed in Luther's thought has reigned throughout Protestantism.

While the Reformed and Lutheran churches could hardly be called loving brothers and sisters in the Lord, they did not wage war against each other. This or that Reformed or Lutheran state might engage in conflict, but usually the conflicts were not religious in nature. Such was not the case in the next division in the Protestant Church.

While the first division of the Protestant Church could be described as a division between two individuals, Zwingli and Luther, the next division would have to be described as a movement, because it occurred with many individuals in many places. This division occurred ostensibly over the issue of baptism. The movement totally rejected as being unbiblical the practice of infant baptism. Because they re-baptized individuals who had been baptized as infants, they were called Anabaptists. The Anabaptists did not accept the appellation of

---

[10]F.E. Mayer, *The Religious Bodies of America* (St. Louis, Missouri: Concordia Publishing House, 1961), pp. 192–228. This is a very low estimate. It does not include the huge number of churches that have again split off from the Reformed or Lutheran churches. For instance, in the small city of Duluth, Minnesota, the small denomination of the Finnish Apostolic Lutheran Church has split into two other churches.

[11]Hans-Werner Gensichen, *We Condemn*, trans. Herbert J. A. Bouman (St. Louis, MO: Concordia, 1967), p. 57.

Anabaptists because they did not accept as valid the practice of infant baptism in the first place. For them, the only legitimate form of baptism was believer's baptism – that is, a baptism administered to a person after he or she made a profession of faith in the Lord Jesus Christ. Menno Simmons (1492–1559), the founder of the Mennonites, and one of the few Anabaptist theologians who were able to systematize Anabaptist thinking and whose work survived the persecutions, described the Anabaptists' problems with infant baptism in the following way:

> Brethren, brethren, how long will you oppose the Holy Ghost? Give the *Word of God its* due praise, and observe that little irrational infants are in baptism not buried with Christ, nor are they raised unto newness of life; for if they die, and if they were buried in baptism, then sin would be so destroyed in them that it would never more vanquish their spirit. Since, then, sin even after their baptism, so powerfully and so abundantly flourishes in them when they begin to come to years of discretion, as may be plainly seen, therefore the proponents of infant baptism must acknowledge that they bury the children alive, which should not be done; or else that they baptize them without faith contrary to the ordinance of Christ. [12]

It needs to be underscored here, even though it is clear in the text when Simmons says, "Give the Word of God its due praise," he is not saying praise to Christ, the living Word, but rather "praise the Scriptures." While it is clear that Simmons shared the same idolatrous view of Scriptures that Luther and Zwingli had, he never reached the level of deprecation of the others' views that Luther and Zwingli did. However, earlier in the work just cited, Menno Simmons asserted, "Little ones must wait according to God's Word until they understand the Holy Gospel of Grace; and then and then only is it time for them to receive Christian baptism as the infallible word of our beloved Lord Jesus Christ taught and commanded all true believers in his Holy Gospel." [13] Thus Luther and Zwingli were not true believers.

Luther countered the Anabaptist position stating:

> . . .In Infant Baptism. We bring the child with the purpose and hope that he may believe and we pray God to grant him faith. But we do not baptize him on that account, but solely on the Command of God. Why? Because we know that God does not lie. My neighbor and I– in short, all men– may err and deceive, but God's Word (the Scripture) cannot err. [14]

Heinrich Bullinger, Zwingli's son-in-law and his theological successor,

---

[12]Menno Simmons, "Christian Baptism," pp. 231–287, *The Complete Writings of Menno Simmons*, edited by John Christian Wenger and translated by Leonard Verduin (Scottsdale, PA: The Herald Press, 1974), 263. Italics are mine. Henceforth, Simmons. "Christian Baptism" was written in 1539.

[13]Simons, p. 241. Throughout Simmons' works, he refers to the "true religion," "true believers," "true brothers and sisters," and "true church." He even wrote a tract entitled: "The True Christian Faith." p. 321 ff.

[14]The Book of Concord, p. 444.

wrote in the II Helvetic Confession:

> We condemn the Anabaptists who deny that young infants of faithful parents are to be baptized. For, according to the doctrine of the Gospel, 'to such belongs the kingdom of God' (Luke 18:16) and they are written in the covenant of God (Acts 3:25). Why, then, should not the sign of the covenant of God be given them? Why should they not be consecrated by holy baptism, who are God's particular people and are in the Church of God? We condemn also the Anabaptists in the rest of those peculiar opinions which they hold against the Word of God (The Bible). (Schaff, Confessions, III p. 169).

This was the reality after the Reformation on the European continent. There were three different Protestant groups. Each reading the same Bible and arriving at three different conclusions. Each believed that its view was the "true faith," and the others' views were of the devil. Of the three, the Anabaptists evoked the greatest hostility. The Reformed and Lutheran leaders saw the Anabaptists not only as a threat to the reformation, but a threat to the very existence of the Protestant states themselves. The Reformed and Lutheran states with the support of their theologians entered into a terrible persecution of the Anabaptists. But it was not just the Lutherans and the Reformed Church. The Roman Catholic Church was equally vicious in the suppression of the Anabaptists. Within the span of nine years (1527–1536), practically all of the Anabaptist leaders and thousands of their followers were killed.

The reaction of the Lutheran, Catholic, and Reformed states was totally unjustified. Not only was the persecution totally inconsistent with Jesus' teachings but, from a very practical perspective, it was unwarranted. Most Anabaptists could not be seen as a threat to the state. Most were pacifists and could not resort to violence of any kind, much less overthrow a government. Some believed that all governments were sinful and corrupt but necessary because of the sinful state of humanity. They, themselves, could not pledge an oath of allegiance to any form of government because they believed that the taking of such oaths to be biblically wrong. Certainly most of them represented no threat to the established authorities! Only two of the early Anabaptists, (1523–1531), Thomas Münzer and Waldemier Hubmaier, believed that governments should be violently overthrown. Münzer and Hubmaier believed that if a government did not perform by biblical principles, the citizens had the right – indeed, the duty, to overthrow that government. That Münzer and Hubmaier were not representative of the Anabaptists did not make a difference for the Lutheran, Reformed, or Catholic states. Anybody who re-baptized was thought to be either an anarchist or just plain anti-government. (Schaff, VIII, pp. 69–87)

This is illustrated by the martyrdom of Felix Manz, who was one of the first Anabaptists to be killed. Manz tried over and over to convince Zwingli and the Zurich fathers that he was not against their government and was not attempting to overthrow them. He stated that he simply wanted to be free to preach and practice his piety. It was to no avail. On June 5, 1527, he was drowned by the Zurich authorities. The following execution notice documents just how threatening Manz and the rest of the Anabaptists were to the Protestant states:

> Because he has baptized, against Christian regulation; because
> it was found to be impossible to bring him back from it through
> any instruction or admonition, because he and his followers
> have thereby separated themselves from the Christian congre-
> gation, and have riotously joined themselves together, as a
> schism, and are trying to organize themselves as a self-made
> sect, under the appearance and cover of a Christian congregation,
> because such doctrines are injurious to the general custom of
> Christendom and lead to scandal, tumult, and rebellion against
> government, to the universal peace, brotherly love and civil
> unanimity, and to all manner of evil.
>
> Therefore Manz shall be handed over to the executioner who
> will bind his hands, place him in a skiff, bring him to the lower
> Huttli, move his bound hands over his knees, and pass a stick
> between his knees, and elbows, and will thus bound cast him
> into the water, and let him die and corrupt in the water . . .[15]

It is really difficult to believe the above mentioned incident happened in
any state, much less a "Christian state." Blaurock, Manz's friend, was drowned
next and then thousands were killed. The masses had a popular expression to
describe the executions. The expression was: "Eintunken, Eingetungt!" It was
a sinister play on words and a diabolical expression. Simply translated, it
meant: "He who dunks, gets dunked (Schaff, VIII, p. 82)." While Luther and
Zwingli never openly endorsed massive persecutions, neither did they speak
out against the monstrous barbarisms. Luther said he would have preferred
to win the Anabaptists by biblical teaching. He, then, gave aid and comfort to
these villainous acts by calling the murdered Anabaptists, "Martyrs of the
devil." Zwingli is not recorded as having stated anything about the persecution.
His silence most likely was interpreted as acquiescence to these heinous
crimes against God.

Both Luther and Zwingli, if they had so willed, could have used their
considerable influence to prevent the atrocities from happening. At the very
least they could have spoken out against the slaughter of these innocent
Christians. After all, both reformers had the courage to stand against the
powerful forces of Rome; they could have strongly condemned these abuses.
That they did not speak out against these abuses is a considerable judgement
against both of these gentlemen. It is difficult for us in a western civilization
in the twentieth century to understand how such pious men as Luther and
Zwingli could commit such monstrous crimes against humanity. It is easy for
those of us who are not invested in defending their theologies to portray them
as villains and totally write off whatever else they may have done.

When, however, a study of the times is made, it is easier to understand
how these pious men could allow such evil things to happen. Under no circumstances can these things be justified or condoned. Just as the evil that happened
in Germany before and during World War II can be understood, it should
never be condoned. The fact that Luther and Zwingli did not vehemently

---

[15]H. E. Dosker, *The Dutch Anabaptists* (Philadelphia: The Judson Press, 1921), pp.
34–35.

condemn the atrocities heaped upon the Anabaptists must be weighed in the same light with the Christians in Germany who did not speak out against the abuses that were heaped on the Jews.

From a human perspective, Luther's and Zwingli's reactions to the Anabaptists are understandable. Unlike our civilization, where it is necessary to tolerate a great many voices asserting that they are endowed with the exact truth, Luther and Zwingli lived in an age where there was no such tolerance. It must be remembered that Galileo's and Copernicus' thinking were still very esoteric. While Columbus had discovered the New World, few people knew it. For most people the world was still thought to be flat. The universe was still thought to be two levels, with heaven above and the ghastly fires of hell below. Life on this earth was particularly difficult for the common person, and getting into heaven was of ultimate concern. The Age of Reason or Enlightenment was a long way off. People's lives from peasant to noble revolved around religion. The Holy Roman Empire was still intact with the emperor still receiving his blessing from the Pope.

Both Luther and Zwingli knew very well that previous attempts to reform the Church were ruthlessly crushed by the Empire. A pious and peaceful group of people called the Waldensians were all but wiped out by the troops of Pope Innocent III, in the years 1198–1216. In the fifteenth century two other reform movements were likewise ruthlessly crushed. These two reform movements were led by two priests, John Wycliffe (1330–1384) and John Huss (1372–1415). John Wycliffe, a graduate of Oxford University, was one of the great intellects of the Middle Ages. Wycliffe translated the Bible into English and believed in the reformed principle of *Sola Scriptura*, that all matters of doctrine and faith must be settled by the Bible rather than by canon law or ecclesiastical hierarchy. John Huss was a popular Bohemia priest who in 1403 defended Wycliffe's theology at University of Prague when the majority of the faculty were condemning it. To Wycliffe's reforms, Huss added the stipulation that at the Mass the cup of wine should also be given to the lay persons. Huss was summoned to Constance, Italy, by the Holy Roman Emperor, Sigismund. There he was arrested and imprisoned. The Council of Bishops and theologians, assembled by Sigismund, condemned Huss to be burnt at the stake. The Council did not stop there. The Council ordered Wycliffe's remains dug up and then burned. The Holy Roman Emperor then waged a holy war against the supporters of Wycliffe, called Lollards, and practically eliminated them. Because of Huss' popularity and the rugged terrain of Bohemia, Huss' followers called Taborites fared better than the Lollards.

Luther and Zwingli believed that if they and the states which supported them were weak, their fates would be similar to the other reform movements.[16] They correctly perceived that the intrusion of the Anabaptists would attract people from the Reformed and Lutheran views and weaken them. The Anabaptists were drawing great numbers by their preaching, and house churches were springing up everywhere, drawing many worshippers away from the Reformed and Lutheran churches. Of course, both Zwingli and Luther argued that the Anabaptists were leading the people away from the true religion to their damnation in a false religion. On this ground and this ground alone, in

---

[16]Indeed, Zwingli was killed by the Papal forces on November 11, 1531, and the Reformed forces defeated, but not destroyed.

there are a wide variety of Baptists. There are the Two Seeds in the Spirit Predestinarian Baptists; The National David Spiritual Temple of Christ Church Union (Inc.), U.S.A. (The Universal Christian Spiritual Faith and Churches for all Nations); the National Baptist Evangelical Life and Soul Saving Assembly of the U.S.A.; Primitive Baptists; Pre-Millenarist Baptists; Post-Millenarists; Duck River Baptists; Adventists; Seventh Day Adventists; and far too many more to list in this small book.[23] Every little group has found some justification in the Bible which was the very word of God, where they had the truth and the other Christians missed the mark.

The situation has been no different for the Reformed Church. While the splinters in the Reformed Church have not been as numerous and exotic or humorous as the Baptists, they are not far behind the Baptists. From the Reformed Church have sprung many variations of the Reformed Church–including the Huguenots in Spain and France; all varieties of Presbyterians; The Christian Churches (Disciples and Independents), and the Church of Christ with its varieties. There is also a Church of God that claims its heritage from the Reformed Church. From this Church came The Church of the Living God and The House of God which is the Church of the Living God, the Pillar and Ground of Truth, Inc.[24]

While there are nowhere near the number of Lutheran branches as there are Reformed and Baptists, that is not because Lutherans are much more saintly than the Reformed and Baptists. It is because there are many fewer Lutherans than there are members of the Baptist or Reformed churches. Until recently, many of the Lutheran Churches have tended to stay within the nationalities of their backgrounds. They did not reach out and evangelize people from other nationalities. Thus, German Lutherans remained German; Swedish remained Swedish; and so on. But the Lutheran Churches have consistently maintained the strong insistence of Luther that they, and only they, had the "pure Word of Truth." Any softening of that position has usually meant a new Lutheran Church springing into existence. Such was the case of the formation of the Evangelical Lutheran Church in America in 1846; The National Evangelical Lutheran Church in 1898; The Evangelical Lutheran Synod in 1918; The Protestant Conference in 1928; The Orthodox Conference in 1951; the Church of the Lutheran Confession in 1959; and the Association of Free Lutheran Churches in 1986.[25] Furthermore, any softening of the Doctrine (that the Bible is the inerrant Word of God) by less conservative Lutherans has resulted in deeper entrenchment of the already very conservative Missouri Synod and Wisconsin Synod Lutheran churches.

From a different perspective, the church in which inerrancy has not been significant has been the church that has split the least. The Church of England, where the Prayerbook is just as important as the Bible, has been the least factious.[26] On the other hand, one of the few splits from the Church of England, the Methodist Church, where inerrancy has been essential, has split over and

---

pacifism.

[23]Mead pp. 19 ff.

[24]Mead, in loc.

[25]Mead, 130–146.

over again. From John Wesley's Methodists have sprung 26 different Methodist and Wesleyan churches and innumerable holiness churches. In this group is found such churches as The Free Christian Zion Church of Christ; The Fire Baptized Holiness; The Pilgrim Holiness Church; and The Christian Nation Church. [27]

And so it goes in the Christian Church. Most of the 2050 divisions of the Christian Church have no dispute over the trinity, divinity, or resurrection of our Lord Jesus Christ. Only a few such as the Unitarians/Universalists, Mormons, and Jehovah Witnesses reject these doctrines. These groups would hardly be accepted by others as Christian anymore. Most of the other groups have found some verse or emphasis within the Bible which they consider their justification for existence.

Thus, the sword dividing the Church is not the Spirit of God which moves people to proclaim the Lordship of Jesus. That which has caused what seem to be insurmountable obstacles and unbridgeable chasms in the body of Christ is none other than the doctrine that the Bible is the inerrant word of God. The doctrine may be wielded by egotists and persons who desire to walk in absolute certainty, rather than by faith; nevertheless, if the Bible were not held in such an idolatrous position the inerrancy doctrine never could have caused the damage it has.

---

[26]In recent days issues such as revising the Prayerbook, the ordination of Women and homosexuals has stretched the bonds of the Episcopalian Church and Church of England to the breaking point.

[27]Mead 108, 173, 69

Chapter III

The Word Of God Is Living And Active

With all the chaos in the Church that has been brought about by the doctrine that the Bible is the inerrant word of God, it should come as no surprise to the Christian that not only is there no support for the doctrine within the early creeds of the church, but the doctrine finds no support in the Bible. It is neither explicitly stated nor is it implied. There are absolutely no statements in the Bible that declare, "The Bible is the word of God," or, "The Bible is the inerrant word of God." This is a simple matter of fact, and takes no further elaboration. The fact that the doctrine is not even implied in the Bible will take a great deal of explanation, simply because so many churches and so many Christians have long thought the doctrine to be based on biblical teaching.

From the very beginning the statement, "The Bible is the word of God," is at conflict with the biblical concept of the word of God. By the 'word of God,' the statement means that the word is the revelation from God. It is the end product of the activity of God's revealing himself. For many conservative Christians there is a slight difference between whether the Bible *is* the literal word of God, or whether it *contains* the word of God. The fundamentalists believe, of course, that the Bible is the literal word of God. Less extreme conservative to moderate Christians believe that the Bible contains the word of God and the exact nature of that word needs to be discovered through study of the times, and the text. However, as appealing as this thought is to more contemporary thinking people, this latter view still is not consistent with the biblical concept of the word of God.

A person does not have to know Hebrew or Greek to find out that not only does the Bible not consider itself the word of God, but that the very essence of the word of God must prevent the word of God from being identified with the Bible. *Webster's Third New International Dictionary* defines "word" as:

> An articulate sound or series of sounds which through conventional association with some fixed meanings, symbolizes and communicates an idea, without being divisible into smaller units capable of independent use: that has meaning when taken by itself... Hence the written or printed character or combination of characters expressing a unit of discourse; as words on the page. [1]

Simply stated, in English 'word' means the use of a letter or letters in combination to communicate an idea or group of ideas. Our brains think thoughts and these thoughts are expressed in words and these words are

---

[1]Philip Grove, ed. in chief, *Webster's Third New International Dictionary* (Chicago: Encyclopædia Britannica, Inc., 1961), Volume III, in Loc.

expressed in language. While 'word' may have colloquial meanings such as one's promise or an oath, its prime meaning is rational, ideational or noetic. In English, there are to be found such expressions as "that person's words moved me to tears," or "I was transported to such and such place by your words." These expressions are to be considered symbolic or metaphoric. Words in themselves have no power. When we speak or write words we do not expect our speaking or writing to produce action. It is human beings, or trained animals or automated machines specifically programmed by humans who will act after words are spoken. Words do not act!

The word: The Creative Force

Genesis 1:3: "And God said let there be light and there was light."

Such is not the case, however, with the biblical concept of the word of God. In the Bible when God speaks it is not like an idea human words convey. It is not a passive thought upon which God or man must act. In Genesis 1, God speaks and when he speaks it is obvious that what he speaks is not for human hearing. In verses 1–25, God speaks eight times. This happens all before God created human beings. After God brings light into existence, the story continues. "**And God said**, 'Let there be firmament in the midst of the waters, and let it separate the waters from the waters. And God made the firmament and separated the waters which were under the firmament from the waters which were above the firmament. **And it was so**" (Genesis 1:6–8). This is the way the creation story proceeds. Every time God speaks some aspect of creation comes into existence and there was no human being to hear God's speaking.

Of God's speaking creation, Martin Luther observed: "The expression is indeed remarkable and unknown to the writers in all other languages, that through his speaking God makes something out of nothing (*Luther's Works*, Volume I: pp. 16–20)." That Luther would input such originality to the whole creation story is not shared by many contemporary critics. Many modern scholars have found elements of pagan mythology within the creation story. Most are quick to point out, however, that biblical narration transforms the stories doing away with the pagan thought.[2] One of the contemporary scholars, Herman Gunkel, points out that in Babylonian and Egyptian myths gods utter magic words and creation comes into existence, but it is the words that unleash the power of creation, and not the gods, themselves. In the creation story, it is God, Elohim, who creates, not some magic formula.[3] God speaks and creation is. Another excellent explanation of differences in creation of the Bible and pagan mythology is found in Gerhard Von Rad's commentary. Von Rad states:

---

[2]E. A. Speiser *Genesis*, Volume I: AB, pp. 16–20. Henceforth Speiser; John Skinner, *Genesis*, revised edition (New York: Charles Scribner's Sons, 1925), pp. iii–xxviii, xxxiv–xliii, 4–19, 41–50; Robert Graves, and Raphael Patar, *Hebrew Myths* (Garden City, NY: Doubleday & Company, Inc., 1969), pp.21–47.

[3]Hermann Gunkel, *Genesis,* 5th (Gottingen: Vandenhoeck & Ruprecht, 1922), pp. 120 ff.

The idea of creation by the word preserves first of all the most radical essential distinction between Creator and creature. Creation cannot be even remotely considered an emanation from God; it is not somehow an overflow or reflection of his being, i.e., of his divine nature, but is rather a product of his personal will... This creative word, in distinction from every human word, is powerful and of the highest creative potency. In the second place, therefore, the idea of creation by the word expresses the knowledge that the whole world belongs to God. It is his creature; he is its Lord... With regard to the history of religions, one cannot deny that there is a connection between this idea and the belief in magic. (The god Marduk, for example, in the Babylonian epic of creation also displays his power before the gods through effective magical words...) But it is also clear that in Israel the idea was purified theologically of every vestige of the magical through centuries of Priestly tradition. This is a good illustration of the fact that in the history of religion terms and ideas obviously related to another occasionally have nothing more than a certain formal similarity...[4]

The Word: God's Relationship with People

Genesis 15:1 After these things the word of the Lord came to Abram in a vision saying:

When God speaks, what he speaks is remarkably different from anything that humanity has spoken or conceived of speaking. It is powerful and it is creative. This fact is borne out almost every time in the Bible the expression "the word of God" is found. The phrase occurs first in Genesis 15:1-20. In the context of the passage it is late in the life of Abram (Abraham). He has left the land of the Chaldeans, the city of Ur, the home of his father and is in a place called Mamre. The text reads, "After these things the word of the Lord came to Abram in a vision saying, "Fear not, Abram, I am your shield. Great will be your reward." What ensues is a conversation between the word of God and Abram. What human word can do that? But the amazing qualities of the word of God do not just end with the Word conversing with Abram.

The picture which the pericope portrays is one in which Abram is in his tent. The text does not tell us whether he is awake or asleep. The Word of the Lord comes to him in a vision. After the Word says that Abram's reward will be great, Abram gets contentious with the Word. He says most sarcastically, "O Lord God, what will you give me, I am childless, and the heir to my house is Eliezer of Damascus." The Word of the Lord responds: "This man will not be your heir, your heir will be your own flesh and blood." Verse five states: "And he took him outside and said, 'Look up into the heavens, and count the stars if you are able to count them, so shall be your descendants.'" It is very clear that the only 'he' that could possibly be referred to here is the 'Word of the Lord.' The Hebrew word, ויצא, which is translated 'brought', is in the

---

[4]Gerhard Von Rad, *Genesis*, trans. John H. Marks (Philadelphia: Westminster Press, 1961), pp. 49–50. Henceforth Von Rad, *Genesis*. For the Babylonian creation epic see "Enuma elis" in ANET pp. 60–72. By permission of the publisher.

Hiphil or causative form meaning 'to cause to go out,' 'to lead out,' 'to bring forth.' The action is strictly that of the word of the Lord. It cannot be interpreted as if 'word of the Lord' was a command of God to Abram, and then Abram went outside on his own accord nor can the action that transpires here be interpreted to be a mental state as a dream or fantasy. Nor can it be interpreted as a metaphorical statement that we might make like, "With his words, he transported me to the land of enchantment." This is the actual physical transporting of Abram from one spot to another spot. The text does not state that Abram was brought outside by God. It specifically states that the word of the Lord is the agent that transports Abram. As Von Rad points out, the word of the Lord is nothing more than the extension of God, God in action.

The occurence of the word of God coming to Abram, speaking and carrying on a conversation with Abram, and then carrying him outside must mean that the word of God here is no mere "abstraction," or "a combination of syllables or letters." It is a personal being. It relates. It thinks. It speaks. It acts. It is God. These characteristics of the word of God are not unique to this one passage. The description of word of God here is the essence of the word of God in the whole Old Testament. The phrase "the word of the Lord" occurs 224 times. The Word is found as an active agent, "coming to a person" 110 times.

The Word: The Agent of Judgment

I Kings 13:1: "A man of God was brought from Judah to Bethel by the power of the word of the Lord."

I Kings 13 contains one of the most interesting narrations of the word of God. Here the word of God is directly instrumental in producing behavior of a person or an angel. The story involves an unnamed prophet and the villainous king Jeroboam. After being brought to Bethel by the Word of the Lord the prophet denounces by the power of the Word of God the altar established by Jeroboam (vs. 2). Through the action of the word of God the altar splits apart and ashes pour out (vs. 5). The man of God refuses to go home and eat with Jeroboam because he states the word of God told him (vs. 9): "You shall neither eat bread nor drink water, nor return by the way you came." When this man of God believes the lies of another prophet and goes home and eats with the other prophet, he is killed because he "disobeyed the word of the Lord (vs. 26; cf. vss. 11–32)."

There is a similar incident that is recorded in I Kings 20:35–36. Here one of the sons of the prophets orders 'by the word of the Lord' another man to strike him (vs. 35). The man refuses to strike the son of the prophets. Because the man refuses to do what the word of God commanded, the man was devoured by a lion. No matter how one interprets this passage, the power still remains with the word of God.

There is other strong evidence in the books of the prophets to support the fact that the word of God in the Old Testament was not just revelatory, but the agent of judgment. In Isaiah 9:8, the prophet states: "The Lord has sent a word against Jacob and it will light on Israel (R.S.V.)." The time is the Syro-Ephraimatic war of 734 B.C.E. Israel has just suffered a stinging defeat at the hands of Syria. Instead of repenting as Isaiah had called them to do, the Israelites say, according to Isaiah: "The bricks have fallen but we will build with dressed stones; the sycamores have been cut down, but we will put cedars in their place (vs. 10)." What the Northern kingdom was saying was, "We will turn this temporary setback into a much better system." They were stating this with the ultimate "arrogance and pride in their heart (vs. 9)." Consequently, the Lord God sent the Syrians and Philistines against Israel (vs. 12). But it would not be the Philistines and the Syrians who would 'burn' and 'consume' the land of Israel. It would be the word of God. The Syrians and the Philistines were simply the agents through whom the word of God was working.

The twenty-third chapter of Jeremiah likewise reveals the distinctiveness, the power, and the destructiveness of the word of God. This passage (verses 9–40) contrasts the false prophets and the faithful prophet. Jeremiah describes the false prophets as "quick in doing wrong and powerful in crime (vs. 10)." They are "godless (vs. 11). They lie, commit adultery, and they are shrewd in supporting evil people in power (vs. 14)." Yahweh describes the false prophets this way:

> I have heard what the prophets say who make their lying prophecies in my name. 'I have had a dream,' they say, 'I have had a dream!' How long will they retain this notion in their hearts, these prophets prophesying lies, who announce their private delusions as prophetic? They hope, by means of the dreams that they keep telling each other, to make my people forget my name, just as their fathers forgot my name in favor of Baal. Let the prophet who has a dream tell his dream as his own. And let him who receives a word from me, deliver it accurately! (vs. 25-28, J B).[5]

This deceptive word of the false prophets (cf. Jeremiah 7:1–11; 6:13–15; 5:12–13) is in sharp contrast to the word of Yahweh. Yahweh states very emphatically and very tersely (Jeremiah 23:29 JB, cf. 5:14): "Does not my word burn like fire—It is Yahweh who speaks—is it not like a hammer shattering a rock?" As the heathen nation of Syria was the agent through whom the word of the Lord worked for Isaiah, so in Jeremiah the agent of the word was "a nation from afar, an invincible nation, a nation whose tongue you (they) do (did) not know... (Jeremiah 5:15)" It was Babylon (Jeremiah 20:4–6; 21:1–10; 24:1–7, etc..). Babylon would consume Israel like a fire (5:14). The proclamation of the word of God by the prophet becomes fire issued forth in the words of the prophet consuming the people of Judah (Jeremiah 5:14). They would 'devour,' 'harvest,' 'food,' 'sons,' 'flocks,' 'herds,' 'vines and fig trees,' and they would 'bring down the fortified cities,' which the Jews believed were indestructible. Babylon would, in short, destroy the 'good life' the Jews had come to know. There would be famine and absolute destruction of Judah

---

[5]While the Jerusalem Bible translation of this passage is excellent and gives the sense of sarcasm, the translation of אֱמֶת, amet, as "accurately" is weak. The best translation in English of amet is "faithfully." While accuracy is indeed part of amet, amet is more than the correct reporting of words. It is the conveying of the message and the passion behind the message. This is why so frequently the revelation occurs through a symbolic event such as the loin cloth in chapter 13; Jeremiah was not to take a wife or have children, 16:1–4; he was not to comfort any mourners, 16:5–7; he was not to feast, 16:8–9; He was commanded to go to a potters house, 18:1–12; he was to break a pot in the valley of ben-Hinnon, 19:1–13; he was given a cup to have the nations drink, 19: 1–38;etc.

as a state (5:10–6:38). Again it would not be Babylon that was doing it, but the word of God proclaimed by the mouth of Jeremiah (5:14; 23:29).

There is a case study of difference between lying prophets and a prophet who is the true agent of the word of God in I Kings 22:1–38. King Jehoshaphat of Judah is asked by Ahab, the King of Israel, to wage war against Syria. Jehoshaphat properly suggests that they first inquire from the word of God whether they should attack Syria (vs. 5; cf. II Cron. 18:4). Then King Ahab assembles 400 prophets whom he knows will tell them what he wants to hear. He asks them: "Shall I go to battle against Ramothgilead or shall I forbear?" The prophets respond: "Go up; for the Lord will give it into the hand of the King (vs. 6, RSV)." King Jehoshaphat sensing that "the deck is stacked" asks whether or not there might be another prophet. Ahab responds that there was and his name was Micaiah. Micaiah, however, never gave Ahab positive advise. But at Jehoshaphat's insistence they consult Micaiah. Micaiah at first mockingly goes along with the prophets, but then at Ahab's insistence he gives the true word of God. The true word was that Yahweh had put a lying spirit in the prophets to entice Ahab to attack Syria who would then destroy Ahab. After that Micaiah is thrown in jail. Ahab disguises himself as a common soldier, and goes with Jehoshaphat who wears the attire of the king to attack Syria. The Syrians first attack Jehoshaphat thinking that he is Ahab. When they find out that they were wrong, an archer shoots an arrow into the crowd and lo and behold, it hits Ahab. It was not the archer who dispatched Ahab but the word of God. (vs. 38).

The Word: Agent of Healing and On-Going Creation.

Isaiah 55:11, "So shall my word be that goes forth from my mouth; it shall not return to me empty, but it shall accomplish that which I purpose, and prosper in the thing for which I sent it."

God's word in the Old Testament had not become simply the agent of God's wrath and destruction. According to Psalm 147, God's word was intricately involved in sustaining creation. Verses 15–18 reads according to *The Jerusalem Bible*:

> He (Yahweh) gives an order; his word flashes to earth:
> to spread snow like a blanket, to strew hoarfrost like ashes,
> to drop ice like bread crumbs, and when the cold is unbearable,
> he sends his word to bring the thaw and warm wind to melt the
> snow. (Parentheses mine)

There is no support in the Bible for the Deist concept that once God created the world he set it up to follow natural laws never to become involved in its functioning. The very metaphor that is developed in Isaiah 55 reveals that the word of God was intricately thought to be sustaining creation. Verses 6–13 read:

> Seek the Lord while he may be found, call upon him while he is
> near;
> Let the wicked forsake his way, and the unrighteous man his
> thoughts; let him return to the Lord, that he may have mercy
> on him, and to our God, for he will abundantly pardon.
> For my thoughts are not your thoughts, neither are your ways

my ways, says the Lord.
For as the heavens are higher than the earth, so are my ways higher than your ways and my thoughts than your thoughts.
For as the rain and snow come down from heaven, and return not thither but water the earth, making it bring forth and sprout, giving seed to the sower and bread to the eater,
so shall my word be that goes forth from my mouth; it shall not return to me empty, but it shall accomplish that which I purpose, and prosper in the thing for which I sent it.
For you shall go out in joy, and be led forth in peace; the mountains and hills before you shall break forth into singing, and all the trees of the field shall clap their hands.
Instead of the thorn shall come up cypress; instead of the brier shall come up the myrtle, and it shall be to the Lord for a memorial, for an everlasting sign which shall be cut off. (RSV)

It would be a grave mistake, here, to identify nature with the word of God. It is clear from the text that the word of God is in control of nature. As it was earlier in Isaiah where the word of God used Syria (9:8), the word of God uses nature as the instrument of joy. In verse 13 it is clear that after Israel returns to the Lord (vss. 1–7), that which happens to the land is a direct result of the power of the word of God. In the deserted and forsaken soil of Israel and Judah (Isaiah 5:6; cf. Genesis 3:18) left so by Syrians (and it can be safely assumed Babylonians) who deported the Jews, thorns and briars controlled the landscape. With the return of Israel's heart to the Lord, and because the word of God controls creation, majestic giant cypress and beautiful, fragrant myrtle break forth in the land. The fact that the mountains and hills break forth in singing and the trees clap their hands is not mere metaphor. It is because the word of God controls creation and can make it do anything God wants.

There are some very strong parallelisms in the New Testament. One passage to recall to any Christian's memory is of Jesus' triumphal entry into Jerusalem. The reader will remember that the Jewish authorities attempted to get Jesus to quiet the crowd from singing his praises. Jesus responds: "I tell you if these were quiet, the very stones would cry out (Luke 19:40 RSV)." On another perspective, at the death of Jesus, creation goes into mourning. There was darkness over the land from the sixth hour to the ninth hour. There was an earthquake, rocks split apart, and the curtain in the temple split (Matthew 27:45–54). In his *Anchor Bible Commentary*, John Mckenzie gives a very compelling exposition of Isaiah 55:11. He stated:

In Hebrew "word" and "deed" are expressed by a single word; the unity of the two ideas is most impressive when it is the word of Yahweh, for Yahweh's word is the externalization of his person. Yahweh's words are acts; his acts are also words, for they are intelligible, and meaningful, even if, as is stated in vss. 8–9, they escape the comprehension of man. This is the paradox of the word of God, that it is both the most meaningful and the most mysterious of words. (AB, 20, p.144)

The problem in the history of the Protestant church, contemporary fundamentalism, and much of conservative Christianity, as this book abundantly points out, is that too many of these Christians believe that they have totally comprehended the word of God. This, as McKenzie stated, is totally impossible and his comments on vss. 8–9 are worth observing. He wrote:

> Yahweh's saving purpose can be grasped and must be accepted; but no one should be so rash as to think that he comprehends its entire scope. Yahweh cannot communicate his whole purpose to man, for man is too small to understand it. Man must surrender to the truth that there are dimensions to the ways of Yahweh that lie beyond revelation. Yahweh never stoops to the level of man, or to the lower level of human prudence. (AB, 20, p. 144)

Another contemporary commentator, A. S. Herbert, not quite as profoundly but much more succinctly, wrote: "What the all powerful Lord decrees will be effected in the created world or in the life of his people. His word is full of power of him whose purposes are beyond man's grasp..."[6] The nineteenth century theologian and biblical scholar, John Peter Lang set forth a very compelling explanation:

> The word is no mere sound or letter. Emitted from the mouth of God, it acquires form and in form it conceals the divine live by reason of its divine origin and so it runs alive of God endued with divine power, charged with the divine commission as swift messenger through nature and the world of man.[7]

On Isaiah 55:10 Luther wrote:

> Here you hear that He is speaking of ways and thoughts which have to do with the Word. He (God) is not speaking sublime thoughts... He does not say "our (preacher's, apostle's, or prophet's) works and thoughts do this," but, "my Word"... So our building and promotion of the Church is not the result of our works, but of the word of God which we see everything is produced by the word of God. (*Luther's Works*, Volume 17, in loc)[8]

---

[6]A. S. Herbert, *The Book of the Prophet Isaiah Chapters 40–66* (Cambridge: Cambridge University Press, 1975), in loc.

[7]John Peter Lang, *A Commentary on the Holy Spirit,* trans. by Philip Schaff (New York: Charles Scribners' Sons, Inc., 1878), in loc.

[8]It is obvious from the above that Luther did not share the view of transcendence of the word that the other three commentators shared. While Luther would totally deny that he, himself, possessed the word, he is quick to point out that a great many others–the Papists, the enthusiasts, the Sacramentarians, the Anabaptists, and those who followed Erasmus' thinking, the Reformed Church, and thus those who likewise followed Zwingli's thinking, did not have God's Word. Luther put it this way in interpretating vs. 8, "For My thoughts are not your thoughts:"

> And I, Martin Luther, know that I am feeble. Many think that they have faith when they have made a specter of faith for themselves, but when they are in danger, they slip. So the Sacramentarians babble with regard to the words of the Lord's supper, but they forsake the Word and labor with their own thoughts...Thus all Sacramentarians and Anabaptists are Pelgians...

In other words Luther's faith was by God and the others were of their own doing. It did

The word of God as found in Isaiah as well as the rest of the Old Testament is the power of God working in the World. While this or that person may be the agent of the word of God, the word does not remain with or upon this or that person. There is no possible way to limit or tie the word of God to even the Jews. The word of God is independent. The word of God creates, comes, speaks, consumes, destroys, breaks, builds up, and heals. The word of God is living and active.

The Word: Jesus the Christ

John 1:1, "In the Beginning was the Word and the Word was with God and the Word was God ."

On a superficial level it would appear that in the New Testament the whole tenor of the word of God has changed. The expression, "the word of God came and said" and all of its corollaries that occur so frequently in the Old Testament is almost totally missing from the New Testament.[9] The word does not seem to be the driving force of the anger of God. In the New Testament, if there is an agent of the anger of God it is the result of man's own sin (Romans 1:18–32) or it is apocalyptic judgment unleashed by four horsemen (Revelation 6), or by angels (Revelation 7, 8, 9, 10, 11) or the Son of man, or Jesus (Matthew 13: 41–43; 25:31–46; John 5:22).

Yet it is very clear from the New Testament that the dynamic and powerful nature of the word of God of the Old Testament is the very present. The word of God has just taken on a slightly different description but almost every Christian theologian would contend that this description is inherent within the Old Testament itself. Every child in Sunday School and almost every Christian knows by heart: "In the beginning was the Word and the Word was with God, and the Word was God. He was in the beginning with God; all things were made through him and without him not anything made that was made (John 1:1–3 RSV)." In Christianity, there is universal agreement that the "Word" here is none other than Jesus.[10] It is very clear that John has every intention of equating the word of God that created the World in Genesis 1 and Psalm 33:6–8 and the word of God that came and spoke to the prophets with Jesus.

---

not matter whether the Anabaptists, Sacramentarians, or Papists believed in God the father, or Jesus Christ, they all had forsaken the "Word and labored by their own thoughts."

[9]There are only two occurrences of the expression in the New Testament. The first is found in Luke 3:2. Here it is simply stated that the word of God came to John and then it is stated that he went into Jordan. In this one very brief thought, it is possible to infer a great deal. It would seem clear that Luke did not accept the later belief that there was no inspiration after Ezra. It could possibly also be inferred that Luke perceived John as the last of the Old Testament prophets, and that now the word of God was to be found in Jesus. The second occurrence is found in John 10:38, but then that is a reference to an Old Testament passage.

[10]The only real dispute over the verse has been on the nature of which Jesus was God. Arius (250–336), as was pointed out in the introduction p. 5, believed that because Jesus was called "the begotten Son τον υιον τον μονογενη"in John 3:16, he therefore must be a lesser being than God the Father. Likewise Charles Taze Russell (1852–1916), the founder of the the Jehovah Witnesses, argued that because in John 1:1 the article ο was omitted in front of Θεοσ that it should be translated,"the word was a god" not "God" and therefore Jesus was not equal to God the Father. .

Hebrews 4:12, "The word of God is living and active, sharper than a two edged sword, piercing to the division of soul and spirit, of joints and marrow, and discerning the thoughts and intentions of the heart."

Hebrews 4:12 is another definition that would equate the word of God of the Old Testament with that of the New Testament. Unlike John 1:1 there is not unanimous support for one interpretation of Hebrews 4:12. Because of various interpretations and the role this verse has played in the support of inerrancy, it has to be dealt with extensively. There have been basically three or four types of interpretations of Hebrews 4:12.

Most of the early Church fathers believed that the word of God in Hebrews 4:12 was identical with the word of God in John 1:1.[11] St. Ambrose, one of the heroes of the fourth century and bishop of Milan, Italy (374 C.E.) interpreted the passage in the following way:

> The Son, as the Word, carries out the will of the Father. Now, a word as we understand and use it, is an utterance... But the words we speak have no direct efficacy in themselves, it is the word of God alone, which is neither an utterance nor an "inward concept," as they call it, but works efficacious, is living and has healing power.
> Wouldst thou know what is the nature of the word of God—hear the scriptures, "For the word of God is living and mighty, yea, working effectually, sharp and keener than any sharpest sword, piercing even to the sundering of soul and spirit, of limbs and marrow"... Thou hearest Him called the living word, the healing word—seek not to compare Him with the word of our mouth...[12]

The second and the predominant interpretation of the Hebrews 4:12 passage has been that the word of God was equated with the proclaimed gospel message. The great preacher and reformer in Geneva, Switzerland, John Calvin (1509–54) interpreted the word in Hebrews 4:12 to be the preached word. Calvin in his usual clarity and preciseness makes sure that it is understood that the preached word does not have independent existence outside of God. His comment on Hebrews 4:12 was as follows:

> Further we must notice that the Apostle (Paul) is here discussing the word of God which is brought to us by the ministry of men. Those notions that the internal word is certainly efficacious that which comes from mouth of men is dead and lacking any effect, are crazy and even dangerous. I admit the efficacy does not come from the human tongue, nor does it lie in the sound

---

[11]Brooks Foss Westcott, *The Epistle to the Hebrews* (Grand Rapids, Michigan: Wm. B. Eerdmans and Company, 1970), p. 101 ff. Henceforth Westcott, Hebrews.

[12]St. Ambrose, Nicene and Post-Nicene Fathers, X, 271. In the seventeenth century, John Owen, a Cambridge University scholar and theologian, likewise identified Jesus as the word. He did a masterful study of the Greek language and the Old Testament and concluded that the Bible could not be meant. His work is worth looking at for its excellence in scholarship. *An Exposition of the Epistle of Hebrews* (London: James Black, 1815), in loc.

itself, but ought to be wholly ascribed to the Holy Spirit; but this does not prevent the Spirit bringing the power in the word that is preached.

Calvin believed that the power of the word was displayed also in the fact that when it was preached it would make listeners 'fidgety' and they would run from the word.[13] Many modern scholars have likewise interpreted the word of God the proclaimed word pronounced by the prophets of the Old Testament or the Christian preachers.[14]

The third interpretation likewise occurred in the same time frame as the interpretation of Ambrose. It comes from the pen of Augustine (354–430), the famous bishop of Hippo in Northern Africa. Augustine uses Hebrews 4:12 to interpret Psalm 149:6–7 which reads: "May the praise of God be in their mouths and a double-edged sword in their hands, to inflict vengeance on the nations and punishment on the peoples." (NIV) Augustine picks up on the sword in verse six and states:

> "And swords sharpened on both sides in their hands." This sort of weapon contains a great mystical meaning, in that it is sharp on both sides. By "swords sharpened on both sides," we understand the Word of the Lord: it is one sword, but therefore are they called many, because they are many mouths and many tongues of the saints. How is it two-edged? It speaks of things temporal, it speaks also of things eternal. In both cases it proveth what it saith, and him whom it strikes, it severeth from the world. Is this not the sword whereof the Lord said, "I am not come to send peace upon the earth, but a sword"? Observe how he came to divide, how he came to sever. He divideth the saints; he divideth the ungodly... The word of God cometh, and severeth the son from the father... Wherefore then is it in their hands, and not in their tongues? By "in their hands" he means in power. They received then the word of God in power, to speak where they would, to whom they would, neither to fear power nor to despise poverty. For they had in their hands a sword; where they would they brandished it: and all this was the power of the preachers.... Lastly we can understand these "hands" another way also. For they who spake had the word of God in their tongues, they who wrote, in their hands. (NF (1st), VIII, 679)

It is obvious that now the word of God, this two-edged sword, is not only the preached word but it is the word of God written. This becomes very clear

---

[13] Calvin, Hebrews in loc.

[14] J. H. Davies, *A Letter to Hebrews* (Cambridge: Cambridge University Press, 1967) in loc.; James Moffatt, *Epistle to the Hebrews* ICC, in loc.; Hugh Montefiore, *The Epistle of Hebrews, Harper's New Testament Commentaries* (San Francisco: Harper & Row, Publishers, Inc. 1964), in loc.; Markus Barth, "Old Testament in Hebrews" in *Current Issues in the New Testament,* edited by Wm. Kassen (New York: Harper Brothers Publishers, 1967), pp. 53–78; also Markus Barth, *Ephesians,* Volume 34 A, AB, pp. 687–699; 775–777; 779–780, henceforth M. Barth, Ephesians 34 or 34A. Brooke Foss Westcott, *The Epistle to the Hebrews* (Grand Rapids, MI: Wm. B. Eerdmanns Publishing Company, 171), p. 102. Henceforth, Westcott, Hebrews.

in the next two sections. In these two sections, Augustine discusses how the Christians "inflict vengeance on the nations" (as Psalm 149:7 reports the Jews doing to the gentiles). The way they inflict vengeance on the nations is by incorporating the word of God into their lives. Of course, at that time every Christian did not have a copy of the Scripture. The way they incorporate this sword was because they were "nourished in the Church." In the Church Christians heard "God's Word read," and thus were able to incorporate the word of God, the scriptures, into their lives. With the Scriptures (the two-edged sword) incorporated into their lives, the Christians were able to beat back and slay the temptations of the world, and thus "inflict vengeance on the nations." (NF (1st), VIII, 680)

It almost goes without saying that most modern conservative and fundamentalist commentators interpret the word of God in Hebrews 4:12 to be the Scripture. Homer Kent Jr., one of the most recent of these stated it this way

> The word of God is not a reference to the personal logos, but describes the revelation of God enshrined as Scripture. The argument in context has been based on certain Old Testament passages, particularly ones showing that God opens his rest to believers but denies it to unbelievers. Now the author reminds the reader that God's Word continues to distinguish between the believers and the unbelievers. [15]

E. C. Wickham, in his Westminster Commentary on Hebrews, states it similarly: "The word of God is not in the sense of John 1:1 but equals the utterance of God: i.e. the warning, promises, and teaching of Scripture."[16] It would be a fair assumption to make that by "the warning, promises and teaching of Scripture" Wickham means the same thing as Kent's phrase "the revelation enshrined in Scripture," and "the warning, promises and teaching of Scripture" are for them the description of Scripture.[17] As to how the Scriptures are living Simon J. Kistenmaker asserted:

> The writer (the author of Hebrews) reminds the reader, the word of God cannot be taken lightly; for if the reader does not wish to listen, he faces no one less than God, himself (see Heb. 10:31; 12:29). The Bible is not a collection of religious writings from the ancient past, but a book that speaks to all people

---

[15]Homer A. Kent, *The Epistle to the Hebrews* (Grand Rapids, Michigan: Baker Book House, 1970), 89.

[16]E.C. Wickham, *The Epistle to the Hebrews* in *Westminster Commentaries* ed. by Walter Lock (London: D. D. Methuen and Company, Ltd., 1922) in loc.

[17]The following commentators fall into this perspective: A. C. Hendricks, *The Epistle to the Hebrews* (New York: Charles Scribner, 1868) in loc.; Philip Hughes, *A Commentary on the Epistle to the Hebrews* (Grand Rapids, MI: Wm. B. Eerdmans, Inc., 1977; Simon J. Kistemaker, *Exposition of the Epistle to the Hebrews* (Grand Rapids, MI: Baker House, 1984); Charles F. Pfeifer, *Hebrews* (Chicago: Moody Press, 1969) in loc.; Oliver B. Green, *The Epistle of Paul the Apostle to the Hebrews* (Greenville, S. C.: The Gospel Hour, Inc., 1969) in loc. A. T. Synge gives a slightly different slant from a more scholarly position. He suggests that what the writer has in mind is not the Scripture, but rather a collection of sayings that the Church fathers had compiled to help the Jews accept Jesus. *Hebrews and the Scriptures* (London: S.P.C.K., 1959), pp. 53–58.

everywhere in nearly all languages of the world... Nothing remains untouched by Scripture for it addresses every aspect of man's life.[18]

There is a fourth interpretation of the word of God which this author brands as mystical. This view is represented by Luther. In his exposition of Hebrews 4:12, Luther gives two interpretations of the word of God. In the first he states:

> In the first place, "it is living," it gives life to those who believe. Therefore we must hasten, lest we perish in death. In the second place, it is "powerful," because it makes those who believe able to do everything. In the third place, "it is sharper than any two-edged sword," because it is nearer and more available than things are to themselves. In Jer. 23:23–24 we read: "Am I a God at hand... and not a God far off?... Do I not fill heaven and earth? says the Lord."... Therefore since the Lord is present everywhere, one should believe in Him with all confidence; for he can help us everywhere, even if everything forsakes us everywhere. (*Luther's Works*, 29, 164.)

Luther's statement is far from clear, but I believe that it is closer to an accurate understanding of the word of God in Hebrews 4:12 than gained by most Lutherans and Protestants since his time. In the first sense it sounds as if Luther is interpreting the word of God as the Gospel message: it is living because it brings life to the believer and through it the believer is able to do everything as Jesus states in Matthew 17:20 "If you have faith as a grain of mustard seed... etc." But then it would appear to be God himself. Luther stated that the word of God is "nearer... than the thing itself," and then to buttress the nearness of the word he quotes from Jeremiah 23:23–24.

In the second interpretation, Luther sounds closer to John 1, and his terms sound like Paul's description of Christ in Ephesians 1:15–25 and Revelation 1:16.

> Therefore since the word of God is above all things, outside all things, with all things, before all things, behind all things, and therefore everywhere, it is impossible to escape to any place. But since it is "living" and therefore eternal, it is impossible for the punishment or cutting to ever cease. But since it is "powerful," it is impossible to resist it. Finally, since it is "sharper than a two-edged sword," it is impossible to hide or be concealed. And thus unbelievers will be tortured with endless, eternal, and incurable cutting. (*Luther's Works*, Volume 29, p.165)

In terms of today's more exacting hermeneutics, it would appear that Luther was taking considerable liberties with the text and that he was imposing elements into the text that the author of Hebrews did not have in mind. The author of Hebrews does not state that the word of God "cleans" and "purifies", and that the unbeliever is subjected to "endless, eternal and incurable cutting." Those elements have to be imported from other concepts in scripture or from

---

[18]Simon J. Kistemaker, *Exposition of the Epistle to the Hebrews* (Grand Rapids, MI: Baker House, 1984) in loc.

Luther's own thinking. Nevertheless Luther's concept of the word of God is close to the understanding of Hebrews 4:12. This will be clear from a totally different passage of Luther's works, which will be cited in this author's exegesis of the passage later in this chapter. It certainly is not clear in Luther's exposition of Hebrews 4:12.

Hebrews 4:12 is one of the many texts in the Bible the exact meaning of which may escape us until the second coming. However, because of our knowledge of Greek, it is possible to rule out one of the above four interpretations. The one that is the easiest to eliminate is number three, that the Bible is the word of God. The reason for this is the two adjectives that describe the word of God; *living*, ζων and *active*, ενεργης.

The definitive reason the Bible cannot be implied here is the use of the Greek term ζων for "living." In Greek there are two verbs used to describe the process of living, ζαω and βιοω. Βιοω and its noun βιοσ imply not so much the principle of life but rather the mundane operation within the specific creature. Life in these terms is understood as the universal principle of all people and living things and distinguishes them from inanimate, inorganic or just plain dead things, whether they had life or lost it. But even more ζωη is the soul of the person, φυχη or in Hebrew, נפש. As God breathed into humanity the breath of life and humanity became a living being, so the ζωη is this very breath of life (Gen. 2:7). So when in the New Testament that which is described as living ζων it has a soul and it lives. If the writer wanted to make a metaphor that the sword, i.e. the Scriptures, gave life to the reader, by reading them and through them the reader finds life eternal; he would have used a form of βιοω. (TDNT, II, 832–874.)

A good example of how in the New Testament what would seem to be an abstraction in English but which is, indeed, alive is found in I Peter 1: 3, "Blessed be the God and Father of our Lord Jesus Christ! By his great mercy we have been born anew to a living hope through the resurrection of Jesus Christ from the dead (RSV)." Here "living hope (ελιδα ζωσαν, accusative singular participle of the verb ζαω)" is not some metaphor like 'Hope springs eternal," or "His memory lives on in his work." This hope lives because this hope is Jesus Christ who was raised from the dead and is the hope of all Christians and all people.

The very next adjective that the author of Hebrews uses to describe the word of God corroborates the fact that the word can not in any way be considered the Scriptures. The writer states that the word of God is active. The Greek word that is used is ενεργης. Ενεργης does not occur in the Bible as frequently as ζωη, but its interpretation is easier to grasp. Ενεργης is derived from the verb which means to be operative, be at work, put forth power, ενεργω (Thayer). Ενεργω is a composition of two Greek words. The first is simply the preposition which is the English translation "in". The second is εργεω meaning "I work." The etymology of the English word "energy" is found in the Greek word ενεργεω. The difference in the meaning between the Greek word ενεργεια/ενεργεω and the English word "energy" underscores why the Bible cannot be considered the word of God. In English energy means: "Internal or inherent power; capacity of acting, or producing an effect, whether exerted or not (Webster)." Objects such as coal, gas, and oil are considered energy. These elements are all passive, that is to say they have to be acted on, ignited, to produce power that is inherent in them. Thus these objects and

42

this definition do not qualify for the Greek ενεργεω/ενεργεια. These objects and the English definition of energy are more descriptive of another Greek word, δυναμις. Δυναμις implies having the ability to produce energy. Ενεργεω/ενεργεια is action, it is that which is in motion, it is that which produces. The Bible cannot on its own work or carry out any action or produce anything. It therefore does not qualify for the word of God that is ενεργης, active. Furthermore, *The Theological Dictionary of the New Testament* points out that ενεργεω is largely used in relationship to God or spiritual powers such as demons (II, 652–655). This is all the more support for the fact that here in Hebrews 4:12, the word must be Jesus .

The most troubling aspect of Hebrews 4:12 must be examined. How is it possible that a biblical writer could compare "the lamb of God who takes away the sins of the world" with a sword? The initial observation is that the author does not state that the word of God is a sword. The author is comparing the word with a sword. It must be assumed that the sword is a metaphor. But even assuming that, talking about Jesus "piercing to the division...of joints and marrow" is bothersome.

In the New Testament the metaphor of a sword is very infrequent. There is one place where the sword is found in connection with Jesus in the gospels. There Jesus says that he came not to bring peace but the sword (Mt. 10:34; cf. Lk. 12:51). The sword here is not Jesus but rather faith in Jesus that brings division between blood-related brothers, sisters, mothers, fathers, etc. In Ephesians 6:17 Paul admonishes Christians to take "the sword of the Spirit which is the word of the Lord." This verse will be examined in great detail in the next chapter. None of the other references to sword in the New Testament help us understand how the author could possibly consider applying the metaphor to Jesus. Even Revelations 1:16 where the "son of man" appears in all his "radiance" Jesus is not compared to "the two-edged sword" which issues from his mouth.

If, on the other hand, we turn to the Old Testament there is an oversupply of metaphors dealing with God and the sword. In Deuteronomy 32:41–42 the Lord says that if he is forced to by the disobedience of Israel, he would "whet" his "glittering sword" in judgment. The sword, itself, will "devour flesh." In Isaiah 31:8 the Assyrians fall from a sword that in no way belongs to man, but is solely the agent of God. In Zechariah 13:7 the Lord speaks directly to the sword saying, "Awake my sword against my shepherd." Jeremiah speaks directly to the sword. He does not, however, ask the sword to strike an enemy of Israel. He pleads with the sword saying: "Ah sword of the Lord! How long till you are quiet? Put yourself into your scabbard, rest and be still! (47:6)" The prophet realizes dejectedly that this is not to be the case. He answers his lament rhetorically: "How can it be quiet, when the Lord has given it charge. (47:7b)" In all Israel's struggles with its enemies, it is, according to the Old Testament, God or his sword who delivers Israel from its enemies. When Israel puts its confidence in its own military armaments or a military alliance with another nation, Israel is bound to fail and be doomed to destruction (Jeremiah 2:15–18). When other nations are used by Yahweh to punish Israel for its unfaithfulness, and the nations themselves take the credit or exalt themselves over Israel, they in turn are broken by Yahweh.[19]

---

[19]Isaiah 34:5–6;Psalm 14:13 Ezekiel 14:12–19; 25:1–7, Walter Eichrodt, *Theology of the*

It must be emphatically insisted that the sword of the Lord is no magical instrument working capriciously and independently of the Lord. The sword of the Lord is simply another of the many and rich variety of expressions used in the Old Testament to depict the power and presence of the Lord. It must be considered a synonym or alternative to expressions such as "the hand of the Lord," "the face of the Lord," and, indeed, "the word of the Lord."[20]

While there is not found in the Old Testament a direct connection of the word of God with the sword or "cutting" action, there is abundant evidence to support that the word of God was another synonym for the judgment of God. In Isaiah 49:2 the prophet, speaking of the word of the Lord that came to him, stated: "He made my mouth like a sharp sword." In Jeremiah 23:23–32, the Lord God compares his word to that of the false prophets and he states: Is not my word like fire,... and like a hammer which breaks the rock in pieces (vs. 29). Isaiah states: "The Lord has sent the word against Jacob and it will attack Israel. (My translation from Mt. text, 9:7; R.S.V. 9:8). There is another, similar, metaphor used in Isaiah 11: 3b–4 that is descriptive of the Messiah. The prophet states:

> He shall not judge by what his eyes see,
> or decide by what his ears hear,
> but with righteousness he shall judge the poor,
> and decide with equity for the meek of the earth;
> and he shall smite the earth with the rod of his mouth,
> and with the breath of his lips he shall slay the wicked. (R.S.V.)

It can be safely assumed that when the prophet states that the Messiah will "smite the earth with the rod of his mouth, and with the breath of his lips he shall slay the wicked" he has in mind the word of God. The type of judgment that is reflected in this passage would seem to be almost identical to that judgment expressed in Hebrews 4:12. As the word of God discerns "the thoughts and intentions of the heart" in Hebrews 4:12, so the Messiah does not judge by what the eyes see and the ears hear in Isaiah 11:3b.

Old Testament, trans. by J. A. Baker (Philadephia: Westminster Pres, 1960), II, 72 and Markus Barth, Ephesians AB, 34A, 799–800)

[20]The Psalmist begs that the Lord deliver his life from the wicked by the Lord's sword (14:13). In the very next verse (14) he begs to be delivered from men, but this time it is the hand of the Lord that is requested to do the delivering. In Ezekiel when the Lord stretches forth his hand, he stretches forth his sword (14:12–19). In Ezekial 25:1–7 the word of the Lord is reported as telling the Ammonites that because they were happy when the temple was profaned and Israel uprooted the hand of the Lord was "stretched out against" them and by it the Lord would "cut them off from the peoples (vs.7)." Job begs God to use his hand and cut him off so that he might be relieved of his misery (Job 6:9). The sword and the hand are not alone in doing this activity of "cutting." At least two times the face of the Lord is found cutting. Psalm 34:16 (MT. 17) states, "The face of the Lord is against evil doers, to cut off (לְהַכְרִית) the remembrance of them from the face of the earth." Jeremiah records the word of the Lord as saying: "Therefore thus says the Lord of hosts, the God of Israel: Behold I set my face against you for evil, to cut off all Judah (Jeremiah 44:11; cf. Lev. 17:10; 20:3–5; Dt. 31:17)."

In many places the hand does the same sort of activity that the sword does, "it cuts (כרה)." In these passages there is no attempt to place the sword in the hand of the Lord, as if the hand of the Lord was doing the cutting through the instrument of the sword, rather it is the hand of the Lord that is doing the cutting. In Exodus 9:15, Yahweh commands Moses to tell Pharaoh that if He, Yahweh, had put forth his hand, Pharaoh would have been "cut off from the earth."

It is not difficult to see how the author of Hebrews could perceive in the Old Testament that the word of God was alive and active, and at the same time compare it to the sword. The creation of all that was by the power of the Word and all is sustained by that word (Hebrews 1:3). Israel defeated its enemies not by its strength but from the force of the word of God. The armies of Babylon, Egypt, Assyria, Syria and Persia were raised up and destroyed by the power of the word of God. As the governments and peoples were weighed in the balance and judged by the word of God, so ultimate judgment was in the hands of the word of God.

It is hard to imagine with all this evidence surrounding the word of God that any person could apply the word of God to words written on pages of paper and included in a book, even if that book be called the Bible. The argument clincher, however, is found in the very next verse Hebrews 4:13: "And before Him no creature is hidden, but all are laid bare to the eyes with whom we have to do." While it is true that there are some problems in translation, almost all translations designate properly that it is the word of God who does the judging. The parallelism by the author of Hebrews is highly intentional. As the word of God distinguishes between the soul and the Spirit, and judges the inner-most thoughts and secrets of the human heart, so everything is revealed before the eyes of God. God and the word of God are not separate entities but in reality *the one and the same.*

This does not necessarily mean that the writer of Hebrews has in mind Jesus as the word of God as does John, but it does not rule out the possibility. It does rule out the possibility that the Bible is the word of God. It would also rule out the possibility that the proclaimed gospel message is the word of God if that gospel message consists simply of human words. No matter how eloquently or brilliantly it is presented; no matter how precisely the message fits the details of Scripture, if the proclamation does not have the presence and force of God, it cannot qualify for the word of God in Hebrews 4:12. The only way that the gospel message, the good news of the rest of God (Hebrews 3:7–8; 4:11) qualifies for the word of God of Hebrews 4:12 is if God, himself, is leading the captives into the throne of God (Hebrews 5:1 ff.).

The Word of God is the Gospel Message

**I Peter 1:23 : "You have been born anew, not of perishable
but of imperishable,
through the living and abiding word of God (RSV)."**

With I Peter 1:23, there is no question about what the word of God is, for the text goes on to state, "For, 'All flesh is like grass and all its glory like the flower of the grass, the grass withers, and the flower falls, but the word of the Lord abides forever.' (Isaiah 40:6-8) That word is the good news preached to you." (Verses 24-25, RSV). The question, however, is naturally raised, How can the gospel be "living?" In the earlier discussion of Hebrews 4:12, I pointed out that one of the identifications of the word of God was the gospel message, but I pointed out that the biblical evidence pointed in that direction only if Christ was alive in the message. Or, if the message was filled with the power of God that message could qualify as "living." This is a difficult concept for western minds to grasp, much less accept. One of the great exegetes of the century, Edward Gordon Selwyn, Dean of Winchester College, and fellow at

Cambridge University, probably best expressed modern thought on the passage:

> The supernatural origin or source from which believers have been begotten again is not the Word...but God's creative grace, the Word being the means of their regeneration...This significance of God's word is brought still further by the participles that qualify it; it is "living" and "abiding". It is "living" because it is the instrument of God's creative grace, cf. Is. 55:11; the fact Christ, the word fulfilled, is not simply brute fact but fact that is full of generative power...And it is abiding because the Kingdom of Christ is abiding...in contrast with transiency of all human things.[21]

Thus for Selwyn the Word does not live but because God and his grace are living and because the Word evokes life in its hearers, it can be described as "living." The qualities of "living (ζῶντος)" and "abiding (μένοντος)" are not inherent within the word itself. They are the end product of the proclamation of the Gospel.

Clearly, however, with the inclusion of Isaiah 40:6-8 in verses 24-25a I Peter intends the proclamation of the Gospel to be identified with the powerful word of God of the Old Testament. As was stated in this work the Old Testament sees the word of God as descriptive of the power of God. Thus we must ask how is it that I Peter can perceive that the Gospel message proclaimed by Jesus' disciples was "alive." For some readers to understand this it may take a little suspension of the modern need to analyze, criticize dissect, and control and perceive that early Christians held as many today hold, a more mystical view of faith. I believe that when it comes to understanding I Peter 1:23 Luther is most instructive. Luther describes how we are born anew by the "living and abiding word" in the following way:

> God lets the Word, the gospel, go forth. He causes the seed to fall into the hearts of men. Now where it takes root in the heart, the Holy Spirit is present and creates new man. There an entirely new man comes into being, other thoughts, other words and works. Thus you are completely changed... But this seed cannot be changed; it remains eternally. But it changes me in such a way so that I am changed into it and what evil there is in me because of my nature disappears completely... (*Luther's Works*, Volume 30, p. 44)

What Luther means becomes even more clear in his exposition of verse 24:

> Thus when I hear that Jesus Christ died, took away my sin, gained heaven for me, and gave me all that he has, I am hearing the Gospel. The Word is soon gone when it is preached; but when it falls into the heart and is grasped by faith, it can never slip away. No creature can invalidate this truth. The depths of hell can do nothing against it; and even if I am already in the jaws of the devil, I must come out and remain where the Word

---

[21]Edward Gordon Selwyn, *The First Epistle of St. Peter* (New York: MacMillan, St. Martin's Press, 1969), in loc. Henceforth, Selwyn.

remains. (Luther's *Works*, Volume 30, p. 45).

There is another passage from Luther that may also be helpful in understanding how the proclaimed word, the gospel message can be living. This is taken from a sermon that Luther delivered on October 19, 1522. Luther said then:

> How, then do we have Christ? After all, he is sitting at the right hand of the Father; he will not come down to us in our house. No, this he will not do. But how do I gain and have him? Ah, you cannot have him except in the gospel which he promised to you... Since Christ comes into our heart through the gospel, he must also be accepted by the heart. As I now believe that he is in the Gospel, so I receive him and have him already. (Luther's Work, 51, p. 113)[22]

In this century Karl Barth, better than I, described the mystical qualities of the Word of God. He wrote,

> For according that we know of the nature of the Word of God one thing is barred; it cannot be an entity which we could delimit from all other entities and thereby make it into an object...God's speech is different from all other speech, God's action is different from all other action...(Dogmatics I, 1, p. 186)

> The language of God is and remains God's mystery above all in its worldliness [translator Thomson's note: in the sense of belonging to the world: and so here passim] When God speaks to man, this happening is never so marked off from the rest of what happens that it might promptly be interpreted as a part of this other happening.[23] The Church in fact is also a sociological entity with definite historical and structural features...Jesus Christ in fact is also the Rabbi of Nazareth, historically so difficult to get information, and when it is...a little common place along side more than one founder of a religion...(Dogmatics I, 1, p. 188) [] Brackets mine.

> We ought not to conceive the worldliness of the Word of God as, so to speak, as a disagreeable accident some day to be removed in whole or at least in part. In this worldliness, and therefore in this twofold indirectness, we have to do with a genuine and

---

[22]I am not sure that anyone really understands Luther's thought. But I surmise that even though Luther would insist that there is *one word of God* (which "is taught from the beginning of the World." *Luther's Works*, 35, p. 153). Luther has two different concepts of the word. The first is a scholastic and very dogmatic approach which was obvious in his struggles with Zwingli and the Anabaptists. In those struggles, Luther used the Bible as the word of God, but most particularly he used his interpretation, and particularly those verses that he felt supported his interpretation to refute or ignore those who used the same Scriptures to support their views. The second interpretation of the Word, I believe, included in the above quotes is the mystical and that view I believe is closer to the biblical view of the word of God.

[23]The reader wil;l remember the Pentecost story, (Acts 2:1-13) That some people heard the gospel proclaimed in their own language, and others perceived the same event and thought the disciples were drunk.

inseparable attitude of the Word of God itself. Revelation means the incarnation of the Word of God. But the incarnation means entry into worldliness. We are in this world, we are thoroughly worldly. Were God to speak to us in a non-worldly way, he would not speak to us at all. (Dogmatics I, 1, p. 192)

By permission.

For the author of I Peter, for Barth and, I believe, for Luther the proclamation of the Gospel is an event (see p. 8 and 9 of this book) where the resurrected encounters us and grasps us. When a person hears the gospel message and through the power of God accepts it, Christ comes in and lives within that person. Christ, himself is mystically present within the message about him and therefore the message is imbued with the power of God. The Message is living because Christ himself is living in it.

In Acts the proclamation of the Gospel is described as "the word" in 8:4; in 15:35, "the word of the Lord"; in 10:36 "peace through Jesus Christ who is the Lord of all"; and in 13:32, "the fulfillment of the promise made to the fathers." However, four times — 5:42; 8:35; 11:20; and 17:18 — it is not the *word or message about* Jesus Christ that is proclaimed, but Jesus Christ *himself*, who is proclaimed.

This also is the impact of Paul's statement in Galatians 1:15–16. There, Paul stated: "But when he who set me apart before I was born, and had called me through his grace, was pleased to reveal his Son to me, in order that I might proclaim him among the gentiles." The sequence of events is important here. On the road to Damascus when the Lord confronted Paul, it was not a message about Jesus which was communicated to Paul. It was Jesus who appeared to Paul. Then Paul does what he was set apart to do; bring Jesus to the gentiles.

It is apparent from the New Testament the means through which Paul and the other disciples brought Jesus to the gentiles and to the Jews does, indeed, contain verbal communication. There are several messages or extractions of the messages in the book of Acts of attempts to communicate Jesus to unbelievers (Acts 2:14–36; 3:12–26; 4:8–12; 5:28–32; 7:1–53; 10:34–43; 13:16–43; 16:31–32; 17:21–31; 22:3–22; 24:10–21; 26:2–23). In most Western theological thinking, including most contemporary Lutherans, the proclamation of Jesus would be interpreted to be equal to words about Jesus. In the New Testament and, indeed, the first three centuries of the church, this was by far not the case. Even the apostle Paul denigrates the power of words. He states in I Corinthians 2:1–5 (New International Version):

> When I came to you, brothers, I did not come with eloquence or superior wisdom as I proclaimed to you the testimony about God. For I resolved to know nothing while I was with you except Jesus Christ and him crucified. I came to you in weakness and fear, and with much trembling. My message and my preaching were not with wise and persuasive words, but with the demonstration of the Spirit's power, so that your faith might not rest on men's wisdom, but on God's power.

This, indeed, is the essence of the New Testament word of God. It is why it is living and active, and why it remains forever, because it is not just words, it is the power of God. Because in much of Christianity the word of

God has become equated with dogma, "correct thinking," "correct believing," and words written on paper–the Bible. The correction may be painful and difficult, but will be necessary in order to achieve a long overdue faithfulness to the truly dynamic and living Church.

The first place to begin with the understanding of the New Testament word of God is with Jesus' promise in Matthew 18:20. He stated there: "Where two or three are gathered in my name there I am in the midst of them." According to Jesus, then, he is not just as Luther stated at the right hand of God the Father, but where two or three are gathered in his name there he is in the midst of them. This is why in the New Testament the disciples were sent out in sets of two: Peter and John; Paul and Barnabas; Paul and Silas, etc.

The proclamation of the Gospel in the early church was not, as it is in most contemporary churches, the result of a single erudite, scholarly, charismatic preacher, who has labored long and hard on a text, or maybe just a Saturday evening "rush job." The proclamation of the gospel in the early Church was an event that grew out of the presence of Christ among at least two people. The proclamation of the gospel is found in power, and it usually is accompanied by "great signs and wonders" (Acts 4:33; 8:13; 5:12; 6:8; 19:11–12; cf. 2:1–13; 3:1–10; 4:10; 9:32–42; 13: 4–12, etc.). It was not the disciples who performed these great wonders and signs. It was Jesus, the resurrected Lord, who was in their midst who performed the miracles. Likewise the word which they proclaimed was "alive" because Christ "the word of God" was alive in that proclamation (See Acts 3:11–25).[24]

---

[24] The fact that the man is healed in the name of Jesus and by faith in that name (Acts 3:16) must not be interpreted as meaning that the name of Jesus is a magic formula if pronounced over a person, making that person well. Rather "the fulness of the being and work of Jesus (T.D.N.T., V, 272–280)" is there. Otherwise the healing is conducted by Jesus who the Jews crucified out of "ignorance" (vs. 17) but who is nevertheless present in their midst (vs 26).

Chapter IV

The Word Of God Is Growing

The Christian Church has proclaimed uniformly throughout its history and among all but a few sects that Jesus was God. And while he has been honored and respected as a great saint and the builder of the gentile Christian church, never has any sect (to the knowledge of this researcher) asserted the divinity of Paul. Yet, through the doctrine of inerrancy, Paul's thinking has been elevated to a level equal to, or even above, the words of Jesus. Consequently, the writings of Paul require inordinate attention.

Paul did not often use the phrase "the word of God" but when he did it is apparent that he had in mind the gospel message: that Jesus was God in man reconciling humanity to God (I Cor. 14:36; II Cor. 2:17; 4:4; 6:7; Gal. 6:6; Phil. 1:14; Col. 1:25; I Thes. 1:8; 2:13; 4:15; II Thes. 3:1; II Ti. 2:9; and Ti. 2:5). However, there are two verses where this is not at all clear. Because of this ambiguity, these two verses are among the most misinterpreted and distorted texts in the Bible.

The Word: The Sword of the Lord

Ephesians 6:17

**"And take the helmet of Salvation,
and the sword of the Lord which is the word of God."**

The Distortion: The Bible – the Sword of Contention

The dogmatists in the Church have long identified "the sword of the Lord which is the word of God" in Ephesians 6:17 as the Bible. In the history of the struggles within Christianity, they have used the Bible as the "sword of Spirit," to carve out from their midst all those who held differing opinions. This has been well illustrated in the works of the reformers and the Anabaptists cited in the second chapter of this work. The concept that the Bible is the sword of the Spirit is so entrenched within large segments of Christianity that challenging the interpretation might seem like a most formidable task. Many who were raised in conservative churches might remember attending Sunday School classes, released-time Bible schools, and summer Bible camps during which there would be a Bible Drill. "Raise your swords!" The leader would command, and all the children would immediately lift their Bibles over their head. Book, chapter, and verse would be shouted out, and the first child to find the verse was proclaimed "victor." Those who have watched television evangelists and listened to the radio preachers will have heard great exhortations to take up the sword of the Bible against the evils of the world and against the Godless liberals.

The demonic way the Church used the Scriptures was so very apparent during the reformation; Luther, himself, was a paramount example of how the Church had perversely interpreted Ephesians 6:17. In exposition of Psalms 45:3 "Gird your sword upon your side..." Luther used Ephesians 6:17 to exhort the Christians, "The Lutherans" to use the Scriptures against "the heretics,"

> For this reason war breaks out with the devil, who will not let God's people go, just as Pharaoh refused to let the Jews go and fought against Moses (Ex. 5:2 ff.). The same is true with us this very day. When we want to lead God's people out, Pharaoh swells with anger and rises up against us. The power of the Word is shown in this, that Christ fights in us with His armament, "with the breastplate of faith and the sword of the Word" (Eph. 6:16,17). So we strike the enemy on all sides, first by laying bare his deceit and lies in the heretics, then by snatching up and defending our men so that they may persevere in holy faith and life. This warfare goes on interminably, and there is no hope for peace....The lying teachers, however, we will overcome not by patience and silence, but against them we must draw the two-edged sword (Heb. 4:12) with which "we destroy all knowledge that exalts itself against the knowledge of God." (2 Cor. 10:5).
>
> ...You, therefore, brethren and fathers, who someday will administer the affairs of the churches, should be armed and trained not only to teach and instruct the good who think correctly in the faith, but also to combat and reprove the adversaries. Otherwise the churches will soon be scattered if there are not people who fight the battle front and refute the adversaries, men who expound the passages and ideas of Scripture that the enemies have stolen, and defeat the truth....This is our war; no matter how dangerous and difficult it may be; it is still most joyous because the victory remains ours. (*Luther's Works*, Volume 12, pp. 216–217).

This "enemy," these "heretics," were not persons who denied the divinity of Jesus. They believed that Jesus was Lord and believed it of paramount importance for the Christian to follow his teachings. They fully accepted the Trinity. They applauded Luther for the Reformation. They believed, with Luther, they were justified by faith and by faith alone. By the criterion of the early Church councils they were orthodox, but they disagreed with Luther over the nature of Communion and Baptism. Because of these disagreements they became "the adversaries" of the "truth."

The type of intolerance to difference that Luther presents in this passage has been so typical of the dogmatic preachers who are the correct thinkers and who think they have "the truth" on their side. They believe that to challenge them is to challenge God. However, when Luther and those like him use Hebrews 4:12 and Ephesians 6:17 to justify severing people with differences they show gross perfidy and inability to read the scriptures. The warfare in which they engaged against fellow-believers finds no justification in the texts they cite.

This paranoia and dogmatism is, of course, not just confined to Christianity. Other religions, such as Islam, are just as intolerant or even more intolerant than Inerrantist Christians. Islam, while accepting Judaic and Christian predecessors totally rejects interrelations with those who do not accept

Mohammed as the final and ultimate prophet and Allah as the only true God (Koran, Surah VIII). Furthermore, while there is not in the Koran a description of armor, there are plenty of passages in the Koran that permit or allow the use of force to extend the cause of Allah and to justify the forced conversions across Asia and Africa (Koran, Surahs VI–XII). The Koran is filled with passages like the following: "Fight against those who have been given the Scripture and believe not in Allah...and follow not the religion of Truth...(Surah IX, 29)"

There is an important difference in the quotes from the Koran and from Luther. When the Koran says "We" Allah is implied. When Luther says "We" he means either himself or the ministers that accept his teachings. Thus his cause is the Lord's and the Lord's cause is his. The sword of dogmatism has worked havoc in the World.

It is hard to find parallels anywhere to Paul's spiritual armor. There is, however, found in Jewish sectarian literature a description of military paraphernalia which when contrasted with Paul's spiritual armor underscores the fact that Paul's armor is of a totally different nature. The description of this paraphernalia is found in the Qumran Communities' *The Scroll of the War of the Sons of Light against the Sons of Darkness*. The Scroll was drawn up by a very pious Jewish Essene some time from sixty to eighty years before Paul.[1] As is apparent from the title of the scroll this was a description of an ultimate cosmic and apocalyptic battle. This military paraphernalia would have better fitted Luther's purposes. Today this community is called Qumran. Among the instruments of war were banners and trumpets that carried religious or spiritual denotations. The banners were to have one of the following ascriptions: "Truth of God," "Justice of God," "Glory of God," and "Judgment of God." As they began the battle they were to write on each one of the banners the following expressions: "Right hand of God," "Appointed time of God," "Panic sent by God," or "slain by the right hand of God." After the battle was over they were to write: "Exalt thou God," "Magnify thou God," "Praise of God," or "Glory of God." The most important instrument of war, as it was for Joshua at the Battle of Jericho (Joshua 5:13–6:21), was the trumpet. Each trumpet likewise had an ascription written on it. Some of these were as follows: "Those called by God," "Peace of God in the encampment of His saints," "God's mighty deeds to scatter the enemy and to put to flight all opponents of justice," and "Disgraceful retribution to the opponents of God."[2]

The whole tenor of the Scrolls is that the Sons of Light, who were the faithful Jews, of whom the author was one, would wipe out the Sons of Darkness. Yigael Yadin, in the Introduction to the Scroll, suggests that included in the Sons of Darkness are the Romans and those fellow Jews who sided with the Romans or did not side with the Essenes.[3]

While Luther or other Christian theologians do not go into such vivid

---

[1]Yigael Yadin, ed., *The Scroll of the War of the Sons of Light against the Sons of Darkness*, trans. by Batya and Chaim Rabin (Oxford, Oxford University Press, 1962), p. xi., Henceforth *The Scroll of War*.

[2]*Scroll of War*,III:4, 1–7, pp. 266–269; IV:6,6–8, p. 274; III:4, 1–7, pp. 266–269.

[3]Yadin, Introduction to *Scroll of War*, p. 18 ff.; I:2, 8–12

details describing the weapons, strategy, and slaughter of the infidel and heretics by the hands of believers, through their dogmas and preaching, they inflamed the passions of the people and the civil authorities to bring about the same results. Their sword has been the sword of the Bible, to use Luther's words to "strike the enemy on all sides."

Of course down through the years conservative scholarship rallying to the cause of dogmatism has mostly interpreted "the sword of the Spirit" to be Scripture. Here again I have to ask the lay reader to bear with the process. The ongoing section is utterly necessary to show how Scripture has been twisted in support of a doctrine that should not exist. The first interpretation that I intend to deal with is that of Scottish biblical scholar, John Eadie, (1810-76), who wrote of Ephesians 6:17:

> By "the word of God" we understand the gospel or revealed will of God and to us it is in effect Holy Scripture. And this weapon "the word of God" is "the sword of the Spirit" who supplies it. By special influence of the Spirit, plenary inspiration was enjoyed, and God's ideas became, in the lips and from the pens of apostles and prophets, God's word. [4]

The reader will note that nowhere in his text does Eadie state why "we understand" that "the gospel or revealed will of God and to us it is in effect Holy Scripture" is "the word of God." If he had simply stated that the word of God was the gospel, he would have had plenty of verses to support that claim (I Cor. 14:36; II Cor. 2:17; 4:4; 6:7; Gal. 6:6; Phil. 1:14; Col. 1:25; I Thes. 1:8; 2:13; 4:15; II Thes. 3:1; II Ti. 2:9; and Ti. 2:5). When he adds, "or revealed will of God and to us it is in effect Holy Scripture" he transgresses the rules of exegesis and places his own prejudices in the text. The problem is then compounded by his adding, "By special influence of the Spirit, plenary inspiration was enjoyed, and God's ideas became, in the lips and from the pens of apostles and prophets, God's word." Nowhere in the text are there any such ideas even hinted.[5]

In the following conservative scholarship, the Gospel gets totally left out and the sword becomes completely identified with the Scriptures. Such is the case with conservative biblical scholars E.K. Simpson and F.F. Bruce, in *The International Commentary* on Ephesians :

> The Epistle to the Hebrews employs the same figure (4:12, the sword); to set forth the trenchant power of Scripture, its scimitar edge, capable of sundering the joints and marrow and dissecting the intents of the heart. This soul-searching quality makes it the chief medium of conviction, far more availing than the subtlety or eloquence of the preacher. A Bible text smites the conscience point blank or floors self-righteousness as no weapon of moral fabrication would do.

---

[4]John Eadie, *Commentary on the Epistle to the Ephesians* (Edinburgh: T. & T. Clark, 1883, reprinted by Zondervan Publishing House, Grand Rapids, MI), in loc.

[5]The phrase, "plenary inspiration" has a life of its own. I quoted earlier in this work (Introduction, p. vii, footnote, #3) B. B Warfield as stating that we must trust "a plenarily inspired Scripture," At Niagara on the Lake, Ontario, the birth place of Fundamentalism, in 1878 one of the five fundamentals of the Christian was the belief in the "verbal plenary inspiration of the Bible".

Again there is no justification in Simpson and Bruce's exposition how they know this to be an accurate interpretation. Simpson and Bruce do not stop simply with the identification of the sword with the Scripture. They take the opportunity to attack theologians and biblical scholars who advocate Biblical criticism:

> The clairvoyants of modern criticism, do with doubt treat the word of God as a half erased or overwritten, the original purport is only to be detected by a lavish use of chemicals; or they read the contents asquint or upside down in their process of hypothetical re-concoction, proudly misstyled scientific. They split the seamless robe into shreds and patches in order to mend its texture. But a mutilated Bible is what Moody dubbed it, "a broken sword." [6]

Similarly Francis Foulk in his Tyndale Commentary on Ephesians identifies the sword with the Scripture but he adds another feature, typical of conservative hermeneutics. Foulk wrote, "The Lord's use of the word of Scripture in his temptations (Mt. 4:1–10) is sufficient incentive for the Christian to fortify himself with the knowledge and understanding of 'the word' that he may with similar conviction and power defend himself by it in the onslaughts of the enemy." [7] Here the element of vilification is added to the dimension of the opposition. When a person or a group disagrees over a passage or interpretation of faith, they become opponents. In their opposition they place themselves on the side of the devil. Therefore as Jesus "dispatched the devil," these opponents can be dispatched with a quote or two from the Bible. Thus Luther dispatched the Anabaptists and all others who disagreed with him. Likewise countless other demagogues have dispatched those who dissented from their views. These religious zealots, like Luther, often perceived the opposition to their views as coming not from mere mortals. It was fomented by the devil, the ultimate evil. Consequently, every means of purging the dissension, the evil, had to be used, burning at the stake, drowning, beheading, or countless horrendous acts of cruelty, all in the name of Jesus.

The Restoration: The Gospel – Creating the Kingdom of Love and Forgiveness

It will be apparent by the end of the following exposition that there is absolutely no support in the text for the assumption that the Sword of the Spirit is the Scripture. When it comes to the actual text of Ephesians 6:17, it is not, contrary to Simpson and Bruce, the "clairvoyants of modern criticism" who reconcoct the Scriptures, but the fundamentalists and conservatives who insist on inerrancy, who distort the Scriptures by imposing preconceived ideas on it.

In the complete text of Ephesians 6, the Scripture – the Bible – is not mentioned nor is the Bible even quoted. Since most uniformly in all other references, Paul has referred to the proclaimed gospel message as the word of

---

[6] E. K. Simpson and F. F. Bruce, *A Commentary on the Epistles of Ephesians and Colossians* (Grand Rapids, MI: Eerdmanns, 1957), in loc.

[7] Francis Foulk, *Ephesians, Tyndale Commentaries* (Grand Rapids, Michigan: Wm. B. Eerdmans, 1963), in loc.

God, one could safely assume that if somehow he meant something entirely different here, he would have made his point clear. Would he not have written: "Take the sword of the Spirit which is the word of God, the Holy Scripture." This, indeed, would have cemented the conservative point of view. That he makes no such statement is compelling proof that he has not changed what he means by the word of God, and that for Paul the word of God is always the gospel message.

When the complete text, Ephesians 6:10–20 is examined, one comes to the realization that the whole purpose of the Christian attire that Paul is describing is just the opposite of the purpose used by the church. Rather than being for confrontation and division, it is for transformation and protection.

In Ephesians Paul is not concerned with the struggles against false teaching as he is in the Corinthians and Galatian letters. The letter to the Ephesians is filled with affirmation. The struggle that Paul envisions, furthermore, is different even than the horrific final destruction of the Apocalypse of John (Rev. 6:8 ff.) where the followers of the beast are dispatched to everlasting damnation or that of the Qumran War Scroll where the sons of darkness are destroyed. The purpose of the armament that Paul describes is not to dispatch human beings to their death or to hell. The text specifically states that the struggle is not against human beings. The Ephesians were not, and we their successors are not struggling against flesh and blood (vs. 12), but "against the principalities," "powers," "the world rulers of this present darkness," and "against the spiritual hosts of wickedness in heavenly places." While Christians in their daily life might face derision, rejection, and persecution, ultimately it was not their friends, neighbors, relatives, or civilian or military authorities that were responsible for their problems but the spiritual forces that were aligned against God and his servants.[8]

According to Markus Barth in his Anchor Bible Commentary, while it was true that Paul described the Christian as "contending (παλη, wrestling)...against the principalities, and powers" Christ had secured the victory (Ephesians 6:12). This struggle was because these powers or forces did not know that the battle was over (see Barth). They were limping around the universe inflicting as much damage as possible before they were ultimately destroyed. The task of the Christian was to put on the armor that proclaimed the victory of God and protected the Christian from the wrath of the defeated evil powers. By "the helmet of salvation (vs. 17)," Barth suggests that Paul most likely had in mind the fancy dress helmet that was worn in the victory parade. By the expression "girded up your loins with truth" meant having put on the Belt of truth, which in the Roman Legion would have had a fancy insignia in silver or Gold identifying the Officer rank and legion, however, in Paul's system it identified the Christian as belonging to the legion of the Messiah. The other paraphernalia, as the shield of faith and the breastplate of righteousness were all defensive. According to Barth, the only really offensive part of the paraphernalia was the foot wear called the Gospel of peace. These were battle boots that only allowed the foot soldier to move forward, they did not facilitate retreat. The picture Barth believes that Paul wants the Christian to perceive is the Christian, him/herself plodding through the world of chaos pressing forward with the Gospel of peace (AB, 34A, pp. 759-808).

---

[8]H. Berkhof, *Christ and The Powers*(Scottsdale, PA: Herald Press, 1962), pp. 3 ff.

When it comes to the issue of the sword, Barth makes a very telling point. The sword, μαχαιραι, referred to in Ephesians 6:17 was not an offensive weapon. If an offensive weapon had been meant, Barth asserts, the Greek term ρομφαια, implying a large broad sword used to devastate the Roman enemies, would have been the expression designated. Μαχαιραι was a small defensive sword, used to thrust into a person who might come over the shield. It was also used to carve up an animal in preparation for cooking or eating. It was not an attack weapon. Consequently, Christian theologians have erroneously used Ephesians 6:17 as justification to attack those who disagree with them (AB, 345A, p. 776).

When it comes to the issue of "the word" Barth again makes a telling point that in Greek there are two terms that are translated as "word"– λογος and ρημα. Usually, but not always, λογος is used for a broader concept such as in John 1:1; "In the beginning was the word (ο λογος)." In the Prophets "the word of God" is most uniformly translated ο λογος του κυριου. But here in Ephesians 6:17 the term ρημα is used. According to Gerhard Kittle in the Theological Dictionary to the New Testament, ρημα means: "...The sense is clearly non-durative," "to state specifically," "saying," "treaty," "definitely stated," "expressly laid down (TDNT, IV, pp. 75-76)." Dealing specifically with ρημα Barth stated: "The term rhema (ρημα), which here and in 5:26 denotes "word" means in Pauline diction a specifically weighty, be it creative, revelatory, prophetic, or likewise binding pronouncement (AB, 34A, p. 777)."

To state it simply, if Paul had meant the entity of Scripture or that the entirety of Scripture was the word of God he would have definitely written λογος. Now λογος can be substituted for ρημα, meaning a word or words, but ρημα does not substitute for λογος in its more abstract and conceptual nature. Ρημα is not an abstraction. In the case of Ephesians 6:17 it is very specific. This word is the proclamation: "Jesus Christ, the very Son of God, who was crucified and buried, is raised from the dead and all who believe and follow him shall have life eternal." This proclamation, this word, is not now and has never been limited to a few select persons, prophets or apostles, who have been especially chosen to transmit it inerrantly. This word of God is every Christian's to proclaim. Barth, put this so eloquently: "...All the saints in Ephesus can wield the sword of the word only because they are inspired (AB, 34A, p. 777; see also pp. 799–800)."

The Spirit of God possesses all the Ephesian Christians because they are "in Christ Jesus." That the sword of the Spirit was not Paul's private possession or that it was not derived from his inspired thinking is underscored in Ephesians 6:19. Here Paul asks that the Ephesians pray for him, also that he might be given "a word" so that he might "proclaim the mystery of the gospel." It is obvious that the word he seeks is the proclaimed gospel message and it is also apparent that Paul does not know the exact nature of that "word." Paul need not ask the Christians to pray that he might know the Scriptures. He was trained as a rabbi. He knew the scriptures intimately. Furthermore, there are indications in Acts that he may not always have used a Scripture passage when he proclaimed the gospel. In Acts 14:15–17 and 17:22–31 Paul is recorded as citing no biblical text at all, and in 17:22–31, Paul even has the gall to include two quotes from Greek philosophers. Paul did not need to ask the Ephesians to pray that he might know the gospel message. Ever since he had encountered Christ on the road to Damascus (Acts 9:3 ff.), Paul knew the gospel. Professor Barth's insightful interpretation of Paul's request is appropriate: "The gospel he preaches is the unchangeable 'gospel of Christ' (Gal 1:6–8; Eph 2:17), however personal and variable his formulations and accentuations (AB, 34 A, 780)."

Paul's request was heartfelt and sincere. He needed the Ephesians' prayers because he did not arrogantly assume that he was so endowed with the Spirit in every occasion and moment that he would know exactly what God wanted him to state or how he should state it. The overwhelming evidence from his writings is that for Paul knowledge of God comes from a deep abiding relationship with Christ in which Christ himself lives in the person or dwells in that person (Romans 8:1–17; I Cor. 1:4–9; 2:1–5; 3:16–23; 4:9–13; 5:3–4:6:13–15; etc.). It does not come from knowledge of the writings of a few chosen persons who have been guided inerrantly by the Spirit. Nowhere in all of his correspondence with churches does Paul insist that as Christians they must study or memorize the Scriptures. The sword of the Lord, then, can not be equated with the Scriptures. The sword of the Lord is the gospel message. Putting the sword in the context of the spiritual armor, it is the power of God severing the person from the kingdom of darkness, of selfishness, and hate and inserting the person into the Kingdom of God; the Kingdom of love and forgiveness. Paul never meant the sword to be interpreted as a weapon to separate Christians from one another.

The Word: The Gospel Message from all Eternity

Romans 9:6

**"For it is not as though the word of God failed.
For not all who have descended from Israel belong to Israel."**

It is not clear here, what Paul means by the Word of God. At first impression it would appear that Paul has something other than the Gospel in mind. Romans 9:6 is part of a lengthy section, chapters 9 through chapter 11, where Paul deals with the problem of why the Jews rejected Jesus. While the whole pericope will be in consideration, Romans 9:1–13 will be specifically discussed.

I am not acquainted with anyone in the history of hermeneutics who has interpreted the word of God here to be the Scriptures. On the other hand, there has not been a great deal of disagreement on the interpretation of the word of God in this passage. Most commentators in the past have interpreted the word of God to be the promises or the covenants given to the patriarchs Abraham, Isaac, and Jacob, recorded in the Scriptures (Genesis 15:1–21; 17:1–22; 22:15–18).[9] Leon Morris' commentary on Romans is an excellent

---

[9]There are some very notable exceptions to this. The first and foremost being in Karl Barth's classic commentary: *The Epistle to the Romans* trans. Edwyn Hoskyns (London: Oxford University, 1933) where he wrote:

> Now, the veritable anguish of this human concern with God proceeds from the fact that the Word, round which all this busy human endeavor revolves, is not a fortuitous, transient, human word, but the eternal and absolute Word of God... The Theme of the Church is very Word of God-the Word of Beginning

summary statement of interpretation of Romans 9:6[a:] :

> Paul begins by denying that God's purpose has failed. *God's word* here means all God's promises to Israel. It is not often used in this sense in the New Testament (being more commonly a way of referring to the gospel), but there is no doubt to the meaning here. Paul has earlier said that "the promise" is by faith and that it is sure to all Abraham's seed, not only those "of the law" but also those "of the faith of Abraham" (Rom. 4:16). [10]

Most of the recent translations convey this thought also. The Jerusalem Bible translates it, "Does this mean that God has failed to keep his promise..." The New English Bible translates it, "It is impossible that the word of God proved false..." The Today's English Version translates it, "I am not saying that the promise of God has failed..."

The above commentator along with most commentators and translators have taken considerable liberty with the text. Within each of their approaches to the text is the view that Paul has in mind – a text or texts of the Scripture in which God has made a promise to, or a covenant with, Israel. The hermeneutic behind the belief is derived from the Western stress on the ideational rather than on the text itself. The argument that will be set forth here is that Paul has not changed the meaning of the word of God; that the word of God for Paul here and always is the gospel message, and that here is further evidence as stated in the last chapter, that for Paul, Christ was present in and with the message about him, making that word powerful.

The first heremeneutical error that most commentators and translators uniformly commit is splitting Chapter 9 into two divisions, verses 1–5 and verses 6–33. In Paul's chief theological work, Chapters 9–11 must be perceived as a single theme. Even grammatically speaking the conjunction "but," δε, in the first clause is not an extraneous word or idiomatic expression.[11] It forces the reader back to the previous thought. Here Paul was agonizing over why Israel or much of Israel had rejected the Gospel message. He wrote:

---

and End, of the Creator and Redeemer, of Judgement and Righteousness: but the theme is proclaimed by human lips and received by human ears. The Church is the fellowship of MEN [People] who proclaim the Word of God and hear it... p. 341

Similarly, Martin Franzmann:

If the word of God can fail, the Church has no ground for faith and hope. For the word of God, only the word of God, has called the Church into being; and the Church lives and dies in the power of the Word. Paul looks into the history which the Word of God has made and sees there the revelation of God's will that will solve the enigma of Israel...The Word of God creates the people of God and defines the people of God. The Lord spoke and his will was done...Martin Franzman, *Concordia Commentary-Romans* (St. Louis, MO: Concordia Publishing House, 1968), p. 171.

[10]Leon Morris, *The Epistle to the Romans* (Grand Rapids, MI: Eerdmans Publishing Co., 1988), in loc.

[11]C.F.D. Moule, *An Idiom-Book of New Testament Greek* (Cambridge, England: Cambridge University Press, 1960), pp. 106-107. Henceforth Moule, Idiom-Book. de oti, places stronger emphasis on the previous thought.

I am speaking the truth in Christ, I am not lying; my conscience bears me witness in the Holy Spirit, that I have great sorrow and unceasing anguish in my heart. For I could wish that I myself were accursed and cut off from Christ for the sake of my brethren, my kinsmen by race. They are Israelites, and to them belong the sonship, the glory, the covenants, the giving of the law, the worship, and the promises; to them belong the patriarchs, and of their flesh is the Christ. God who is over all be blessed for ever. Amen (R.S.V.)

The "Amen" at the end of verse five is not the conclusion of the thought, like a period, but rather the typical affirmation: "It is so," "So be it," "God is Faithful" or simply "Yes," "I proclaim it," or "Amen!" In verses 4–5 Paul says that God had given all the gifts to Israel, and in verse six he asks rhetorically why then had not the gospel message incorporated his brothers and sisters of the flesh. Was the Gospel message ineffective? Did the Gospel message fail?

If Paul had meant that the word of God was simply the promises made to Israel he would have quoted the original blessing of Abram in Genesis 12:2–3. There, God says to Abram: "And I will make you a great nation, and I will bless you, and make your name great, so that you will be a blessing. I will bless those who bless you and him who curses you I will curse; and by you all the families of earth will bless themselves." Or He would have quoted God's statement to Moses in Exodus 6:7:" And I will take you for my people, and I will be your God..." There are several passages (Ex. 19:5–6; Lev. 26:11–13; Dt. 7:1–15; 26:18 –19; 28, etc.) which Paul could have quoted if he had meant the word of God was a promise. It is apparent that the verses that Paul quotes (7, 9, 13, 15, and 17) are not the promise but the textual proof that the word of God did not fail.[12]

There is one important clue that has most invariably been overlooked by the commentator and should have alerted translators to the meaning of the word of God. The clue in the text is the verb, εκπεπτωκεν, which the R.S.V., J.B., and the T.E.V. translate as "failed." Paul's connecting that Greek term with the word of God should have immediately reminded translators of another passage where the same verb is connected with the word of God. This is the Septuagint (LXX) text of Isaiah 40:7–8[13], where εκπιπτω occurs in such a close relationship to the word of God that Paul must have either consciously or unconsciously had it in his mind.[14] The R.S.V. translation of Isaiah (40:7–8)

---

[12]In a 1984 article in *The Journal for the Study of the New Testament*, "Romans 9:6–29–A Midrash," William Richard Stegner argues that the reasoning of Romans 9:6–29 follows a typical rabbinical (Tannaitic and Amoraic rabbis, c. 200 C. E.) practice. Following the work of Earl Ellis (1957), Stegner suggests that verses 6–8 are the "theme and initial text," Genesis 21:12. If verse 9 was a secondary text, Genesis 18:10 and verses 10–28 were the "exposition containing additional citations" and verse 29 was the final text referring back to the initial text with the word "seed." The Prime text, "the word of God," in Stegner's (Ellis) interpretation is then "Through Isaac shall your descendants be named." But the text is clear this not the prime text but the reason why not all of Israel is Israel; some of Abraham's seed are the sons of Esau.

[13]Εκπιπτω is derived from πιπτειν which meant "to fall," "to commit a sin," "to perish," "to come to an end," or "to cease." Εκ is the simple preposition meaning from, out of, away from (ex) This brings an added force to πιπτω. Εκπιπτιεν then means "to fall down from," "to burst forth," "goes forth," "to digress," "to deviate away from," "to be omitted," "to be lost," "to be deprived of." (TDNT, VI, 161).

is, "The grass withers, the flower fades (το ανθοσ εξεπεσεν, third person singular Second Aorist indicative of εκπιπτω) but the word of the Lord remains forever." In the last chapter I pointed out that I Peter picks up on the same verses from Isaiah with a few modifications, and quotes the LXX directly in 1:24–25. With I Peter it was clear that by the word of God the Gospel message was meant. It is not as clear with Paul because he is dealing with the opposite side of the issue. He was not writing about the inclusion of the gentiles, but about why his "brothers and sisters of the flesh (vs. 3)," had not accepted the gospel message. After all, according to Isaiah (40:9), Zion and Jerusalem were to be the "proclaimers of good news (ευαγγελιζομενος LXX)," but not only did Paul's kinfolk crucify the giver of life, they were rejecting the very news of the resurrection and of salvation through Christ Jesus. Paul was rhetorically asking: "Does this mean that the very powerful Word of God that could bring down nations and create the world could not include the people of God in the kingdom of God, making that Word ineffective?" In light of Isaiah 40:8 another paraphrase of Paul's statement is in order: "But it is not possible for the word of God to become corrupt or of naught like the grass of the field; for not all Israel is Israel."

The whole issue that is being dealt with in Romans 9–11 is the agony and pathos that Paul feels – why his brothers and sisters of the flesh have not accepted the Christ. The question was why the powerful word of God, the gospel message, was not able to include the Jews. Did the Word of God fail?

The Word of God is Dynamic

Because I believe the stress historically has been placed on interpreting the word of God as the promises of God, the richness and depth of Paul's thought has been overlooked. In Romans 9:4-5 the promises and covenants were only part of the history of Israel. In what must be described as a summary statement of the people of Israel, it is apparent that Paul was far from being a biblical literalist. Furthermore, it is apparent that Paul was not a revolutionary who was out to make radical changes in the people or reject them. He had a deep love and appreciation for his people and of how God or the word of God interacted with the people of God.

Paul takes great pains to encapsulate the life of Israel, and, in doing so, he never quotes Scripture. While much of what he states "the giving of the Law," "the covenants," and "the patriarchs," are spelled out within the Scriptures, the other phenomena mentioned were not defined within the Scriptures. To find the depth of what Paul had in mind one has to explore the wealth of literature that had built up after "the closing of the Hebrew canon" or what is now considered the intertestamental period. This material is called the Apocrypha, the Pseudepigraph, and the rabbinical literature.

Paul's first and foremost descriptive term of Israel is perplexing. The term "sonship [υιοθεσια]" never occurs in the Old Testament or the Septuagint's translation of the Hebrew canon. Furthermore, it never occurs again in the New Testament. Sonship could hardly be called a central descriptive concept of Israel. Israel is seldom called God's son. A notable exception is when Yahweh tells Moses to tell Pharaoh to let his first born son go in Ex. 4:22–23.

---

[14]Richard B. Hays, *Echoes of Scripture in the Letters of Paul* (New Haven. CT: Yale University Press, 1989), ix–33.

As poignant as this statement is, outside of two small references in the prophets (Jer. 31:20 & Hos 11:1), Israel is not called Yahweh's son again in the Old Testament. There are indeed references to Yahweh as Father (Deuteronomy 32:6, 18, and Jeremiah 3:4), and Israel is described as being sons and daughters of Yahweh (Deuteronomy 14:1; 32:5, 19; Isaiah 43:6; 45:11; Hosea 2:1), but not as a designation of sonship. But then the stress could hardly be described as being central to the Old Testament. The stress on Israel being Yahweh's son really blossoms, after Israel returns from exile.

The pseudepigraphic work, the Book of Jubilees, written in Palestine in Hebrew about 161–140 B.C.E. (Charlesworth II, pp. 43–44), after describing how Israel was too disobedient, the Lord is purported to have made the following statement to Moses, "I will purify them (vs. 23)...And they will do my commandments. And I shall be a father to them, and they will be **sons** to me and they will all acknowledge that they are my **sons** and I am their father in uprightness and righteousness. (Jubilee 1:24b–25, Charlesworth)" Even though the Book of Jubilees is pseudepigraphic (false writing) and therefore most would consider the oration of Moses to be spurious, it is obvious the person who wrote this was a very pious and well-meaning person. He was most likely a Hasidic priest (Charlesworth, 38), and this was his vision for Israel. To command the greatest audience for his vision he places the words in Moses' mouth. It is hard to think that Moses would disagree with the above statement. There are many similar statements in the Pentateuch: Ex. 19:38; Lev. 26:3–15; Dt. 4:32–40; 7:1–15; 10:12–11:32; 26:18–19; 28:1–14; 29:13–30:20, but none of these statements call Israel God's son. Throughout the other literature of the "intertestamental" times there are so many references to Israel as sons of God that it would be a safe assumption that by the time of Paul "sonship" was a central concept in Judaism.[15]

If Paul had wanted to be more consistent with the Old Testament, he would have chosen other concepts that seem to be more central in the Old Testament. More prevalent are the concepts of "the nation of God (Genesis 35:9–11; 46:3, 19; 48:19; Exodus 19:6; 32:7–14; 33:12–16 etc.)," and "God's people (Exodus 3:7–10; 6:6–8; 7:4, 16; 8:1 etc.)."[16] It is understandable, however, why the concept of nationhood and peopleness was no longer dominant in the thought of Judaism by the time of Paul. After all, Israel was no longer a

---

[15]Testament of Levi 3:9–4:4; 18:1–14; Testament of Levi 18:1–14. Testament of Judah 24:1–6; IV Ezra 5:57–59; Sirach 36:11, cited in TDNT, VIII, 359. The works of the rabbis refer constantly to Israel being sons of Gods. The following are just a few references from the rabbinical literature cited by Professor Eduard Lohse in his *Theological Dictionary to the New Testament* article:

> Rabbi Agiba stated, "Beloved are the Israelites: for they are called the sons of God. It was declared to them as a special love that they are called God's sons." Rabbi Jehuda ben Shalom records that God said, "You have the wish to be singled out, that you are my sons? Busy yourselves with Torah and observances of the commandments, so all will see that you are my sons." Another Rabbi stated, "When the Israelites do God's will they are called sons; when they do not do God's will they are not called God's sons" (VIII, 359–360).

[16]The concepts of the "Nation of God" and "the people of God" are almost non-existent in the Pseudepigraph and the Apocrypha. The same is the case with the rabbis. Outside of a prayer by Rabbi Joshua in Beracoth 4:4 and a few quotes from the Old Testament, the Mishnah does not refer to Israel as God's People or his nation.

nation. A familial concept such as "sonship," that transcended territorial boundaries would be much more descriptive of the reality of Israel as it existed in the time of Paul.

The next attribute that Paul ascribes to Israel is "glory [δοξα]." For the knowledgeable scriptural reader, this is an incredible shock wave which Paul creates, and immediately passes on with no explanation. The New Testament speaks of "the Glory of God (Mt. 6:13; Lk. 2:9, 14; 17:18; 19:38, etc.)" or the "Glory of the son (Mt. 16:27; 24:30; 25:31; Mk. 8:38, Lk. 9:26)," "the Son of God (John 1:14;11:4, 40)," and "Jesus (John 2:11; cf. 17:5, 22, 25)."[17]

There is only one time when Israel is described as having glory. This is found in the Prayer of Simeon that is delivered when the baby Jesus is presented in the temple. Simeon prayed,"...My eyes have seen your salvation, prepared for all peoples, a light of revelation to the heathen, and glory of your people Israel (Luke 2:30–32, RSV)." Simeon is referring to the prophesies in Isaiah 42:6 and 49:6 where Israel is described as being "a light to the nations." The grammatical parallelism (φως εις αποκαλυφιν ..και δοξαν) leaves the impression that the glory is not presently part of Israel. It will come to Israel as revelation has come to the gentiles from the fact that salvation has come to the peoples. This, of course, is because God's Messiah has come, and he will establish God's reign and God will bestow his glory on Israel.

Paul's statement, on the other hand, implies that the glory was part of Israel's past and present, rather than something to come to Israel through some future event. Did Paul then mean that Israel has glory like God? If he meant that Israel had Glory, it would be totally unacceptable in terms of the Old Testament. There the overwhelming usage of glory [כבוד] is reserved for the Lord God. No place in the Old Testament is it stated that Israel has an inherent glory or even one that Yahweh bestowed on Israel. There is no possible way that Israel could share the glory of Yahweh, יהוה אלהינו אתכבדו [Dt. 5:24 (MT. 21) see 5:22–27].[18]

Such modern commentators as Ernst Käseman,[19] Sanday, and Headlams (ICC, in loc) suggest that, by the concept of "the glory of Israel," Paul has in mind the concept of the shechinah that finds its roots in the Old Testament

---

[17]TDNT, II, pp. 232–237. Only a few times in the New Testament is δοξα used in one of its primitive meanings to be applied to transient phenomena such as wealth or a popular reputation. Solomon is described as having 'glory (Mt. 6 :29; Lk. 12:27),' it is clear there that this is descriptive of Solomon's wealth and power rather than a spiritual state. The Devil describes the nations as having Glory (Mt. 4:11; Lk. 4:5). Of course, this glory could not be compared to God's, but must be looked on as earthly power and wealth that so frequently corrupts humankind.

[18]BDB, in loc. Hebrew has similar mundane meanings to that of the Greek δοξα, but its derivation is much different than Greek. Whereas in Greek δοξα is derived from δοκεω which means "to believe", a typical Greek noetic etymology, Hebrew כבוד is derived as are most Hebrew words, from the concrete. The root word is כבד. and it means to be heavy or weighty. Its usage is found in a rotund gentleman. Because of its origins in the concrete כבוד has a very rich variety of usages. See Genesis 31:1; 45:13; Exodus 28:2; 28:40; Esther 5:11; Job 19:9; 29:20; Ps. 4:2;16:9; 106:20; 108:1; Isaiah 9:8–10:3; Jeremiah 2:11.

[19]Ernst Käseman, *Commentary on Romans*, trans. and ed. by Geoffry W. Bromiley (Grand Rapids, MI: William B. Eerdmans Publishing Company, 1980), 258–259. Anders Nygren properly places this glory in the Holy of Holies, but he does not demonstrate how he got from Glory to the Old Testament concept of the Holy of Holies. *Commentary on Romans*, trans. by Carl C. Rasmussen (Philadelphia: Fortress Press, 1949), 353–360.

but is developed most fully by the rabbis. Shechinah is the English transliteration of the Hebrew word שׁ which means settle down, abide, or dwell (BDB). The rabbis identified the glory of the Lord with whenever and wherever the Lord related to humankind.[20] For the Jews Yahweh's place of ultimate contact for Yahweh was in the Holy of Holies, the innermost part of the temple. This is, indeed, the essence of Solomon's statement at the dedication of the temple in I King 8:13 where he stated to Yahweh, "I have built thee an exalted house, a place for thee to dwell (שׁ) for ever... (R.S.V.)" The destruction of the temple created major problems for the rabbis. Did this mean that the Spirit of Yahweh was forever removed from Israel? Some of the rabbis believed that the survival of part of the western wall of Solomon's Temple, (what is known today as the wailing wall) meant that the Spirit of Lord still remained (Midrash, Exodus, pp. 47-48). Other rabbis believed that through Moses and David's "shepherding" Israel, through Israel following the Law, Yahweh continued "to test" Israel and in that testing Israel the Most High was still present above Israel. In another passage it is learned when someone spoke slander the Shechinah immediately retracts into heaven (Midrash, Dt, p. 111). When a gentile was converted, that person is brought under the wings of the Shechinah (Midrash Lev, pp. 28–29; Num, p. 43). Otherwise the person was brought under the gaze of Yahweh, under 'His eyelids.'

This is most likely what Paul meant by "the Glory" of Israel. Paul did not mean that Israel had any Glory, but that Israel was under the eyelids of Yahweh. The Shechinah of God dwelt with Israel because God's Glory was part and parcel of Israel's history. While this is implied in the Old Testament, it is not stated. It is only developed by the rabbis and to understand what Paul means one needs to know the rabbis' thinking.

The covenants, the promises, and the giving of the law are spelled out in the Old Testament and in Paul's own writings. (see Romans 4:1–25; 5:12–14; 11:1–2, 25–32; Galatians 3:1–25; 4:21–31) On the other hand, when Paul says that the worship belongs to Israel, he is not referring to practices spelled out in the Old Testament. While many of the feasts and services of worship are prescribed in the Old Testament, the methods of worship and feasts were not. Through the ages both took on rich depths of meaning and practice, a richness that Paul participated in, enjoyed, and had in mind in Romans 9:6. It would be a grievous mistake to be dogmatic or too emphatic about the conclusions to which this leads. The one thing that we can be certain of is that the Word of God does not mean the Scripture. It would likewise appear that Paul has in mind a more dynamic and powerful word of God like that of the Old Testament.

Paul Completes 'The Word of God'?

Colossians 1:24-27: Now I rejoice in the suffering for you, indeed, I complete in my flesh what is lacking in Christ's affliction for the sake of his body the church, for which I became a servant by divine commission which was given me for you to complete the word of God, the mystery hidden in all eternity and for

---

[20]Midrash, Genesis, p. 160. Here is a humorous insight. The rabbis report that of all species, only humans, fishes (whales), and snakes copulate face to face. The reason for this is that God spoke the shechinah to the man and the woman and the snake. He also spoke to the Fish when he told the fish to spit Noah up.

generations, but now he (God) has revealed to his saints, to whom God willed to make it known among the gentiles, the glorious wealth of God's Glory, which is Christ in you the hope of Glory.

Does Paul mean something substantially different than the word of God as Gospel? If Christ is alive and lives in the very word proclaimed about him, as was suggested as a possibility in the discussion of I Peter 1:23, it might be that Paul believed that the dynamic word of the Old Testament and the Gospel were the same. This would place Paul and the prologue to John as identifying the Word of God to be Jesus. There is much in Paul that commends this understanding. I am going to suggest that the above quote from the Epistle to the Colossians leads precisely in that direction.

Colossians 1:24-27 is one of the most unique passages in the New Testament. It has created great problems for theologians and uniformly led to mistranslations. Even for a person with limited theological knowledge, the problems of interpretation of this text are transparent. How could Paul consider that there might be something lacking (υστερηματα) in Christ's affliction, his suffering (θλιψεων) or how could Paul complete the word of God? The uneasiness that theologians and commentators feel with this passage is very evident in the translations or mistranslations that have been produced. J.B. Philips, an excellent Greek Scholar, translated vs. 23b–26:

> I myself have been made a minister of the same gospel, and though it is true at this moment that I am suffering on behalf of you who have heard the gospel, yet I am far from sorry about it. Indeed, I am glad, because it gives me a chance to complete in my own suffering something of the untold pains which Christ suffers on behalf of his body, the Church. For I am a minister of the Church by divine commission, a divine commission granted to me for your benefit and for a special purpose: that I might fully declare God's Word. [21]

William Beck puts a different slant on verses 24 and 25:

> I delight to suffer for you now and in my body am enduring what still need to be endured of Christ's sorrow for his body, which is the church. God made me its servant when he gave me this work among you in order to do everything God meant to do by His Word.[22]

While Beck maintains the active emphasis upon Paul, he completely destroys the grammatical structure of the Greek so that his translation becomes not a translation but a paraphrase. There is nothing in the text that states that the affliction is for the Church. The Word of God becomes totally twisted into what "God meant to do by the Word" implying that God was not able to complete the work, but needed Paul to finish the job.

The Jerusalem Bible likewise maintains the action but its normal clarity of translation likewise degenerates into a paraphrase here also: "It makes me

---

[21]J. B. Phillips, *The New Testament in Modern English* (New York, MacMillan, 1958).

[22]William F. Beck, The New Testament in the Language of Today (St. Louis, MO: Concordia Publishing House, 1964), in loc.

happy to suffer for you, as I am suffering now, and in my own body to make up all; that has still to be undergone by Christ for the sake of his body, the Church. I became the servant of the Church when God made me responsible for delivering God's message to you." The New English Bible likewise totally transforms the verse. In its translation Paul's suffering becomes a dramatization, not a completion of Christ's suffering. The completion of the word of God becomes as with the J. B.[????], the delivering of God's message only "in full."[23]

While Paul's poor use of Greek does not add clarity to the text,[24] a rudimentary knowledge of Greek demonstrates that all of the above translations are flawed. Getting as close to the literal translation as possible seems to be most helpful in understanding Paul's thinking on the word of God. The first observable fact from the grammar is that the subject doing the acting is first person (I). It is Paul who gives thanks (χαιρω). It is Paul who "fills up" (ανταπληρω). It is Paul who becomes (γενομην) a servant (διακονος). The second fact is that the receiver of the action or the accusative is (υστερηματα), deficiency or lacking. (TDNT, VIII, p. 592.) The third observation is that the modifiers of deficiency are affliction (θλιψεων,) and Christ, Χριστου. The deficiency, thus was not Paul's or the Church's but the affliction of Christ. Fourth, the remainder of verse 25 describes Paul as the servant διακονος. These two major descriptive clauses clearly are, 1. by divine commission which was given me for you κατα την οικονομιαν του θεου την δοθεισαν μοι

---

[23]θλιψις is never used in the Bible to describe Christ's suffering and death. Θλιψις is derived from the Greek verb θλιβω, which originally meant: to press, squash, hem in, to kiss, to press together. (TDNT, III, 139) The basic idea of affliction is derived from martial practices, not so much of killing although killing may be part of the tactic, but of creating the mental attitude of fear, anguish in the opponent, or when opponents have been conquered, of keeping them in fear and anguish. The sense of groaning "under the heel of the Romans" is the essence of the meaning. (TDNT, III, 139–143)

The fact that Paul does not mean Christ's death here is borne out in the rest of Paul's works. He used θλιψις 24 times and in none of the times is death explicitly described. θλιψις, affliction, is a state also in marriage that Paul would have single people avoid (I Corinthians 7:28). But the passage that is most descriptive of Paul's usage of θλιψις and a passage that must be used to understand Colossians 1:24–1:27 is II Corinthians 1:3–7. Here Paul uses θλιψις twice, and the verb, θλιβω, once.

Praise be to the God and Father of our Lord Jesus Christ, the Father of compassion and the God of comfort, who comforts us in all our troubles (επι παση τη θλιψει), so that we can comfort those in any trouble (θλιψει) with the comfort we ourselves have received from God. For just as the sufferings (παθηματα) of Christ flow over into our lives, so also our comfort overflows. If we are distressed (θλιβομεθα), it is for your comfort and salvation; if we are comforted it is for your comfort, which produces in you patient endurance of the same sufferings (παθημα) we suffer (πασχομεν). And our hope for you is firm, because we know that just as you share in our sufferings (παθηματων), so also you share in our comfort.

[24]C. F. D. Moule describes the grammar of I:15–23 as being "lax," and this is one of the reasons he stipulates that so much of the translations and interpretation of the passage is "subjective." Moule, *The Cambridge Greek Testament Commentary: The Epistles of Colossians and to Philemon* (Cambridge: The University Press, 1962), p.61. This is also true of vss. 24–27. "Lax," however, is too gentle, too "British" of a term. Poor is a better word for Paul's grammar in 1:15–23, as well as 24–27 to speak nothing of the rest of Colossians, but that is indeed a sign of Pauline authorship.

εις υμας, 2. to complete the word of God πληρωσαι τον λογον του θεου. It was Paul that was commissioned and it was Paul who fills up. Now this sounds very un-Christian and very egomaniacal and all the commentators and translators try to avoid those implications, but in their doing so I am afraid they look in the wrong direction. They look outside the text to broader Christian theology.

The Answer:

Christ in You the hope of Glory!

Within the text itself there is a major clue uniformly overlooked by most commentators and translators, to the interpretation of Colossians 1:24–25 and the dynamics of the Word of God for Paul. While it is not good Greek grammar, it is no accident that verses 24–27 are one run-on sentence. Paul has one continuous thought and all the clauses are interwoven.

In verse 24 it can be safely assumed that Paul is not referring to Christ's suffering and death on Calvary. Paul does not see the deficiency in Christ's atonement (ICC, in loc.).[25] While it is clear in this and other passages (II Cor. 4:7–15 and Phil. 3:10–11) that Christians share in the suffering of Christ, nowhere is Christ's suffering on the cross identified with that of the Christians. Christians may reflect in some way Christ's suffering and even his death. (II Cor. 4:7–15; Rom. 6:5–7) Paul uses the verb πληρω to describe completing the sufferings of Christ and the Word of God,[26] because the thoughts, the actions, are interconnected and inseparable. Likewise is the case with verses 26–27. Without so much as taking a breath right after "the word of God," Paul writes: "the mystery hidden through the ages and from generations, but now revealed to his saints, to whom God intended to make known how rich the glory of the mystery among the gentiles, which is Christ in you, the hope of Glory:"

Here is the essence of it all – it is "Christ in you!" How does Christ come to live in you? It is through the Word of God (vs. 25). Therefore we can understand "to complete...the word of God" in the senses in which more and more persons accept the Gospel, more and more persons come into Jesus Christ, the Word of God, when his reign becomes larger and larger, or in terms of Romans 11:25d: "until the full number of Gentiles come in." This is what Paul means, "to complete...the Word of God."

To cement the argument, right after Paul stated, "Christ in you, the

---

[25]In verse 24 the cognate ανταναπληροω is used. It appears very rarely in the existing literature. It is never used in the LXX. The TDNT (VI, 307) only cites four references to the word in classical literature. TDNT defines the word as supplementing or replacing. The word only occurs once and that is here in Colossians 1:24. Paul certainly does not perceive his suffering as replacing Christ's suffering. Consequently, it must be interpreted that Paul means something in the nature of supplementing, or the basic root word of to fill up or bring to completion. It may be that he wants to emphasize the ongoing work of the Church. But without Paul interpreting the word it is impossible to be emphatic.

[26]The fact that Paul uses the aorist infinitive may indicate that he himself expected to see "the full number of Gentiles" to be brought under the reign of the Word of God (Romans 11:25) in his own ministry. After all, it is very apparent from I Corinthians 15:51 and I Thessalonians 4:13–5:11 that Paul expected to see the return of the Lord in his lifetime.

hope of Glory," he wrote: "Whom we proclaim." He does not state that it is the message about Christ he proclaims, but the person of Christ. Paul states the same thought in II Cor. 4:5, "For it is not ourselves we proclaim but Christ Jesus, the Lord, ourselves are your servants through Jesus. "

Thus the gospel was not just the message about Christ, but it was Christ, himself. I must underscore here that when Paul says he "completes the word of God", this is not a statement of an egomaniac. Paul saw himself, as the above statement asserts, as a servant. He was the vehicle through which Christ reached the world. He states in Galatians 2:20, "It is not I who live but Christ who lives in me." Thus it must be concluded that through Paul the resurrected Lord makes his appeal to other people.

As it is with the word of God so it is with the statement that Paul "completes what is lacking in Christ's afflictions." The best way to conclude this discussion I believe is to quote from the article on θλιψις, affliction, in TDNT. Heinrich Schlier connects suffering/affliction with the proclamation of the Word. Schlier was dealing with II Corinthians 4:8f. I will include verses 7–12, because I believe it will be helpful in understanding Schlier's comments and Colossians 1:1:24–28:

> But we have this treasure in earthen vessels to show that the transcendent power belongs to God and not to us. We are afflicted (θλιβομενοι) in every way, but not crushed; perplexed, but not driven to despair; persecuted but not forsaken; stuck down, but not destroyed; always carrying in the body the death of Jesus, so that the life of Jesus may also be manifested in our bodies. For while we live we are always being given up to death for Jesus' sake, so that the life of Jesus may be manifested in our mortal flesh. So death is at work with us, but life in you. (R.S.V.)

Schlier's comments are:

> The apostle experiences in his own physical existence the death suffered by Jesus. For he is given up to death for Jesus' sake. For Jesus' sake, however, his sufferings take place in the wholly concrete sense–the context shows this quite plainly–that they are experienced for the sake of preaching his Gospel, in which Jesus is present. The apostle sets himself under the Word of the death of Christ. He represents by giving up his own life to the claims of men. The Lord present in the Word is thus set among men through the obedient apostle, who bears the afflictions suffered by Jesus Christ who fulfills here and now the tribulation experienced by Him (TDNT III, p. 144).

Seen in this light, the sequence is as follows: As Paul or the disciples proclaim the gospel in the power of the Holy Spirit and in the presence of the Son of God, more and more people accept Christ. He comes into their lives, so that it is not they who live, but Christ who lives in them. Thus, rather than "to complete the word of God" in Col. 1:25 Paul means "to make more full" or "to fill up more completely."

The Word of the Lord Grows

There is confirmation that this dynamic attitude towards the word of God was shared by others in the New Testament. In Acts (6:7; 12:24; 19:20) the word of God is described as growing (ηυξανεν/3rd. person sing. imperf. αυξανω). It is typical of modern scholars to note that Ernst Haenchen, in his commentary on Acts states,"The Word of God here appears to be a living reality; we should probably say "Christianity spread."[27] Haenchen does not so much as offer a reason why the Word of God which grows, must be translated as "Christianity spread." One can only hazard a guess that Haenchen considered the word of God a message about Jesus, a way of thinking about Jesus that was aimed at converting people to Jesus. It is obvious for Paul, Luke, and the rest of the New Testament, that the proclamation of the Gospel was much more than a simple proclamation of words about Jesus. Jesus was in that word; that word was indeed living and active, and because Jesus was living in more and more people, the Word of God was growing.

Putting this all in perspective, particularly now with Romans 9:6, it would appear that the Word of God for Paul is the power of God transforming humanity. Jesus is in that word, if he is not that word of God from all eternity. He is God relating to man; he is God in man. While there is a great deal of room to disagree with some of the above conclusions, the fact that there is no support in Paul for considering the Bible to be the word of God is beyond dispute. When Paul states that it is not as if the word of God failed, he means that it is not as if God in all his activities relating to his people, failed to include them into his kingdom. He reasons that not all persons in Israel who claim to be Israel are true Israelites, but those who hear the Word of God and accept Him into their lives are Israel.[28] As far as Israel of the flesh is concerned, their rejection is only temporary. According to Romans 11:25–26a, Paul asserts: "Lest you (the gentiles) be wise in your own conceits, I want you to understand this mystery, brethren: A hardening has come upon Israel, until the full number of Gentiles come in, and so *all Israel will be saved*...(Bold italics mine)" The purpose of Israel's rejection of the Good News was so that the Gentiles would accept the good news, and then **"All ISRAEL WILL BE SAVED." The Word of God is effective. He is living and powerful.**[28]

---

[27]Ernst Haenchen, *The Acts of the Apolstles* (Philadelphia: Westminster Press, 1971), p. 264. Henceforth, Haenchen.

[28]In the most plausible interpretation of Romans 9–11, Mary Ann Getty in "Paul and the Salvation of Israel: A Perspective on Romans 9–11" in *The Catholic Biblical Quarterly* (50:1988), pp. 456–457, emphasizes that chapter 9 stresses the election of God and not Israel's guilt for the rejection of Jesus. Accordingly, the purpose of the rejection of the Jews, is not for the destruction of the Jews, but so that the "full number of Gentiles may be saved. (11:25)"

Chapter V

The Minority Report

As is apparent from the preceding chapters, the overwhelming evidence from the Bible is that the Word of God is filled with the power of God.

In two passages of Scripture this is not evident. These two passages are Matthew 15:1–6 and Psalm 119.

The Word: The Law
Psalm 119

Containing 176 verses, divided into 22 strophes, with each verse of the strophe beginning with a consecutive letter from the Hebrew alphabet, Psalm 119 is the longest Psalm in the book of Psalms and the longest Chapter in the Bible. One of the great Hebrew scholars of this century gave this Psalm just about the worst review a piece of literature could receive. The late Moses Buttenwieser of Hebrew Union College wrote, "Biased by the high regard in which Psalm 119 was held in the past by church and synagogue alike, some interpreters consider it a great, profound psalm. Yet it is anything but this, being void of essential qualities of literary creation—spontaneity and originality. There could not be in anything as artificial as this Psalm..."[1] Even the most conservative reader, if she or he is honest, could hardly help but find this Psalm one of the most boring pieces of literature within the whole Bible and all of literature.

If it seems boring in English, in Hebrew it is doubly so. If it was a chant recited in the temple worship, it most likely was the ultimate sleeper. If it was a didactic tool, it must have been the worst torture for young minds. The Psalm does not teach the law. Its sole purposes were to praise God for the law, to proclaim how well he, the Psalmist, follows the law and lament how others do not follow, and these themes are repeated over and over. While the thematic repetition is tedious, the Psalmists lexical redundancy is unbearable. Eight synonyms for the law are monotonously intoned verse after verse. Two almost identical verbs are repeated forty-four times: נָצַר, to watch, to guard, or to keep (23 times); שָׁמַר, to watch, to keep, or to preserve (21 times). Another verb לָמֵד, to teach or to learn, is used 12 times. Two of the eight synonyms that the Psalmist uses for the law are likewise two Hebrew synonyms for 'word,' אִמְרָת. אִמְרָה and דְּבָר. אִמְרָת used fifteen times and variously translated 'promise' or 'word' but in Hebrew its pronunciation does not change (vss. 11, 41, 50, 67, 103, 116, 123, 133, 140, 148, 154, 158, 162, 170, 172). דְּבָר is repeated twenty-two times (vss. 16, 17, 25, 28, 42, 43, 49, 57, 65, 74, 81, 89, 101, 105, 107, 114, 130, 139, 147, 160, 161, 169). דְּבָר is the Hebrew word that is most frequently used in the rest of the Old Testament for 'word of the Lord', דְּבַר יהוה.

Whereas in the rest of the Old Testament the word of God was the power of God bringing about creation; the word of God raised up the nations, and

---

[1] Mose Buttenwieser, *The Psalms* (Chicago: University of Chicago Press, 1930), p.860

then destroyed them; the word of God might possess the prophet; it was never his personal possession. Such is not the case with the Psalmist who composed Psalm 119. The Psalmist, himself, has the power to "hide the word of God in his heart" בלבי (vs. 11). While the Word is always Yahweh's (yours), and the Psalmist seeks Yahweh with his whole heart (vs. 10), seeking Yahweh to teach and help him understand the law, this seems to be theological lip service. The prophets would have said, "Yahweh, you put your word in my heart." The prophet would be empowered by the Spirit of God. This psalmist is empowered by his correct understanding of the law. (vss. 18, 26, 27, 28, 32, 36, 64, 66, 68, 71, 73) In verse 9, the Psalmist asks, "How can a young man keep his way pure?" He does not respond, "by the Spirit of God" or "the power of Yahweh." He responds, "By guarding his ways according to your word בִדְבָרֶ-·." Here the Psalmist does not mean that the young man has such a relationship with Yahweh that in every situation Yahweh tells the young man what to do. He means that the young man has to immerse himself in the law in such a way that he knows exactly what the law requires and then does that.

Instead of being the power of God sustaining and maintaining the universe and the force of God relating to people, the Word of God is 'fixed נִצָּב' forever in heaven (vs. 89). In verse 109 the Psalmist makes an outrageous statement: "I hold my life in my hand and I do not forget your ordinances." It does not take a theological genius to figure out that this verse has a serious theological problem. Even a confirmed believer of human free-will would believe that his or her life is in the hands of God. Most of the other Psalmists would agree. Psalm 27:1c asserts, "The Lord is the stronghold of my life..." Psalm 63:7–8 sings to Yahweh, "....For thou hast been my help and in the shadow of thy wing I sing for joy. My soul clings to thee; thy right hand upholds me." The Psalms are filled with such thought. But here it seems that the Psalmist has the power to control his life by following the law. Daily, he has the choice of following the law or not. If he chooses to follow the law he lives; if he chooses not to follow the law he dies. This is clear from strophe teth ט, verses 65–72.

> You have done well with your servant,
> Yahweh, according to your word
> Teach me right judgement and knowledge
> for I believe in your commandments.
> Before I was brought down because I went astray,
> but now I obey your word.
> You are good and what you do is excellent,
> teach me your statutes.
> The arrogant besmear me with lies,
> but with my whole heart I keep your precepts;
> Gross-fat is their heart,
> but I am consumed (besmeared· שָׁעַשְׁעָתִי) by your Torah
> (תוֹרָתְךָ).
> It was good that I was brought down,
> to better learn your statutes.
> Better to me is the law
> than all the silver and gold in the world.

From this passage it is apparent that God's mercy was not dependent on God but on the Psalmist first being obedient to the Law. This is crucial for interpretation of this Psalm. Everything is dependent on the law of God. The law gives life, and the law heals. Of course, it is God working through the Law or the healing comes through God bringing a better understanding to the Law, but nevertheless it is through the Psalmist storing up the law in his heart that he escapes the trials and tribulations in the world. The very attitude that the Psalmist displays is comparable to that of an athlete in preparation and participation of an athletic contest.[2] He studies the law arduously and he looks to God for understanding of the Law. In the end, it is his obedience to the law and not the power of God that triumphs. His sorrow and affliction now is because of those persons who do not follow the law. The ultimate eschatological event for this Psalmist will be when all arrogant people with 'gross-fat hearts' are no more and all follow the law of God.

Modern critical scholarship has dated the Psalm late after the exile and after the return.[3] While Artur Weiser does not place a date on the Psalm, he states that this Psalm "carries with it the germ of development that was bound to end in the self-righteousness of the Pharisees and scribes."[4] A commentary, written in 1959 by W. O. E. Oesterly, reflects some of the best understanding of the text:

> ...There are a number of passages which bear witness to the existence of a difference of religious outlook; the forceful language which is sometimes used may be the echo of the bitterness of controversy with those of differing views, who, in the eyes of the psalmist, were sinners and enemies of the Law because they did not observe it in the strictness which he held to be right. In other words, the psalm seems to reflect a clash of views within Judaism. There is nothing to suggest that the writer had gentiles in mind when speaking of his adversaries; indeed, the whole way in which their enmity and hatred are spoken of precludes this; they are Jews like the psalmist; and this psalm reflects the opposition between two religious attitudes among Jews which in a later day issued in the formation of parties. The beginnings date back to the return from Babylonian exile; it was then that the stricter and more orthodox form of Exilic Judaism, held by those who returned, was opposed to the laxer religious outlook and practice of those living in the homeland. Through the centuries of the antagonisms, then formed,

---

[2] The Hebrew verb שעע occurs in verses 14, 16, 24, 47, 70, 92, 143, and 174. It is one of the most interesting words in the Hebrew language. The R.S.V. translates it "delight." It translates verses 14 and 16: "In the way of thy testimonies, I delight as much as all riches." "I will delight in thy statutes; I will not forget thy word." "Delight" is a very weak translation. The verb is derived from the word that means "to smear over," "to be blinded by." It came to mean that kind of passion that an athlete would participate in, preparing for his games and, indeed, the passion in which the athlete would have during the games themselves.

[3] C. A. Briggs, *The Book of Psalms (ICC, 1906)*, II, p, 417; Mitchell Dahood, *The Psalms*, (AB) III, in loc.; Elmer Leslie, The Psalms (New York: Abingdon-Cokesbury, 1949), p.176; J.W. Rogerson and J. W. Mckay, Psalms 101-150 (Cambridge: Cambridge University Press, 1977), p.89.

[4] Artur Weiser, *The Psalms*, trans. Herbert Hartwell (Philadelphia: Westminster Press, 1962), in loc.

continued, and ultimately there arose the definitely constituted and opposed parties of the Sadducees and Pharisees. Our psalm reflects these conditions as they existed in the middle of the third century...[5]

The whole emphasis of modern interpretation is that the Psalm displays the type of piety of the Pharisees or it is a precursor of that piety, [6] and there is support in the rabbis that Psalm 119 was, indeed, central to the life of Judaism in post-exilic times. In Berakoth 4b, it is stated:

R. Eleazer b. Abina says: Whoever recites [the Psalm] Praise of David (145) three times daily is sure to inherit the world to come. What is the reason? Shall I say it is because it has an alphabetical arrangement? Then let him recite, Happy are they that are upright in the way (Psalm 119), which has an eightfold alphabetical arrangement. (Parentheses () mine)

Even though Psalm 145 has the artificial or imposed structure of an acrostic poem, it is a beautiful hymn of Praise to Yahweh and is well worth reciting three times a day. On the other hand, Psalm 119's sheer length of one hundred seventy-six verses makes it a considerable task to recite three times a day. But Psalm 119 with its total focus on the Torah and the repetition of eight verses fed essential elements of rabbinical Judaism's preoccupation. Not only was the Torah the central focus of the rabbis but because of that focus every little nuance within that Torah took on special meaning. Misspelled words, concepts or objects, or expressions that had lost their meaning, and particularly numbers, had mystical meanings.[7]

While the central focus and, indeed, the only focus of Psalm 119 and the rabbis was the Torah, neither the rabbis nor the psalm rise to the level of idolatry of worship of the law that Christians have risen to in the worship of the Bible.[8] It is clear from this psalm and from all that we have from Judaism, this psalmist, and the rabbis, that the Torah was Yahweh's creation and it would always be connected to Yahweh.

Having stated that, it likewise must be reiterated that "self-righteousness," bristles from almost every line. This is the same type of self-righteousness that the gospels portray as being the hallmarks of the Pharisees and Sadducees who confronted Jesus.

This attitude of Psalm 119 is in stark contrast to the penitent spirit of

---

[5]W. O. E. Oesterly, *The Psalms* (London: S. P. C. K.:, 1959) in loc. Used by permission

[6]Recently, James Luther Mays, in an article, "The Place of the Torah-Psalms in the Psalter" *Journal of Biblical Literature* (106:1, 1987, pp.3–12, henceforth, Mays), has suggested that instead of being extraneous to the canon such Torah psalms as 119 (1 and 19) were pivotal psalms around which the psalter was formed. While his thesis is commendable, Mays is a far distance from rescuing Psalm 119 from the "self-righteous, single minded legalism" of the Pharisees. Considering the fact that the rabbis who formed the canon most likely were Pharisean descent, it would not be surprising to find that they indeed formed the Psalter around the Torah Psalms.

[7]The number eight was of particular importance to the rabbis. Rabbi Samson Hirsch, The *Psalms* (New York: Robert Feldheim, Inc. 1966), II, 322.

[8]See Burton's hymn to the Bible, does offer worship to the Bible, Introduction to this manuscript, p. v.

Psalm 51: "Be merciful to me ...(vs 1), Wash away my evil...(vs. 2) I recognize my faults...(vs. 3) TEV. The remorse that is expressed in Psalm 119 is not expressed because the psalmist feels inadequacies in following the law. His remorse is over other people's disobedience to the laws. (vss. 28, 53, 81–88, 113, 115, 139, 150, 153–157), or because of his own obedience to the law he is persecuted by the unrighteous and those who disdain the law (vss. 22, 39, 42, 51, 56, 69, 70, 78, 84–87, 92, 95 etc.). The remorse, the psalmist feels, is not sorrow and pity for people who are going the wrong direction and don't know it, as is apparent in Paul's lament for his kinfolk in Romans 9:1–5. His remorse is, as Mitchell Dahood translates it, "indignation" to their callowness for that which is right (vss. 53, 56, AB, Volume 17a, in loc.). This fellow is not only angry with the wickedness and his own personal mistreatment but begs Yahweh to show no mercy to the wicked (vs. 155).[9] Furthermore, if James Luther Mays is correct that Psalms 2, 18, and 118 were "intentionally coupled,"[10] then the self-righteousness is doubly underscored. Not only does the psalmist feel superior to the Jews who are not faithfully observing the law, but he arrogantly exults himself over the nations and looks forward to their suppression.

The Word: the Commandment

Matthew 15:1–6: Then Pharisees and scribes came to Jesus from Jerusalem and said, [2]"Why do your disciples transgress the traditions of the elders? For they do not wash their hands when they eat." [3]He answered them, "And why do you transgress the commandment of God for the sake of your tradition. [4]For God commanded, "Honor your father and mother," and, "He who speaks evil of father or mother, let him surely die." [5]But you say, "If any one tells his father or mother, What you would have gained from me is given to God, he need not honor his father." [6]So by your traditions you have <u>made void the word of God</u>.

The attitude expressed by Psalm 119 is totally different from that expressed by Jesus in the Gospels (Mt. 8:5–13; 11:20–24; 12:38–42; 15:21–28; Mk. 7:24–30; Lk. 7:1–10; 10:29–37; 17:11–19). Jesus would have called the person who wrote Psalm 119 a hypocrite and castigated him for his self-righteousness and arrogance (Mt. 15:7; 16:3; 22:18; 23:13, 14; Mk. 7:6; Lk. 12:56; 13:15). While it is true that in the above recorded incident Jesus, like the Psalmist, refers to one of the ten commandments as the word of God (Matthew 5:6 and Mark 7:13), Jesus could hardly be found sharing the Psalmist's veneration of the law. In this incident, the Pharisees and scribes displayed the same self-righteousness and arrogance as the Psalmist. However, both texts that report the incident, Matthew 15:1–20 and Mark 7:1–23, are fraught with problems and these problems have been instrumental in creating distortions of reality.

---

[9]Dahood most properly translates רְחוֹק as an imperative. Thus 155 is a command to Yahweh to remove Salvation far from the wicked.

This fits well within the whole attitude of the Psalm. Dahood, in loc.

[10]Mays, p. 11.

The texts report that the Pharisees and scribes "make void" the law of God by their "traditions." The clear implications of the texts are that the Pharisees and scribes are unfaithful to the law and change the law. At the end of the next chapter, the study of Jesus and the law is completed. The reader will know that when it comes to the Old Testament Law it was not the Pharisees and the Sadducees, Jesus' antagonists in all of the gospels, who reshaped and remade the Law. All the biblical evidence points to the fact that it was Jesus, himself, who reshapes and remakes the law. It should be clear that the Pharisees and the Sadducees were the staunch supporters of the law and that Jesus was reinterpreting the law and a legal innovator. In today's terms the Pharisees and the Sadducees would be the biblical conservatives and fundamentalists. Jesus would be the biblical radical.[11]

The incident in which Jesus reported calling the fifth commandment the word of God is found in Matthew 15:1–20 and Mark 7:1–23. The incident revolves around the confrontation of the Pharisees and scribes over the issue that Jesus' disciples do not wash their hands before meals. In this section the pericope Matthew 15:1–20 will be examined and then primarily verses 1–6. This is because verses 1–6 contain the essential information about the incident and the Pharisees and Scribes without going into the editorializing that Mark does.

Obviously the commandment, "Honor your father and mother" here is considered to be the word of God. Many of the ancient scribes, including the scholarly Origen, sensing the conflict between the essence of the biblical word of God and the statement in verse 6 changed τον λογον, the word, to την εντολην, the commandment, which then made verse 6 consistent with Jesus' statement in verse 3, or they changed τον λογον to τον νομον, the law. The overwhelming number of the manuscripts support the change, but because the most reliable manuscripts have τον λογον it has been the accepted version.[12]

Matthew 23:1-3a –"Then Jesus said to the crowds and his disciples, 'The scribes and the Pharisees sit on Moses' seat; so practice and do whatever they tell you...'" (RSV).

The antagonists in the hand-washing incident, the Pharisees and scribes, as likewise Sadducees in other sections of the New Testament are little understood and greatly vilified by Christians. Such passages as Matthew 15:1–20 and Mark 7:1–23 do not help to improve the image of the Pharisees and Sadducees. In reality these persons were not God-denying cynics who were sinisterly plotting against the lamb of God. No, indeed! The schools of the Pharisees and Sadducees had a long history of seeking to be obedient to the will of God. While their roots can be traced back to Ezra and Nehemiah, their identity emerges in the period of the Maccabees (c. 167 B.C.E.). Like Nehemiah

---

[11]I hesitate to use the term liberal because today's liberal expositor would be interpreting the scriptures as sociological and psychological phenomena, rather than seeing the outpouring of the power of God. The very essence of the life and teachings of Jesus was in the very power of God.

[12]See Nestles Text Apparatus. The American Bible Society edition of the Greek text gives a fairly strong (B) rating to τον λογον. The stronger, more confident rating would have been an A.

and Ezra they were greatly concerned with Israel's following the laws of their God. They had become greatly alarmed with the great number of Jews who were following pagan ways during the reign of the Seleucids.

The Seleucids controlled Palestine from 321–167 B.C.E. Seleucus was a General of Alexander the Great who had defeated the Persians in 331 B.C.E. Seleucus and his progeny attempted to rule most of the Middle East from two years after Alexander's death in 323 until 64 when the Romans took control. During that period of time, the Egyptians under the Ptolemies kept trying to control the region also. The influential or upper class Jews found their allegiance split between the two dynasties. In that period of time there were a great many of these Jews, who became secularists and many others who had not only become secularists but had taken on Pagan practices. For many Jews being a Hellenist was even a means of achieving influence.[13] Professor Orlinsky described well the split in Jewish Society:

> Increasingly, these Jews spoke Greek instead of Hebrew and adopted Hellenic and Hellenized forms of names. Many laws of Judaism became irksome for them...While the Judean upper class did not oppose the Hellenization of their religion and way of life, the common people, most of them farmers, craftsmen, menial workers, petty merchants, and the like, having little or nothing to gain from collaboration with either Syria (Seleucids) or Egyptians, did not favor it. Why should they give up the Judaism of their fathers for alien paganism? Some of these Jews actively opposed the foreign and brutally enforced attempt to alter their religious and social beliefs and practices.[14]

In 167 B.C.E. Antiochus Epiphanes, the Seleucid ruler, in an attempt to solidify his control over Palestine, and thus prevent the incursion of Roman and Egyptian forces offered a sacrifice to Zeus in the Holy of Holies (Daniel 9:27). The pious Jews were outraged. They rose up under the leadership of a priest by the name of Judas Maccabeus and threw out the Seleucids. The Jews as a nation were then free until Rome conquered them in 64 B.C.E. This was the only time from the deportation of Judah by Babylon in 587 B.C.E. until 1948 that Israel existed as an independent nation.

It was during this time that the Sadducees and Pharisees came into existence. The Sadducees were a group of pious priests and the Pharisees were a group of pious and God-fearing laymen. Both of these groups devoted their lives to the study of the Torah, the law of God, and were keenly interested in helping the Jewish people to be faithful to their God and the Torah. During this period when Hellenization was being forced upon the Jews they gained much favoritism among the Jewish people. Severino Pancaro in *The Law in the Fourth Gospel* gives an excellent description of the important role that the Pharisees and Sadducees played in maintaining the Torah in the life of Judaism. Pancaro wrote:

---

[13]H. M. Orlinsky, "Maccabees, Maccabean Revolt," in Volume III: *The Interpreter's Dictionary to the Bible*, ed. by George Arthur Buttrick (New York: Abingdon Press, 1962); 197–201. While Hellenic is strictly speaking, a term that is restricted to Greek culture, in the first and second century BCE, the influence of Alexander on the Egyptian ruling culture was so considerable that the Ptolemies were Hellenized. Used by permission.

[14]Orlinsky, Maccabees, III, 199.

In Judaism there can be no 'teaching', just as there can be no 'school' (Bet Sefre, Bet Midrash), without the Torah. The teaching office, which before Ezra, belonged to the priestly caste and later became also the task of the scribes (Sadducees, but mostly Pharisees) was centered around the law... 'Teaching' was essentially the imparting of what was considered to be an unchangeable body of tradition (written or oral) which was revealed (taught) directly by God. [15]

So great was their preoccupation, or as Psalm 119 put it 'delight שעע,' for the Torah, that the Pharisees and Sadducees must be described as the first biblical fundamentalists. They believed that what were held to be obvious mistakes in the Hebrew canon of the Torah were not mistakes at all. The mistakes, they believed, were planted intentionally in the text by the most High so that he might impart some deep hidden spiritual meaning.[16] Just a few quotes from the rabbis supports their exalted view of the Torah:

> The Law because it was more highly prized than everything was created before everything was created, as it is said, 'The Lord created me [the Law], as the beginning of his way, first of his works of old. I was set up from everlasting, before the earth was ' (Proverbs 8:22). *Sifre on Deuteronomy*
> Those who deny that the Law is from heaven have no part in the world to come. *Sanhedrin x, 1.* cited by Moore; Soncino, XI, 1, 90[a]
> Even if one said the Torah is from God, with the exception of this verse which Moses, not God, spoke from his own mouth; then applies to him (judgement), 'The word of the Lord he has despised.' *Sanhedrin 99[b]*

Of the two groups, the Sadducees were the most conservative, allowing the least flexibility in interpretation of the law. Hans Lietzmann in *A History of the Early Church* gives an excellent contrast between the Sadducees, represented by Rabbi Shammai and the Pharisees, represented by Rabbi Hillel:

> ...Granted that on the Sabbath no food might be cooked, but could one keep warm food which stood on the hearth where fire was still alight on the Sabbath evening? Yes, if it were a gentle fire of burning stubble, but if the fire was of burning wood, it must be covered with ashes, otherwise the food would begin to simmer – this was Hillel's view. In such cases, Shammai altogether forbade keeping food warm and only permitted water. Could those foods be put back to cook which had been taken away from the fire? Hillel said yes, Shammai, no. Might one eat an egg laid on a holy day by a hen which did not know the law? Shammai permitted it, Hillel did not.[17]

---

[15]Severino Pancaro, *The Law in the Fourth Gospel (Leiden*: Brill, 1975), p.18, pp. 226, 506. Henceforth Pancaro.

[16]George Foote Moore, Judaism, I, 77-78; 88-89, 237 ff.

[17]Hans Lietzman, *The Beginnings of Christianity*, trans. by Bertram Lee Woolff (Cleveland, OH: The World Publishing House, 1949); I, 31. Henceforth Lietzman. The Sadducees

While Professor Lietzmann accurately portrays the differences between the two schools of thought, his almost satirical style reveals his Christian bias. Professor Eduard Lohse of Gottingen University put a much more positive outlook on the Pharisees in particular. Lohse wrote:

> Whereas the Sadducees also sought to keep to a stricter exposition of the Sabbath commandment, the Pharisees and scribes tried to avoid the rigorism in order to bring the Sabbath laws as far as possible into harmony with practical situations and requirements, and destroy the joy in the Sabbath. (TDNT, VII, pp.9–10)

The Pharisees and Sadducees were not trying to be petty. They were just trying to bring adherence to the law. With the state of North Dakota being the last state in the United States to abolish 'Blue laws', or Sunday Observance Laws, it is hard for many people to realize that only sixty years ago in the United States no store would be found open and only essential work would be performed on Sunday which had been transformed in Christian circles to the Sabbath. Then in Christian circles there were great discussions of what was and was not permitted to do on 'the Lord's Day.' Such was the case with the debate between the Pharisees and Sadducees. The Pharisees, particularly, felt if flexibility was allowed in certain areas greater Sabbath observance would be stimulated.

What allows the flexibility in the interpretation is not only the mystification of the text of the Torah, but the whole tradition of the Oral Torah. The rabbis believed that at the same time that Moses received the written Torah, he received the Oral Torah. The Oral Torah was a huge body of traditions handed down by rabbis from generation to generation. This was called the Mishnah. In the Mishnah, the rabbis did not perceive themselves as innovators of the Torah, but simply revealors of that which was either implicit in the Torah, handed to Moses, or given to Moses through oral communication. They were simply the extension of Moses in the World.[18]

Midrash Tanbuma recorded a Rabbi Juda ben Shalom as having stated:

> Moses desired the Mishnah to be also in writing, but the Holy One, Blessed be He, foresaw that the nations of the world would translate the Torah, read it in Greek, and assert: "We too are Israel!" The Holy One, Blessed be He, thereupon said to Moses: "Were I to write for thee the multitudes of my Torah then they would be considered as a Stranger." (Hosea 8:12) Why so? Because the Mishnah is the mysterium of God which he transmits only to the righteous.[19]

Only "the righteous" receive the Mishnah and, of course, those who received the Mishnah were the rabbis of Pharisaic and Sadducean lineage, the same

---

were far from being the most rigid in the interpretation of the Law. The Essenes, the now famous inhabitants of the Qumran community, were by far the most assiduous in their observance of Torah. Professor Lohse characterized the Essenes' zealousness in the following way: "The Essenes kept the Sabbath more conscientiously than other Jews, doing no work, not lighting fires, moving no vessels and not even relieving themselves throughout the day." TDNT, VII, 6–14.

[18]Quoted in Joseph Baumgarten, Studies in Qumran Law (Leiden: E. J. Brill, 1977), p.22. Henceforth Baumgarten.

[19]Quoted in Joseph Baumgarten, p. 24.

people who confronted Jesus throughout the New Testament and in the confrontation over the washing of hands. They and only they received the Mishnah. They, like the Psalmist of 119, had hidden the Torah in their hearts. They, above all people, were righteous. These Scribes considered themselves 'pious and holy'. What power it must have been for a select group of men to possess teachings that were orally transmitted directly from God, generation after generation. What a struggle it must have been for Jesus, a commoner from Galilee trained as a carpenter, to endure the pomposity of these pious elite men. Seen from the perspective of the above quote one can almost feel the sneer in the voices of the Sadducees and Pharisees as they address Jesus as "Rabbi." This same sort of contempt is obvious in the confrontation over washing hands.

Traditionally, it has been argued that this confrontation over the washing of hands was clear evidence that Jesus maintained the Torah of God, the law of God, but rejected the oral Torah that the rabbis had built up through the ages.[20] Professor Frank Stagg of Southern Baptist Theological Seminary wrote:

> The pharisees gave the oral tradition a value as great as that of the written law. They held that Moses received the oral law at Mount Sinai and passed it on to the prophets, who in turn passed it down to the men of the Great Synagogue (Pirke Aboth 1:1). Thus they gave Mosaic sanction to traditions which were actually under development at the time of Christ. Jesus rejected the authority of this oral tradition and thus alienated the Pharisees...
>
> Jesus charged the Pharisees with elevating their tradition above the commandment of God, by which he meant the Scriptures. Jesus reversed this, recognizing the authority of Scriptures but rejecting the oral tradition (BBC, vol. 7 in loc.) By permission.

The reader must have noticed that without a word of explanation Stagg jumped from a particular part of Scripture, the commandment, to the entirety of scripture. Stagg does not state how he knew or came to the conclusion that Jesus did not mean the commandment of God but the entirety of Scripture.

When the hand washing incident is examined in relationship to Jesus' attitude towards the law as revealed in the New Testament and the Pharisees and Sadducees as they are historically documented, there are very strong and persuasive reasons to reject Stagg's interpretation and for that matter much that has been written about this passage. The strongest arguments against such thinking are found in Matthew 23:2–7 cited above.[21] As is apparent, this

---

[20]W. C. A. Allan, *The Gospel according to Matthew* (ICC, 1907) in loc.; William Barklay, *The Gospel of Matthew*; *The Gospel of Mark* (Philadelphia, PA: The Westminster Press, 1956); F. W. Beare, *The Gospel according to Matthew* (San Francisco: Harper & Row Publishers, 1981) Henceforth Beare.; William L. Lane, *The Gospel according to Mark* (Grand Rapids, MI: William B. Eerdmans Publishing Company, 1974); I. R. C. H. Lenski, *The Interpretation of Saint Matthew's Gospel* (Columbus, Ohio: Wartburg Press, 1956). Henceforth Lenski.; C.S. Mann, *Mark* (A.B, 1986); Alan Hugh M'Neile, *The Gospel according to St. Matthew* (London: MacMillan & Co., Ltd., 1961); in loc. Henceforth M'Neile.

[21]The various problems with this text are thoroughly discussed in Gerhard Barth, "The Interpretation of the Law in Matthew" in Gunther Bornkamm, G. Barth, and Heinz Joachim, *Tradition and Interpretation in Matthew*, trans. Percy Scott from *Uberlieferung und Auslegang im Matthausevangelium* (Philadephia: The Westminster Press, 1963);

passage would create some problems for those who share Mr. Stagg's views. Stagg, himself, has to backtrack. He wrote:

> **Moses' seat** seems to refer to an actual chair in a synagogue, symbolizing the origin and authority of scribal teaching. The scribes traced all their teachings back to Moses. The charge that **the scribes and Pharisees** did not practice what they preached is not taken in the absolute sense, as verse five indicates. Jesus did not endorse everything they taught, he recognized that they practiced some of their teachings outwardly. (BBC, vol. 7 in loc.) By permission.

Here again is obvious distortion of the text. Jesus stated in the text of the Pharisees and scribes, "so practice and do whatever (παντα, all) they tell you." Stagg interprets this as, "Jesus did not endorse everything they taught..." Acknowledging that Jesus might have accepted some rabbinical teaching Stagg goes on to discount that by stating, "they practiced some of their teachings outwardly." This implies that even if one accepted the possibility that some of their teaching was right, one could overlook that because their practice was wrong. While Jesus does excoriate the scribes and Pharisees for their hypocrisy, he does not in this text discount their teaching. As far as "the seat of Moses" is concerned, there is no evidence in the rabbis that there was such a seat in the synagogue;[22] there is no clear evidence in the Talmud that there was a seat in the synagogue that was called "Moses' seat." In his commentary, F. W. Beare is correct in his interpreting "Moses' seat" as "—the post of teaching authority... simply a metaphor; the scribes and Pharisees are those responsible for declaring to the people what the law of Moses required of them." In loc.

There is abundant evidence in the rabbis that the scribes considered themselves to be the heirs to Moses. They thought that through the generations of scribes the Law had been passed down from Moses to them. Even their interpretation of the law was not expansion and reinterpretation of the law, but given to Moses by Yahweh. The Talmud reports Rabbi Isaac as stating:

> The textual reading as transmitted by the soferim (scribes), their stylistic embellishments, [words] read [in the text] but not written, and words written but omitted in the reading are all halachah (teaching) from Moses at Sinai.
> Nedarim 37[b], (Parentheses mine; [] textual corrections.)

Likewise it reports Rabbi Hiyya as stating:

> What is the meaning of the verse, *And on them was written all the words which the Lord spoke to you in the mount* (Ex. 23:20). It teaches us that the Holy One, blessed be He, showed Moses the Minutia of the Torah, and the minute of the Scribes, and the innovations which would be introduced by the Scribes...
> Megillah 19[b]. Parentheses mine.[23]

---

cited henceforth as G. Barth, Interpretation; David E. Garland, *The Intention of Matthew 23*, Volume III *Supplementum Novum Testamentum* (Leiden: E. J. Brill, 1979); henceforth Garland.

[22]Albright and Mann, (AB, 26) in loc. M'Neile, in loc.: "the Seat of the president of synagogue"

[23] There are abundant other references in the Talmud to the belief: Nazir 56[b]; Sotah 21[a];

These Sopherim (scribes) knew the law of Moses by heart. They knew the prophets and the writings, but they also knew what other rabbis had said in previous generations, and they 'pontificated' what God 'expected' in their generation. This was the oral tradition, and it was this that Matthew 23:2 states "to do and observe."

Elsewhere in the New Testament, as Robert Banks points out, there is abundant evidence that Jesus accepted the teachings of the rabbis and the oral tradition. He attended the Synagogue for which there is no injunction to do in the Torah (Stipulated in Berakoth 6ᵃ–8ᵇ; Mt 4:23; 9:35; Mk 1:35; Lk 4:15, 44; 13:10). At the last supper, he blesses both the bread and the cup (Stipulated in Tos. Ber. 4.1; Pesahim 10.7 69ᵇ ff. Also see Mt 26:26–27; Mk 14:22–23; Lk 22:14–18). These blessings were not both stipulated in the original Passover feast (Ex 12), but came about through the teachings of the rabbis.[24] He pays the temple tax (Mt 17:24–27), another practice that finds no support in the written Torah, but stipulated in the Oral Torah which was written down in the Babylonian Talmud.[25]

Banks likewise suggests that Matthew 9:14–15 is a parallel passage to Matthew 15:1–20. Here the question is raised by disciples of John the Baptist why Jesus' disciples do not fast. Jesus responds, "Can the wedding guests mourn as long as the bridegroom is with them?" From that initial response one could suppose that Jesus was not in favor of fasting, but Jesus goes on to state that the time was coming when the Bridegroom would be taken from them and then the Disciples would fast. Consequently, it is apparent that Jesus was not opposed to fasting. Indeed, in the Sermon on the Mount, Jesus gives guidelines on how to fast. He stated, "When you fast, do not look dismal, like the hypocrites...(Mt 6:16–17)" From this statement it is obvious that Jesus was not opposed to fasting but he was opposed to doing it out of wrong motives and in a false manner. There is, however, no command or directions in the written Torah for Israel to fast.[26] It must be assumed that fasting had been developed throughout the Oral tradition.

There is at least one indication in the New Testament that the disciples at least occasionally observed the rabbinical principle of washing their hands. In the portrayal of the last supper in the gospel of John (13:1–35), it is stated, "Jesus...rose from supper, laid aside his garments, and girded himself with a

---

'Erubin 21ᵇ; etc. The whole Mishnah of Aboth basically deals with the transmission of the Oral Torah from Moses through the rabbis.

[24]Robert Banks, *Jesus and the Law in the Synoptic Tradition* (Cambridge: Cambridge University Press, 1975), 89–96. Henceforth Banks.

[25] Derrett, *The Law*, 248-253, cited by Banks, 89-96.

[26] However, by the time of Ezra and Nehemiah, it is very apparent that fasting had become an essential part of rabbinical teaching. Ezra proclaims the first public fast as he leads the people back to Jerusalem (Ez 8:21). The rabbis believed that in Babylon there was not and could not have been a public fast because there was not a Sanhedrin or governing council of rabbis (Tannith 11ᵃ, Talmud, p.50, footnote #6.) In Babylon there was only private fasting. The fast had become an essential part of Jewish thought because the rabbis believed that with the destruction of the temple the gates of prayer were closed to prayer (Berakoth 32ᵃ⁻ᵇ). But if the Jews suffered enough along with their prayers "the gates of crying," the Lord would answer their prayers (Tannith 11ᵇ ff.; Berakoth 32ᵇ). On serious fasts of seven days one was not to wash or anoint oneself (Tannith 13ᵇ–14ᵃ). Of course Jesus teaches just the opposite, and totally rejects public fasts, but he still supports the principle of the fast which is supported in the Oral Torah.

towel. Then he poured water into a basin and began to wash the disciples' feet (vss. 3–5)." The event is made all the more poignant if one realizes that the disciples were most likely getting ready during the Seder meal to perform the rabbinical practice of washing hands (Pesahim 105^a–107^b). The rabbis would have never washed somebody else's feet — such a practice would be self-degradation.

There is abundant evidence in the rabbis that they considered washing hands an essential practice of Judaism (Str/Biller, II, 694 f.). For the rabbis and the scribes, the reason for the washing of hands is never quite clear. It is considered a "meritorious act," but the failure to perform it could have disastrous effects. The rabbis knew of situations where the failure to wash one's hands led a Jew to eat pork, another to divorce, and finally even one to commit murder (Hullin 105^a–108^b). During a meal there could be as many as three washings. At the beginning, in the middle, and at the end. The middle one could be dispensed with but the other two were required (Berakoth 52^{a-b}, Hullin 105^{a-b}). The practice is considered so intrinsically part of the Torah that the rabbis do not even attempt to find textual proofs for justification of the practice. But if they had so desired they could have found plenty of support in the Torah for the practice of washing hands. The rabbis most likely would have begun with a text where Yahweh commands the Israelites "to consecrate" themselves (Lv 20:7); then they would have pointed out that Yahweh commanded Aaron and his sons to wash their hands before he entered into his presence (Ex 30:17–21), and that David washed his hands before he danced before the Lord (Ps 26:6). Of course, one could support the rabbis' argument from modern sanitary practices, much as our parents would have done for us and we for our children, but then the rabbis did not think in terms of germs. Their sole concern was ritual and ceremonial cleansing. They believed that they as a people were to be clean before Yahweh. They were to be a consecrated people.

The issue of Jesus' acceptance of the traditions of the Pharisees and Sadducees or the oral tradition is by far not the most serious problem in Matthew 15:1–20 (Mk 7:1–23). The most serious problem is in the accusation against the Pharisees in vss. 3b–6 that the duty to the parents could be dispensed with, by saying it was "given to God." The expression "given to God" or "Corban" as it is found in the Markan account (7:11) is a valid Rabbinic concept. In Hebrew it is transliterated Korban from קָרְבָּן which means "sacrifice." For something that was given to God could never ever be used for any other purpose (Nedarim 2^b ff.). Consequently, even if a man could declare that his support for his parents was korban, he could not use it for himself. In reality, however, not once in the extant Rabbinic literature is korban used to allow one to dispatch one's obligations to one's parents.

Everything that is presently known of the Pharisees and Sadducees would sustain the idea that they would heavily support the commandment to honor the parents and never under any circumstance allow its suspension.[27] The

---

[27]Stagg, in his commentary on Matthew suggests that Nedarim 9:1 allowed a man the right to cancel a vow to his parent. If Professor Stagg had read the Talmud more closely he would have realized just the opposite was so. The text suggests that if there is an "opening (absolution)" to the vow to honor one's father and mother then there would be "an opening" to the vow of honoring God. In short "There would be no vows." And a person who did such a thing would have been considered "impudent."

rabbis are very emphatic about this. Kiddushin 30[b] states, "For us [Jews] honoring our fathers and mothers is the same as keeping the first commandment." A few sentences further Kiddushin continues, "...There are three partners in man, the Holy one blessed be He, the father, and the mother. When a man honours his father and his mother, the Holy One, blessed be, says, 'I ascribe [merit] to them as though I had dwelt among them and they had honoured me.' (30[b]) Kiddushin also states:

> Our rabbis taught, It is said, Honour thy father and thy mother (Exodus 20:12), and it is also said, Honour the Lord with thy substance (Proverbs 3:9): thus the Writ assimilates the fear of parents to that of the Omnipresent. It is said, 'Ye shall fear everyman his father and his mother (Deuteronomy 6:33)' and It is also said, The Lord thy God thou shalt fear, him thou shalt serve; thus the Holy Writ assimilates the fear of parents to the fear of God...(30[b])[28]

For the rabbis only one thing was more important than the honoring of one's parents and that was the study of the Torah — and then the study of the Torah produced greater devotion to one's parents (Megillah 16[b]).[29] Rabbi Brad Bloom in an excellent article entitled: *"Honor Thy Father and Thy Mother" The Scope of Filial Responsibility in Talmudic Literature* offers the following example how the rabbis would not allow a person to dispatch his responsibility to his parents:

> Rabbi Yannai and Rabbi Jonathan were sitting together when a man came up and kissed Rabbi Jonathan's feet. Rabbi Yannai asked, "What did you do for this man that he repays you so? Rabbi Jonathan answered, "Once this man came to me and complained about his son that he would not support his father. I told him 'Go gather the congregation together in the synagogue and·publicly shame him.'" Rabbi Yannai asked, "And why did you not compel the son to support his Father?" "Can you compel that?" Rabbi Jonathan responded. Rabbi Yannai answered, "You don't know that?" From that point on, Rabbi Jonathan taught, "One may compel a son to support his father." Rabbi Yose said, "Would that I was certain of all my traditions as I am that one, that 'one may compel a son to support his father.'"[30]

It is apparent that the issue here is not whether the son can or can not dispense with the obligations to support his father. The only question is how

---

[28] Cited by Moore, II, 132. In the Zohar, which is another valid indication of rabbinical views, compares "the Holy one" to the human father, and the human mother to the nation Israel. See Harry Sperling, Maurice Simon, Paul P. Levertoff, trans. and ed., *The Zohar* (London Soncino Press, 1933); III, 276–281.

[29] While honoring one's parent is equal to observing the Sabbath, honoring one's parents does not take priority over Sabbath observance. Otherwise, if a parent asks a son to do something on the Sabbath that is forbidden, the son should not honor the request. Yebamoth 5[b].

[30] Brad L. Bloom, "Honor Thy Father and Thy Mother" The Scope of Filial Responsibility in Talmudic Literature," *Central Conference American Rabbis Journal, Immanuel*, (Winter, 1993), p. 15. Henceforth Bloom, *Filial Responsibility*.

to make the man do what the Torah expects: whether he can be forced to do it or whether he must be shamed into doing it from social pressure. The rabbis respond that the man may indeed be forced to support his father. These words do not sound as if they were written by a person or a group of persons who could even tolerate allowing a person to suspend his obligations to his parents. Rabbi Bloom summarizes well the ancient history of Judaism in its attitude towards 'Honoring ones Parents.' Bloom wrote:

> What we see from these texts is that rabbis realized that they could not command people to feel love for their parents. They could, on the other hand, command children to preserve the dignity of their parent in a variety of different contexts. Their primary concerns were making sure that children were respectful through their responsibilities to financially sustain their parents. The rabbis were focusing their energies on creating a code of conduct, a proper ethical system for governing intergenerational relations. This ethos is, however, rooted in a very intense spiritual commitment to interpreting what God expects from us in our conduct with other human beings.[31]

The reader may object to using quotes from the Talmud as criteria for what the rabbis of the first century C.E. believed. However, Hebrew scholars such as Robert Gordis[32] and J. Duncan Derrett,[33] who is one of the foremost experts in Near Eastern studies, stipulate that the Talmud is excellent grounds to determine what the rabbis believed in the first century. Derrett likewise asserts that a rabbi as late as Moses ben Maimon (Maimonides c. 1180) is not too remote to be used as an interpreter of Palestinian Judaism of the first two centuries C.E. Derrett emphatically stated:

> ...The continuity of Jewish juridical thought, down to minute details, was still beyond question. The law was added to and developed, but remained essentially the same for the Jewish community as it had been from the time of the last great crisis in the 130's intensely self-absorbed and defensive, and had cherished its Torah as the symbol of its identity and hope of its redemption. Room for innovation was restricted, and even innovation took the cover of revealing the past through accurate interpretation. [34]

Derrett stipulates that if something is found in the Mishnahs, the Talmud, and Maimonides, then proving that it did not exist in first century Palestinian Judaism is almost impossible.[35] From the same perspective, finding something

---

[31]Bloom, *Filial Responsibility*, p. 17.

[32] Robert Gordis, *The Word and the Book* (New York: KTVA Publishing House, Inc., 1976); p.4.

[33]J. Duncan Derrett, *Law in the New Testament* (London: Darton, Longman Todd, 1970); p.xxviii–xxxvi. Henceforth Derrett.

[34]Derrett, xxxv.

[35]Derrett, xxxiv-xxxvi. Derrett's insight must be accepted about Palestinian Judaism,

in a non-Jewish source concerning something as important as the fifth commandment and then not finding it in the Mishnahs, Talmud, and Maimonides, would force one to question the accuracy of that non-Jewish source. Otherwise, two places in the New Testament would hardly be enough evidence to substantiate a devastating argument that the Pharisees permitted the doing away with one of the ten commandments.

"Doing away" is in reality a mild translation of the Greek word, ηκυρωσατε in Matthew 15:6, and the R.S.V. translation, "you make void" is likewise mild. Ακυροω is the Greek root word, and it is about the harshest word that could be used of the Pharisees. It means "to make invalid, to rob of force." (TDNT, III, 1099) Ακυροω is by the addition of the prefix A, a negation of the Greek word κυροω which means, "to enforce," "to confirm," "to validate." (TDNT, III, 1098) But κυροω finds its genesis in an even more basic Greek word κυριος and its verb derivative κυριευω. Κυρις is the Greek word that is uniformly translated Lord in the New Testament. It finds its genesis in words that meant "strong," or "brave." It came to mean "having power," "having legal power," "lawful," "empowered," or "important." The noun finally evolved to mean the ultimate authority of the emperor or then even God, and so the verb means ultimate validation or confirmation by authority. Addition of the "a" in Greek is the negation of the root meaning. Instead of confirmation and validation the meaning becomes complete negation and rejection.

It is not difficult to determine the meaning of the word of God. The Word of God is clearly not the Scriptures but the commandment: "Thou shalt honor thy Father and Mother." Nowhere else in the scriptures except Psalm 119 is the command called the word of God. But it is not difficult to see how Matthew could have applied from the Pharisaic teaching. The rabbis, as we likewise saw in Psalm 119, never refer to the commandments as the word of God, but they call them the "ten words," and it would not be difficult to see how Matthew could mistakenly make the transference of one of the ten words and call it the word of God.

Jesus' accusation that the rabbis "make void the word of God" certainly would have evoked the wrath of the Pharisees more than anything else that Jesus did or said. If one would have been permitted to listen to their response to Jesus, it might have gone something like this:

> Listen, Rabbi Jesus ben Joseph, it is not we who have made void the Word of God. We would never allow a person to dispense with his obligation to his parents by saying, "It is given to God." For us honoring the father and mother is the same as keeping the first commandment. One of our sages has said, "When a man honors his father and mother, God says I impute it to you as if I were dwelling among them and they honored me (Kiddushin 30[b])." Furthermore, we believe that it would be better for a man to go begging than to allow his parents to live in poverty (Peah 15[b]). But such is not the case with you Jesus

---

but thanks to the work of Jacob Neusner (see *Scriptures of Oral Torah* (San Francisco: Harper & Row, Publishers, 1987); 5–25; *Judaism and the Age of Constantine. The Initial Confrontation* (Chicago: The University of Chicago Press, 1987); p. 1 ff.) it is very apparent that up to 350 A. D. there was much more flexibility in Diaspora Jews, even to the extent of their forgetting their Hebrew. With the persecution that developed in the 4th and 5th century the Hebrew identity was regained and Palestinian rigidness became the identity of Judaism.

ben Joseph. You said to your disciples, "He who loves father or mother more than me is not worthy of me (Matthew 10:37)." In the same place you said, "I have come to set a man against his father, and a daughter against her mother... (Matthew 10:35)." Do you remember the time that one of our members came to you saying he wanted to follow you but his father had died and he needed to go and bury him. You said very disrespectfully to him, "Let the dead bury the dead" (Matthew 8:21–22). The crowning disrespect came when your own poor dear mother came to you, and when you were told by your disciples of her arrival, you said, "Who is my Mother and who are my brothers?" And stretching your arm over your disciples you said, "Here are my mother and my brothers. For whoever does the will of my Father in heaven is my brother, and sister, and mother" (Matthew 12:46–50). This we would never state, Jesus ben Joseph. We might consider every man who follows the Torah our brother (Megillah 2ª ff.). But, the most High Blessed be He, set our Mothers and Fathers in a special relationship to us. They are not our equals, but to be 'honored,' and we do that but you, Jesus, stand convicted by your own words. (If Luke 14:26 were used here, the rabbis judgement might be much harsher).

The rabbis did have problems with the severity of the death penalty for cursing one's parents (Exodus 21:17). They stipulated that a person could be put to death for cursing the mother or father only if in that cursing the person uses the sacred name of the Most High (Sanhedrin 66ª). Otherwise the death penalty was not to be enforced. Outside of this occurrence there cannot be found in any of the writings of the rabbis any lessening of the requirements of the parental honor commandment.

It would be difficult to determine the source of the accusation of making void the fifth commandment. Beare in his commentary suggests that the compiler of Matthew's thoughts had in mind a single incident where a rabbi had given permission to a person to dispense with his obligations to his parents and prejudicially prescribed the doing of such to all Pharisees. In loc. Another modern interpreter has suggested that rather than a reaction to the Pharisees, the compiler of Matthew has in mind practices that were current among Christians. People were using Jesus' teachings themselves to justify dispensing with their responsibility to their own parents, and the compiler of Matthew inserted this story just so they could not have that justification.[36] Others have suggested that the conflict between scribes and Pharisees reflects the struggle going on between Jewish and Christian groups in the second half of the first century. The Christians and Jews had become sufficiently isolated from one another so that Christians, particularly, had lost an accurate comprehension of Judaism. But, there was sufficient contact between these groups so that each knew that the other was claiming common roots. The Jews were

---

[36]J. Andrew Overmann's *Matthew's Gospel and Formative Judaism* (Minneapolis, MN: Fortress Press, 1990), p.19 f.; pp. 141-161. Henceforth Overmann. David Garland in his *The Intention of Matthew 23, Supplements to Novum Testamentum*, Volume LII, (Leiden: E.J. Brill, 1979. Henceforth Garland.) suggests that the real reason for Matthew's confusion of Jewish belief is because he no longer cared for the distinction and the reason for his work was an apologetic for why the Jews had rejected Jesus (in toto; 43ff.; 211-215).

accusing the Christians of being law breakers, and the Christians responded by asserting that it was not they who were the law breakers but the Jews, themselves, who were the violators of the Law. Hence this story of handwashing with its inaccurate picture of the scribes and Pharisees. A. J. Saldarini in *Pharisees and Sadducees in Palestine Society* asserts that the common feature that is present in almost every sectarian group is the denigration of the parent group.[37]

There can be no definitive answer to all the historical inaccuracies in this text. Even though the text inaccurately portrays Jesus as rejecting the Oral tradition and the text inaccurately reports rabbinical teaching, there is truth in the incident that transcends the deficiency in historical reporting. The very history of the rabbis, both biblically and extra-biblically, shows that they were tied to a religious rigidity and formalism. While this rigidity and formalism was not as extreme as is often portrayed in Christian circles, it was formidable. Almost everything that Jesus did and said was a threat to the orthodoxy of these pious religious folk. This is reflected on almost every page of the New Testament. Surely there must have been an incident where Jesus and his disciples were confronted for not washing their hands. Surely Matthew can be forgiven for slanting the evidence against the Scribes or Pharisees or for not checking out his sources better. The reader must remember accuracy in reporting is more a phenomenon of the present age, and the wise person must question whether we have objectivity in reporting news in some circles even today. In the first century A.D. there was no attempt at objectivity. The early historians such as Heroditus (c.484 –423 B.C.E.), Josephus (c. 37–c.100 C.E.), and Pliny (23–79 C.E.) knew no such thing as objectivity. Their biases permeated their works. This story is permeated with the clearly shown biases of Matthew towards the Scribes and Pharisees. It is obvious in the Qumran literature that the Essenes vilified the leadership in Jerusalem.[38] Likewise Moshe Weinfeld points out in his article, *The Charge of Hypocrisy in Matthew 23 and in Jewish Sources,* that the rabbis likewise vilified and called their detractors hypocrites.[39]

In concluding this chapter it must be stated that even if one were to deny all the biblical and extra-biblical problems this text creates, the most one could derive from this text is that Jesus calls the commandment the word of God. It again would be a logical fallacy to conclude that because the commandment is called the word of God that the Scriptures were to be called the word of God. It simply would mean that one would add another category to that which is considered the word of God. There would not only be the word of God that was given to the prophets and the word of God that was the Gospel message but also the word of God given to Moses in form of the law. There still is a great amount of material in the Bible that falls outside those categories.

---

[37]A. J. Saldarini, *Pharisees and Sadducees in the Palestinian Society: A Sociological Approach* (Wilmington, DE: Michael Glazier, 1988); p. 3ff.

[38]Yadin, Introduction to Scroll of War, p.18 ff.

[39]Moshe Weinfeld, *The Charge of Hypocrisy in Matthew 23 and in Jewish Sources* CCAR, Winter 1990 p. 52 ff.

Chapter VI

The Law and the Powerful Word of God

It is obvious there are some serious problems. The overwhelming evidence in the Bible has been that the word of God is a powerful and living force, that the word of God is God in power; that the word of God is Jesus, the Christ, from all eternity. But, then there is Psalm 119 and Matthew 15:6. In these texts it is clear that the Word of God refers to the law. While this might be sufficient evidence to establish that the word of God can be passive and be written down in the form of the law, there are sufficient problems with both texts to leave the question open. Is Psalm 119 descriptive of the way that human beings are to receive the Old Testament Law? Perhaps, as the Psalmist wonders, Jesus was God bringing correct understanding to the Law so human beings could be correctly obedient. Did Jesus consider the law the word of God, written in stone, binding in all time and in all places? Is Matthew 15:6 indicative that Jesus accepted two rudimentarily different words of God: one dynamic and the other written in stone in the form of the Law?

I believe that there is sufficient evidence in the Bible to answer these questions. Because the Law is the first pillar of the Old Testament Scriptures and because in the history of the church Matthew 15:6 is of paramount importance for the transference of the concept of the Word of God to the Bible, the next two chapters will deal with Jesus' attitude towards the Law. If it could be established that Jesus considered the Old Testament Law to be God's word, valid for all times and places, then one would be able to assert that the word of God was passive and written.

The Law: Jesus Came to Fulfill the Law

Matthew 5:17: Think not that I have come to abolish the law and the prophets; I have come not to abolish them but to fulfill them.

The place to begin to study Jesus' attitude towards the Law is with the Sermon on the Mount. While there are illuminating incidents or teachings throughout the gospels in which Jesus usually is found in sharp contrast to the legal authorities of Israel (Mt. 12:1–14; 15:1–9; 19:1–12; 23:1–39; Mk. 2:1–12; 2:23–28; 3:1–6; 10:1–12; Lk. 5:17–26; 6:1–11; 11:37–54; 13:10–17; 14:1–6; 18:18–27; John 5:1–47; 7:53–8:11; 9:1–41), the Sermon on the Mount contains the most information in the Gospels directly dealing with the Torah or Old Testament law.

As far as a substratum of literature is concerned, there is more written on the Sermon on the Mount than any other piece of literature. Most of what has been written and said about the Sermon on the Mount has not been in support of Jesus' teachings, I am afraid, but rather to make them socially more *palatable*. Mahatma Gandhi, a Hindu, quite accurately described the Church's attitude towards the sermon when he said, "If I had to face the Sermon on the Mount and my interpretation of it, I should not hesitate to say, 'Oh yes, I am a Christian.' . . . But negatively I can tell you that much of what passes as Christianity is a negation of the Sermon on the Mount."[1] Even contemporary scholarship, while it may enhance our understanding of the historical background of scriptures, often in relation to the Sermon on the Mount, has conclusions that are not dictated by science but rather by class, ethnic, and gender biases.

In this chapter it will be shown that the evidence within the scriptures and in the historical milieu all support interpreting Jesus in radical terms of the early church, St. Chrysostom, St. Benedict, St. Francis, and the Anabaptists. At the same time that the biblical and historical evidence supports the radical Christ, this same evidence destroys the doctrine that the Bible is the inerrant word of God. Specifically, the biblical and historical evidence does not support the idea that Jesus accepted the Old Testament or the law of Moses as the inerrant word of God.

Within the Sermon on the Mount the text that is most frequently used to lessen the impact of Jesus' teaching is Matthew 5:17–20 and specifically verse 17: "Think not that I have come to abolish the law and the prophets; I have come not to abolish them but to fulfill them."

The basic hermeneutical problem of the text revolves around one Greek word, πληρωσαι, translated as 'fulfill.' What does Jesus mean when he states that he "came to fulfill the law and the prophets"? Augustine (354–430), the Bishop of Hippo, allowed that there might be two possible ways of interpreting 'Fulfill': "Either that [Jesus] is going to make it complete by adding what it lacks or he is going to do what it claims. (CF, v. 1, p. 35)" Luther took exception to Augustine's first interpretation. "All by itself, the Law is so rich and perfect that no one needs to add anything to it . . . (Luther's Works, Volume 21, p. 69)" By 'fulfill' the reformer interpreted Jesus to mean that he came to bring proper 'understanding' or 'teaching' of the 'Law and the Prophets.' In Luther's opinion the Sadducees and Pharisees had 'corrupted the law.' Christ came to 'clean the law off,' and 'polish it' (Luther's Works, 21, 67–70). John Calvin's interpretation differed slightly from Luther's. His emphasis was that Jesus came to place the Christians under the full authority of the Law, and bring us to the proper understanding of the law (*Commentary on the Harmony of the Gospels* I, 277–278). In essence what the interpretations of Luther and Calvin did was to assert that there were no contradictions between Jesus' teachings and the Old Testament. Therefore, the Old Testament could be and was used to justify warfare, the compilation of wealth and, coupled with a few verses from Paul, the oppression of women.

Early in this century, scholars saw Jesus' teachings as a radical departure from the law.[2] After Krister Stendal's monumental work, *The School of St.*

---

[1]Louis Fischer, *Gandhi* (New York: The New American Library, 1954), p. 131.

[2]Adolph von Harnack (1851-1930), *The History of Ancient Christian Literature* (1904), Benjamin Bacon, *Studies in Matthew* (New York: Henry Holt & Co., 1930), p. 181, and T. W. Manson recognized the radicalness of Jesus teachings, and indeed that Jesus' teachings were a departure from Old Testament law. They resolved the hermeneutical problems of Matthew 5:17-20 by asserting that the pericope was inserted in the sermon by later editor to show that Jesus was not really contradicting or opposed to the law Adolf Harnack German church historian and theologian, in Benjamin W. Bacon, T. W. Manson, "The Sayings of Jesus," *The Mission and Message of Jesus*, H. D. A. Major, T. W. Manson, and C. J. Wright (New York: E. P. Dutton and Co., Inc., 1938), pp. 515-517; 445-447, see also

Matthew, there has been an abundance of books, monographs and articles,[3] stipulating that, rather than being a radical departure from the Law, Jesus' teachings as Matthew presents them are just another rabinical interpretation among the many interpretations. Consequently, much of modern scholarship ends up in a roundabout way with Luther's and Calvin's conclusions.

Gerhard Barth, of Heidelberg Germany (1955) divided the modern interpretation of 'fulfill' into three different approaches: 1. "set forth the true meaning," 2. "Jesus declares that the law is binding, valid." 3. "Jesus fulfilled the law by doing it". Barth believed, however, that all three approaches were not accurate in their interpretation of 'fulfill'. He believed that 'fulfill' would most properly be understood as Jesus establishing the will of God in the law and the prophets.[4] W. D. Davies and Dale C. Allison in their recent commentary on Matthew in the updated *International Critical Commentary* give a much more comprehensive picture of interpretations of 'fulfil' with nine categories. Most of the categories that they describe do not deal with the inherent problems of Old Testament Law and the contradictions of Jesus' teachings with the Law itself. However, Davies and Allison suggest that two of the categories together present a more accurate understanding of what Jesus meant by 'fulfill'. These categories are: "Jesus 'fulfills' or 'completes' the law by bringing a new law which transcends the old," and, "The 'fulfillment' is eschatological: the telos which the Torah anticipated, namely, the Messiah, has come and revealed the law's definitive meaning. Prophecy has been realized."[5] Thus the law and the prophets anticipated and proclaimed the arrival and presence of Jesus, the Messiah, but his law transcends the Old.[6]

However, from the analysis of the text and historical background of both

---

The Sayings of Jesus (1949), p.152 ff. Henceforth Manson, Sayings. Others led by Hans Windische of Germany (1927), *The Meaning of the Sermon on the Mount*, trans. Maclean Gilmour (Philadelphia: Westminster Press, 1937), p.106. (Henceforth Windische, Meaning) have suggested that 5:17-20 as an anti-Pauline tract.

[3]R. H. Gundry, *The Use of the Old Testament in the Gospel of Matthew*, Supplement No. 18, *Society of New Testament Studies* (Shefield, England: Shefield University Press, 1967). Henceforth Gundry. Geza Vermes, *Jesus, the Jew* (Philadelphia: Fortress Press, 1973); Gerhard Barth, "Matthew's Understanding of the Law," in *Tradition and Interpretation in Matthew* by Gunther Bornkamm, Gerhard Barth, and Heinz Joachim Held, trans. by Gerald Scott (Philadelphia: The Westminster Press, 1976),. Henceforth G. Barth; Robert Banks, *Jesus and the Law in the Synoptic Tradition* (Cambridge: Cambridge University Press, 1975), pp. 1 ff. Henceforth Banks. M. D. Goulder, *Midrash and Lection in Matthew* (London: S.P.C.K., 1974), pp. 3 ff. Henceforth, Goulder. J. Andrew Overmann, *Matthew's Gospel and Formative Judaism* (Minneapolis, MN: Fortress Press, 1990), pp. 6 ff. Henceforth, Overmann; Klyne Snodgrass, "Matthew and the Law", *1988 Seminar Papers of the Society of Biblical Literature* (Atlanta, GA: Scholars Press, 1989), pp. 836-854.

[4]Gerhard Barth, "The Matthew's Understanding of the Law," in *Tradition and Interpretation in Matthew* by Gunther Bornkamm, Gerhard Barth, and Heinz Joachim Held, trans. by Gerald Scott (Philadelphia, The Westminster Press, 1976), p. 67.Henceforth G. Barth

[5]W. D. Davies and Dale C. Allison, *The Gospel of Matthew*, I (ICC, 1989), in loc. Henceforth Davies & Allison.

[6]Eduard Schweizer suggests that the meaning is that Jesus comes to fulfill *what the Law and the prophets only announce*. Eduard Schweizer, *The Good News according to Matthew*, trans. by David Greene (Atlanta, GA: John Knox Press, 1975), p. 107. Henceforth, Schweitzer.

the Old Testament Law and Jesus' teaching, Davies' and Allison's conclusion that Jesus' law 'transcends' the Old Testament law is still weak. When the Old Testament Law is viewed for what it is, and when Jesus' law is contrasted with the Old, it has to be acknowledged that Jesus' Law not only transcends the Old but replaces it. Otherwise their interpretation that Jesus is the Messiah to whom the Law and prophets witnessed, and that he is their proper culmination, is, I believe, the accurate interpretation of what Jesus meant by *fulfill*.

The main reason most interpretations of this passage have been flawed is that the interpreters have started at the wrong place in the equation and asked the wrong questions. The first question that expositors have asked is, "What does it mean to say that Jesus fulfills the Law and the prophets?" Expositors would have been correct if they had asked first: What is meant by *the Law and the prophets*? After answering that question, the question of how Jesus fulfills the law and the prophets might be properly asked.

In the formula, *the law and the prophets*, the commentators have correctly interpreted *the law* to be the Torah, the Law of Moses. The problem, as will be shortly apparent, is that the Law that the commentators envision is fantasized, idealized, and even whitewashed law. Contemporary commentators acknowledge that *prophets* mean the Old Testament prophets. Most commentators totally ignore the prophets in the formula. Because of the identification of 'iota or a dot' in verse 18 with the Torah of Moses, almost the total stress in interpretation has been on *the law*. In fact some commentators have gone so far as to suggest that *the prophets* was a *later addition to the formula*.[7]

I believe that most of the previous interpretations of *fulfill* would have been rejected if the commentators would have been consistent in their interpretation, and they have not been consistent because of the fact that most of the commentators were male. If the commentators had been female and if they had not been indoctrinated by the male gender bias they would have come up with remarkably different conclusions than the theologians historically have.

The prophets, however, are indispensable to the formula. The text does not advocate that Jesus was the fulfillment of individual prophesies, proclaiming the judgment of God against specific kings, Israel or other nations, or that Jesus was the *fulfillment* of specific demands by Yahweh on certain nations or individuals. In Jesus' view, the chief function of the prophets was to proclaim his coming as the Messiah. The other functions of the prophets were simply of secondary importance. Jesus was the end and purpose of the prophesy.

The same thing can be said of Matthew 22:34–40, the great commandment. Jesus did not mean that every law and every prophesy is dependent on loving God and one's neighbor, but the essence of the law and the prophets is found in these two commandments.[8] This is precisely what Matthew 5:17 means by

---

[7]M'Neile, in loc

[8]The Greek word γρεμαται, which the R.S.V. translates as *depend*, is most helpful in understanding Matthew 5:17. Professor Bertram of the University of Giesen asserts that it is an *exact parallel* to πληροσαι, *fulfill*. TDNT, III, p. 921. Bertram wrote:

The particular significance of Mt.'s metaphor of hanging (en [on] not ex [from]) is as follows. As objects hang on a nail, and fall if the nail does not hold, so

the law and the prophets.[9] Jesus did not come to fulfill individual laws, but he came to fulfill the reason that Israel was called into being. Israel had been called to be a nation set apart by the law so that all nations might be blessed through it (Genesis 12:3; Isaiah 11:1–10). Likewise, Jesus did not come to fulfill each and every prophesy but the prophetic hope of Israel for all the nations and people.

For all those who have interpreted *fulfill the law* as *bringing its true meaning into existence*, *declaring it binding and valid*, *doing the requirements*, or *establishing the will of God in the law*, Jesus' very next statement should be confusing, confounding, and even dismaying. He stated, "For truly, I say to you, till heaven and earth pass away not an iota, not a dot, will pass from the law until all is accomplished (vs. 18)."

W. G. Kummel, asserted that κεραια, *dot* (RSV), or *stroke* (JB or NEB), referred to the practice of the scribes when they made little flourishes on the Hebrew yodh (y).[10] Likewise M. D. Goulder in *Midrash and Lection in Matthew* found passages in the rabbis that he felt were identical to that of Jesus. Goulder cites the following two passages: "God spake (the Torah) – Solomon and a thousand like him will pass away, but I will not permit the smallest stroke of thee to pass away" (Sanhedrin, II 20ᶜ). "Heaven and earth have measures, but the law has none: heaven and earth will have an end, but the law will not." Genesis R. 10.1. Goulder's commentary on Jesus' statement *not an iota, not a dot* is much like Kummel's, "The Scribes' love for the text of the pentateuch is very apparent. Not one yodh, the smallest, not one qots, the flourish with which the scribe formed his letter, nothing shall fail of the fulfillment to the end of time. Every commandment must be kept."[11]

If Jesus' statement of verse 18 is interpreted as Kummel and Goulder interpret it, verse 19 ("Whoever then relaxes one of the least of these commandments, and teaches men so shall be least in the Kingdom of heaven, but he who does them and teaches them shall be great in the kingdom of heaven.") would place Jesus squarely in the rabbis' camp. The following are just a few quotes (cited by Str-Bil., in. loc.) of the rabbis that would seem to support such a contention, "Behave towards an easy commandment exactly as towards a difficult one; for you do not know what rewards will be given for the commandments." (Aboth 2:1ᵇ) "The Scriptures make the easiest among the easy commandments equal to the hardest among the hard. (Kiddushin 61ᵇ) Such statements reaffirm the fact that the rabbis were not legal innovators. Any interpretation was to move the Jews into better adherence to the Old Testament

---

that they are essentially dependent on it, so the details of moral conduct or individual requirements of the law are, dependent on the law of love...It means... that the love of God is seen to be the sustaining basis of all human attitudes, and action. But the love of God in men [people], and therewith also the love of men [people], is revealed and actualized in love for one's neighbor. TDNT, III, p. 920. [] Brackets this author. () Parentheses Bertraim's.

[9]Acts 13:15; 24:14; the law of Moses and the prophets, 28:23) refers to the Scriptures. In Mt. 11:13,Lk.16:16–17; *the law and the prophets* refer to an age that existed up to John. Matthew 7:12; & 22:40, the Law and prophets refer to the Scriptures

[10]W. G. Kümmel, "Jesus und der Judische Traditionsgedanke," in *Zeitschrift für neutestamentlich Wissenschaft*, 33 (1934), p. 127.

[11]Goulder, pp. 3 –15.

Torah.

If most interpretations of 'fulfill' that accept "the iota and dot" and "the least of these commandments" as applying to the laws of the Torah, then the commentators advocating these positions would have to acknowledge that Jesus' and the rabbis' attitudes towards the law were essentially the same. Even Augustine's interpretation that Jesus fulfilled the law by doing the *requirements* of the law rather than *his doing the law*, would be essentially the way the Rabbis considered the Law should be performed.

Jesus' Commands and the Old Testament Law

"You have heard it said ... but I say unto you ... "

These arguments do not hold when Jesus' teachings, as they are presented in the gospel, are compared with the Old Testament and rabbinical teachings. While Jesus cannot be described as destroying the law, he cannot be described as maintaining the smallest detail of the law, the stroke and the flourish. It is an undeniable fact that Jesus *establishes the will of God*, as G. Barth asserts,[12] but it is impossible to support that he *establishes the will of God* in the law itself, as it is written and interpreted in the first five books of the Bible. He took the law, reshaped it, and made a totally new law. Most Christians have failed to grasp the reality of this through the ages. Because Christians have failed to comprehend the radical nature of what Jesus did, they have participated in activities that totally deny the Lord and his teachings, and then they have used the Scriptures to justify those activities.

When the Sermon is examined, it is clear that Jesus broadens the implications of three Old Testament laws; one he totally changes so it becomes a completely new law, and two laws he totally abrogates. The three laws that Jesus broadens need no real comments, for one could say that they fall into the category of supporting the law. The rabbis had no problem with broadening the Law. They would consider this placing fences around the law to prevent real violations of the law (Aboth I; Sanhedrin 46ᵃ). Jesus' teachings on anger (verses 21–26) while totally original and profound would be considered broadening of the law. While there cannot be found statements as strong as Jesus' in the Rabbis, there can be found similar pronouncements (Sanhedrin 102ᵇ; Berakoth 30ᵃ; Pesahim 66ᵇ; Yoma 75ᵃ). Likewise his teachings on oath taking (vss. 33–37) may also be considered putting a fence around the Law. Jesus' teaching differed remarkably from the rabbis' teachings in their simplicity, but the Rabbis were terribly concerned that no one in Israel took the Lord's name in vain (Shabbath 33a; Yoma 73a etc.).

Jesus, Man, Woman, and Adultery

Matthew 5:27–28: "You have heard that it was said, 'You shall not commit adultery.' But I say unto you every one who looks at a woman lustfully has already committed adultery with her in his heart."

In Jesus' teachings on male and female, adultery and divorce, he turned the Old Testament laws upside down, and totally changed them. Most Christians have mistakenly interpreted this commandment as being implied in the

---

[12]G. Barth, p. 68.

92

ten commandments or that Jesus brought the proper understanding to the adultery commandment. It is instructive to examine Luther's interpretation of this passage. Not because Luther is so typical of Christian interpretation of this passage, but because the distortion of Christian interpretation is so apparent in Luther. Luther stated:

> In this pinch of salt directed against the teaching of the Pharisees, He discusses two subjects, adultery and divorce. They had interpreted adultery the same way they had interpreted the Fifth commandment and taught that this was only a prohibition of actual adultery. The ardor of the heart with its evil lusts and love, as well as the obscene language and vulgar gestures this produced, they did not think of as sinful, or as harmful to their sanctity . . . Thus instead of teaching God's commandments, they distorted them; instead of making people pious, they only made them worse, opening the door to every kind of sin and immorality. But here you are listening to another Master. He turns their sanctity into sin and shame, illuminating this commandment and arguing that when a man leers at a woman or cracks shady jokes or even thinks about her lustfully, this is an adultery of the eyes or the mouth, and above all an adultery of the heart. (Luther's Works, Volume 21, p.84.)

More recent interpretations have been much more charitable than Luther to the rabbis. In the following, James Stagg wrote one of the best interpretations of modern conservative scholarship:

> The Ten Commandments forbade adultery and also coveting another man's wife (Ex. 20:17; Deut. 5:21). Upon this foundation Judaism built in two directions. It gave increasing attention to the lustful look as sin against one's own marriage. On the other hand, the rabbis tended to reduce the concept of adultery to sin against the property rights of another Jewish man, adultery being limited to illicit sexual relationship with the wife or the betrothed of another Jew. In this view of a single woman or of a non-Jew's wife, intercourse was not considered adultery.
>
> Jesus saw adultery as a sin against any woman, as something destructive to the offender, to the offended, and to marriage, and first of all a matter of attitude or intention . . . [13]

It is hard to imagine how Luther or Stagg derived their accusations against the Pharisees. Jesus does not mention them in this passage. There is nothing in the history of these pious people, these Pharisees, that would permit one to make such accusations against them. The rabbis might even have been found agreeing with Jesus in much of his teaching.[14]

The problem with Professor Stagg's accusation against the rabbis is that

---

[13]Staggs, in loc.

[14] As evidence Samuel Tobias Lachs, in *A Rabbinical Commentary on the New Testament* (*Hoboken*, NJ: KTAV Publishing House, 1987 in loc. Henceforth, Lachs) quotes the following from the rabbis, "He who has a pure heart in love, looks not on a woman with thoughts of Fornication." (Testament of Benjamin) "Unchaste imagination is more injurious than sin itself."(Yoma 29[a])

the concept of adultery as being a "sin against the property rights of another Jewish man . . . " did not originate with them. It is true that rabbis did see women as men's possessions but the rabbis did not reduce adultery to a matter of violation of property rights. They were faithfully interpreting the seventh commandment.[15] In Old Testament law, women were indeed property of men. Adultery was the most serious violation of a man's property rights. The way to discover this is to let the Old Testament speak for itself.

In the Old Testament law, the law of Moses, there are very few places where women receive favorable treatment. To receive this favorable treatment a woman had to become a widow. The one truly positive law concerning women in the Torah is the following: "You shall not afflict any widow or orphan. If you do afflict them, and they cry out to me, I will surely hear their cry, and my wrath will burn, and I will kill you with the sword, and your wives will become widows and your children fatherless" (Ex 22:22–24; cf. Dt. 10:18 RSV).

There could not be a stronger statement anywhere against the abuse or the taking advantage of widows. At the same time, widows were denigrated to the status of scavengers. They could scavenge the fields of the farmers for produce, and the farmers were commanded not to clear harvest produce so that the widows could feed themselves and their children (Dt. 24:19–22).[16]

From the beginning of a woman's life she was inferior to a man, according to Hebrew Law. After the birth of a boy a woman was considered unclean for seven days, and then the boy was circumcised. The mother was then to wait thirty-three days to be purified. On the other hand, if a woman had a baby girl, she was considered unclean for fourteen days. She was then to wait sixty-six days before she was purified (Leviticus 12:1–5). It does not take a genius to figure out that if the Lord legislated these laws, God considered the birth of a female to be a worse event than that of a male.[17] If the very birth

---

[15]Thanks to the insights of Rachel Biale in *Women and Jewish Law* (New Yourk: Schocken Books, Inc., 1984, pp. 3 ff) We know that the rabbis' interpretation helped humanize the Old Testament's attitude towards women.

[16] There has long been a Judaic-Christian bias which has asserted superiority of the Jewish culture over the surrounding cultures in relationship to the treatment of women. The following statement from Madeline S. and J. Lane Miller's *Harper's Bible Dictionary,* are typical of that bias: "The lot of Hebrew women of any age was usually better than that of their contemporaries of Mesopotamia, Arabia or Egypt, unless the latter were royal rank." (New York, NY: Harper & Row Publishers, Inc., 1973), p.821. The existing documents from surrounding culture do not, however support those claims The Hammurabi Law Code of Babylon allowed for women to support themselves through businesses. They could possess and operate farms. (ANET, pp. 163–179; Laws: 107–109; 141; 150). While there is no provision for women to support themselves stipulated within Assyrian Law, and one has to acknowledge that Women are passively dependent on men, Assyrians seem to be much more humane than the Hebrews with regard to the widow. They make every attempt to see that the widow is cared for by her father, her sons, her husband's father, or sons of the husband from other marriages (ANET, p.184, #43; 46). In Middle Assyrian Laws there is a statute that sounds as humane if not more humane than many western nations. This law stipulates that if a poor soldier died in the service of the king, the king was obligated to support the wife. (ANET, p. 184, #45) She would not need to scavenge as a beggar as a soldier's widow would have had to do in Hebrew society.

[17]Here is another good example of interpretation that has been based on projection of one's views on the Bible rather than on the text itself. Ronald Clements is in his Broadmans Bible Commentary states that "childbirth" was "an experience filled with mystery and wonder," but a time of great danger in which "it was necessary that the mother and child

process makes the woman unclean and therefore separates her from the presence of God, she is unclean twice as long for birth of a female child than a male child.

The difference in the time that a woman was unclean after birth of a female or male infant indicates that the uncleanness had nothing to do with health or biological phenomena. There is essentially no difference in labor and trauma that a woman experiences in the birth of a male or female child.[18] However, there is a difference in the fragility of the life of the male and the female infants. Again, the law has nothing to do with the birth process and the fragility of life after birth. It is not the female child that needs the most protection after birth but the male infant. Without the aid of modern technology, male infants have always been in greater jeopardy than female infants.[19]

---

should be properly protected, that due thanks should be given to God, and that proper atonement made lest the forces of evil should bring disaster." Furthermore Clements asserts that *childbirth, maturity, marriage,* and *death* were all *great transitions in life* where *men sensed the awesomeness of the divine presence.* While Clements' words sound wonderful and like a great interpretation, his interpretation is not based on the text but rather on wishful thinking. The text does not state anything about the presence of God; or that God is concerned with the life of the child or the mother. The context, chapters 11–15, is as lenghty series of laws dealing with uncleanness. In chapter 10, after God killed Nadab and Abihu, the sons of Aaron, because they did not bring the proper fire into the presence of the Lord (vv. 1–2), the Lord stated: "I will show myself holy among those who are near me, before all people I will be glorified." In verses 9–11 the Lord tells Aaron that he and his sons should not drink any wine or strong drink before they enter the convocation of the people, *the tent meeting,* because it is their job *to distinguish between the holy and the common, between the clean and the unclean,* and *to teach the people all the statutes.* It is very clear from the text and from the rest of the witness of the Torah that the Jews were called to be a Holy people. Part of being Holy people was being a clean people. Leviticus 11 there is the list of all the living creatures that were unclean and therefore could not be eaten. Right before the discussion of uncleanness of women at child birth is the prohibition against eating any thing that slithers along the ground or swarms along the ground. The reason for this Yahweh says is "For I am the Lord who brought you up out of the land of Egypt, to be your God; you shall therefore be holy, for I am holy." (Verse 45, R.S.V.) With the birth of a child being surrounded with all the other laws on uncleanness that would obviously separate oneself from God, it is hard to imagine how one could possibly conceive that somehow this part of the Torah was concerning itself with the *presence of God* or that these laws dealt with the *awesomeness* or *sanctity of the birth process.*

[18]Thanks to Loraine Turner, M.D., for the confirmation of this fact.

[19]In some cultures the female infant death rate might be high not because of biological inferiority but because of infanticide. While there may have been some improvements in delivery methods in the first part of the twentieth century, the differences from first century methods were not that great. Infant mortality rate was substantial in both eras. A look at the infant mortality rate in the first seven years of this century reveals that female infants have a much greater chance of survival than do males. According to the Bureau of Census: Bicentennial, Colonial Times to 1970 (Washington, D. C.: Department of Commerce, 1975), the following numbers of infants died before they were 1 year old, per thousand:

Year	Female	Male
1900	145.4	179.1
1901	126.1	156.4
1902	124.1	153.4
1903	118.3	146.6
1904	124.2	153.9
1905	125.5	156.6
1906	129.2	160.2

Consequently, the law concerning birth is based not on the natural happening but strictly on the holiness code of Yahweh that favored the male.

The next area of life where the inequity between male and female in the Old Testament Torah is found when a Hebrew man (not man and woman) sells his (not their) son or daughter into slavery (Exodus 21:1–11). After six years a male Hebrew servant must be given his freedom. The female slave was never to be given her freedom.[20] It could be assumed that the woman slave was most likely used as a concubine. Women would never be used in the fields. Because she was a concubine she would be considered damaged property.[21] Her hymen would not be intact and consequently she would not have prospects for marriage. It would be better for her if she remained in slavery, otherwise she would most likely end up as a prostitute.

The next stage in the female's life which the law of Moses deals with is the pre-betrothal and betrothal period. These laws are found in the laws covering adultery in Deuteronomy 22:23–29. I cite the New International Version because I believe that translation reflects the Hebrew accurately:

> [22]If a man happens to meet in town a virgin pledged to be married and he sleeps with her, [24]you shall take both of them to the gate of that town and stone them to death–the girl because she was in a town and did not scream for help, and the man because he violated another man's wife. You must purge this evil from among you. [25]But if out in the country a man happens to meet a girl pledged to be married and rapes her, only the man who has done this shall die. [26]Do nothing to the girl; she has committed no sin deserving death. This case is like someone attacking and murdering his neighbor, [27]for the man found the girl out in the country, and though the betrothed girl screamed, there was no one to rescue her. [28]If a man happens to meet a virgin and rapes her and they are discovered, [29]he shall pay the girl's father fifty shekels of silver. He must marry the girl, for he has violated her. He can never divorce her.

There are some readily observable features in this passage that confirm the Old Testament Torah had an adverse attitude towards women. From the Hebrew, and the above translation, force was the element in the last two copulations, but it may also be implied in the first copulation. The fact that the text indicates that the woman was to be killed because she did not scream out (צעק׳) implies that the man most likely approached the woman with intent to rape her, but the text insinuates that instead of fighting or screaming out, she went along with the act and thus was complicitous. That there is no

---

[20]Here again conservative commentators attempt to justify inequities in the Mosaic law by stating it was superior to the laws of the surrounding area. Roy L. Honeycutt, Jr., in his *Broadmend's Commentary* on Exodus, made the following observation, "Because of the secondary and often unprotected role of women in the ancient world, it is of unique significance that the Old Testament gave specific guidance to Israelite jurists who made decisions concerning the 'amah, the female slave." "Exodus," Volume 1, *BBC*, in loc. Such thinking is totally flawed and does not reflect the knowledge of the surrounding cultures of Israel. The Code of Hamurabi stipulated that both the Babylonian male and female slaves were to be free after three years. (Code of Hammurabi (117), ANET, pp.170–171)

[21]Brevard Child, *The Book of Exodus* (Philadelphia: The Westminster Press, 1974), p. 469.

mention in the law of other possibilities is just another indication of how antagonistic the Torah was to women. It does not take much genius to imagine from what we know of rape today what rape must have been in Old Testament times: how fear may have paralyzed the woman, making it impossible for her to scream out, or how the man may have overpowered her so she could not scream. Yet the woman was assumed to be guilty even though she did not cooperate or comply with the rapist, because she did not scream out. Even if that possibility was not meant in this text, the omission of that possibility from the Scriptures is egregious and the law is defective for the omission.

In the next two rapes the reader must question whether there is any justice in these laws for the assaulted woman. From the second law (vss. 25–27) it is obvious that the execution of the male and the preserving the female was far from humane. It is obvious with the premium placed on virginity in the Hebrew Law (22:13–21; cf. Lev. 21: 7–8, 13–15), the rape most likely destroyed the girl's chances of having a husband. Since being married and bearing children (particularly, boys) was the essence of womanhood, the rape for all purposes may have ended her chances of having a worthwhile life. It may have likewise forced her to be destitute for the rest of her life if her brothers and father refused to support her. In short, the girl's life was over and the text insinuates as much, "This case is like someone attacking and murdering his neighbor (vs. 26)." The girl was effectively murdered. Preserving the life of the rapist and forcing him to support the woman would have been better for the woman.

This is the impact of what happens in the third incident where a man raped an unbetrothed virgin. If this man was caught, he was forced not to just support the girl, but to marry the girl and never divorce her. One has to wonder who was being punished in the incident, the rapist or the girl who had to live the rest of her life with her rapist. Of course, the feelings of the girl did not count. The father was paid off for his investment in his property and would not suffer the financial loss for the ruptured hymen.

Questioning the humanity of laws governing rape is only natural, but even more inhumane are the laws governing virginity (Deuteronomy 22:13–22). In these laws, if a groom claims he did not find proof that his bride was a virgin— *tokens of virginity*— and if her parents could not produce nuptial sheets with blood stains on them,[22] the young woman was taken to her father's house and stoned. Normally, stoning took place outside the walls of the city. In this case the stoning took place in front of the home of the woman's father, because the father had perpetrated *fraud* by selling damaged goods and was guilty of not being a good *guardian of his property.*[23] The law, of course, did not take into consideration that there might be other reasons than intercourse for the ruptured hymen. The girl could have been killed for an accidental happening or a deviation in nature.

---

[22]S.R. Driver, *Deuteronomy* (ICC), in loc.; W. Gunther Plaut, Bernard J. Bomberger, and William W. Hallo, *Torah* (New York: The Union of American Hebrew Congregations, 1981), in loc.; Gerhard Von Rad, *Deuteronomy,* in *The Old Testament Library*, eds. G. Ernest Wright, John Bright, et. al. (Philadelphia: The Westminster Press, 1966), in loc.

[23]Anthony Philips, *Deuteronomy*, in *The Cambridge Bible Commentary*, eds. P. R. Ackroyd, A. R. C. Leaney, and J.W. Packard (Cambridge: Cambridge University Press, 1973), in loc.

If the parents produced the nuptial sheets, and there was blood on them, the bridegroom had to pay a penalty of one hundred shekels of silver not to the bride whose reputation he besmirched but to the father (vs. 19). He then had to live with the bride for the rest of his life. Would the bride consider this to be better than stoning? She was now forced to live with a man who would have impugned her reputation and callously would have had her killed. Many might say this would be a fate worse than death, but then the feelings of the woman did not matter.

It is clear from the above that before her marriage the woman was the property of her father. Normally the groom paid fifty shekels of silver for his property, actually called the *bride price* in Exodus 22:16–17.[24] The groom in the previous case had to pay double to the father because he lied. This case underscores just how unjust the law of Moses was and how anti-woman it was.

After the husband bought his wife, she was no longer her father's possession. She belonged to her husband. A fact confirmed by the tenth commandment. The commandment lists the wife among the possessions of a man his house— donkey, ox, servants, and everything else. Furthermore, the Hebrew expression, describing the marriage process, "to take a wife (לקח אשה Genesis 19:14; 21:20; 24:3, 4, 7, 15, 37, 67; 25:1; 26:34; 27:46; 28:1, 2; 38:6, etc.)" underscores the demeaning attitute of Jews to women. The expression "to take (לקח)" literally means *to take in hand, to grasp* as one would take an object or lead an animal by a leash (BDB). The word is first used in the description for Yahweh's *taking* the rib from Adam and presenting him with a wife, Eve (Genesis 2:20). The term is then used almost every time for the act of seeking a wife or finding a wife. This *to take* (לקח) is used to describe the rape in Deuteronomy 22:25. The term is likewise used to describe the forbidden acts of having sex with a mother-in-law (Leviticus 20:14) and incestuous relations (Leviticus 20:17). Another term used to describe marriage is בעל (Deuteronomy 21:13; 22:22; 24:1). It means *to rule over, or own* and is transliterated *Baal*. This the reader will remember was the Caananite word for God (cf. Judges 2:10–15 or 16:29–33 etc.) The noun-forms mean husband, owner, ruler and Lord (BDB).

Only with this whole attitude towards women in the Old Testament can one understand the adultery commandment. The Hebrew term for *adultery* is נָאַף as it first occurs in the Hebrew Bible in the commandment (Exodus 20:14). The commandment is very simple לא תנאף "You shall not commit adultery." Here there is no definition of what נָאַף means. If one were just reading Hebrew for the first time, had no dictionary and had no previous knowledge of what נָאַף meant, one would not have the slightest idea of what was being forbidden. The next time the term adultery occurs is in Leviticus 20:10 which states, "If a man commits adultery with the wife of his neighbor, both the adulterer and adulteress shall be put to death." Since the context of the proscribed behavior is included in the description of various forbidden types of sexual intercourse, it can safely be assumed that adultery was having sex with the neighbor's wife. The next time the word occurs is in the Deuteronomic recitation of the

---

[24]In this case the father, not the daughter, was given the choice of whether or not his daughter would marry the scoundrel who *seduced* his daughter. If the father chose not to let his daughter marry the scoundrel, the man had to pay the *bride price* anyway. This was because the daughter was damaged property and the father could not resell her. If he did, the laws in Deuteronomy 22:13–21 would then have applied.

commandment (Deuteronomy 5:18). Therefore, from the Torah itself, the most one can assume is that adultery is having sex with a neighbor's wife.

To cement the argument about women as mere property, the biblical record demonstrates that many behaviors traditionally considered by Christians to be violations of the seventh commandment were not considered so in the Old Testament. Having promiscuous sex with women who were not related to oneself, engaged, or married, was permissible. Even paying for sex from a prostitute, while not acceptable and a holy way, did not qualify for adultery and thus did not qualify for the death penalty (see Genesis 38:1–30 Joshua 2:1–24; 6:22–25).

There is no need to do a protracted exegesis on this subject. The reader may simply be reminded of some Old Testament history. David was reported having at least seven wives and at least ten concubines or mistresses. The only time he got in trouble with the adultery commandment was when he stole another man's wife. Granting that polygamy was acceptable, the fact that he had sexual relations with ten women who were not his wives was not considered to be a violation of the seventh commandment. When it comes to Solomon, he could hardly have been tempted to commit adultery, after all, he had seven hundred wives. In addition, he had three hundred concubines—non-paid prostitutes or women who were to gratify his sexual needs. The possibilities would be enough to boggle the mind of the worst pornographer. Adultery was not Solomon's problem according to the Bible. Solomon's problem was that he had chosen foreign wives and had allowed these wives to lead his heart after false gods (I Kings 11:4). This was the reason that his heirs were to be deprived of ruling the Kingdom (I Kings 11:9–13). It was not because Solomon had so many wives and concubines. If Solomon had not gone after foreign wives and concubines and worshiped their gods, Yahweh, as he was presented in the Old Testament, would not have had any problems with seven hundred wives and three hundred concubines. There was no violation of the seventh commandment. There could not be any stronger evidence in the Old Testament Canon that adultery was having sexual intercourse with another man's wife or the woman to whom he was engaged.

When Jesus stated "You have heard that it was said, 'You shall not commit adultery.' But I say unto you every one who looks at a woman lustfully has already committed adultery with her in his heart." The "but" is most definitive, most negative. Jesus not only negates the commandment, he changes the whole attitude towards women.

Jesus' statement differs remarkably from that of the rabbis. For the rabbis a man not looking at a woman with lust was only for his own protection. It was preventing him from committing sexual acts with another man's wife. The demeaning of the woman was in no part of the consideration.

With Jesus, just the opposite is true. Professor Francis Beare, University of Toronto, is correct in pointing out that one of the meanings of the Greek word, Επιθυμησαι, to lust after can be translated to covet. Beare believed that Jesus was coupling the seventh and the the tenth commandments and that the woman that Jesus has in mind is definitely married, and he was saying don't covet another man's wife. But then Beare goes on to confine Jesus' commandment to sex. Beare wrote, "If this is taken as a 'demand' of Jesus, then it must be said that he is demanding the impossible, for it is the universal experience that the sexual impulses are uncontrollable." Beare then goes on to say that this, indeed, may be proof for the Pauline (Lutheran) concept that all *men* fall short of the glory of God. (Beare, in loc.) An even more recent commentator, Frederick Dale Bruner, took exception to Beare (and Guelich, *The Sermon of the Mount*) and states that it is possible to be above lust, and that the Lord will give his disciples the power to be obedient.[25]

Both men make the mistake that the Church has made for centuries, assuming that Jesus' comments are confined to sex. The Church has imposed a huge amount of unnecessary guilt on young men and women for even having sexual fantasies. The text does not state, "If you think (δοκειτε) or you dream (ενυπνιαζετε) of lust you commit adultery with her in your heart." Of the six Greek words used to describe the process of seeing, the word Βλεπω is used the least to describe a metaphorical quality of seeing, such as fantasizing or dreaming. It is most frequently used to describe the physical act. If fantasizing or dreaming had been meant, it would have been more proper to use οραω θεωρεω, or προοραω. Today's English Version, I believe, has established the proper translation, "You have heard that it was said, 'Do not commit adultery.' But now I tell you anyone who looks at a woman and wants to possess her is guilty of adultery in his heart." This is different from looking at a woman and thinking about having sexual relations with her. (Which is natural.) Interpreting the text in this way puts the idea of looking at a woman as a possession back into the biblical Hebrew culture and conveys the true radicalness of Jesus' teaching. The evidence is abundantly clear in the Hebrew culture the woman was just another of man's possessions. When the Bible describes Solomon as having 700 wives and 300 concubines, it is describing a person of extreme wealth and power, not a sex machine or maniac. These women were Solomon's possessions.

Jesus cuts through centuries of abuse in the Old Testament and in many societies. His teaching was not reinterpretation of the commandment or bringing out the true meaning of adultery. Jesus abolished the Old Testament Law and replaced it with something totally new. Adultery was changed from having sex with another man's wife, to not even looking at a woman as a possession. This was a radical position in Jesus' day and still needs to be heard in our day. Jesus' whole attitude towards women was completely different from Old Testament Law and this will be another chapter in itself..

Jesus, Adultery and Divorce

Matthew 5: 31–33: "It was also said, 'Whoever divorces his wife, let him give a certificate of divorce.' But I say to you that every one who divorces his wife, except on the ground of unchastity, makes her an adulteress; and whoever marries a divorced woman commits adultery."

Here Jesus directly connected the issue of divorce with the seventh commandment. In the Old Testament the penalty for sexual indiscretions was not divorce but death (Leviticus 20:10–16; Deuteronomy 22:22–30).[26] Even

---

[25]Frederick Dale Bruner, *Matthew*, Volume 1 (Dallas, Texas: Word Publishing, 1987), p. 182.

[26]Contrary to R. C. H. Lenski, *The Interpretation of Saint Matthew's Gospel* (Columbus,

the suspicion of indiscretion could lead to death for the woman (Numbers 5:11–31). In the text of the Sermon on the Mount it is not clear whether Jesus is expanding Old Testament law of divorce or abrogating it. In his commentary Hugh M'Nielle (in Loc.) points out that the Torah citation concerning divorce, Deuteronomy 24:1–3, does not legislate or allow the practice of divorce. It simply assumes that the divorce practice exists and the Law simply precludes the man who divorces a woman from remarrying her. The text states: "When a man takes a wife and marries her, if then she finds no favor in eyes because he has found some indecency in her and he writes her a bill of divorce . . . "

It can be safely assumed from Matthew 19:8 that Jesus believed that divorce was a valid practice stipulated by the Law of Moses. By the time of Jesus, the meaning of *indecency* had gotten lost. There was a great deal of debate between the rabbis as to what it meant. Again the Sadducees represented by Shammai took a very conservative approach to divorce. They would have re-interpreted the divorce decree with Jesus in Mark 10:11–12; Luke 16:18; Matthew 19:3–9 as implying adultery. On the other hand the Pharisees, represented by Rabbi Hillel would have had a very lenient policy towards divorce. If a wife so much as *spoiled the meal*, she could be divorced (Gittin, 90 [a–b]).

Taken by themselves, Jesus' comments on divorce in the sermon on the Mount are, to use Professor Beare's terminology, *peculiar* (in loc.). It is understandable that marrying a divorced woman could be construed as adultery because she already had been married to another man. How can a man make his wife an adulteress when she did not commit any act at all, and it is he who divorces her—not her divorcing him? This question may not be able to be answered. It can also be assumed that Deuteronomy 24:1 must have been granted for something other than adultery because in the Old Testament the penalty for divorce was death.[27]

Taken in the context of other teachings of Jesus in Mark 10:11–12; Luke 16:18; and Matthew 19:3–9, Jesus categorically is not found supporting *the iota or the dot* of any divorce law. He totally does away with the divorce law. The divorce Law is now applied to the law on adultery so that the law on adultery is likewise changed. No longer are women killed for adultery (John 8:2–11). They are divorced from their husbands. While I believe the Church in past ages has properly understood that Jesus' law opposed divorce, it totally distorted his teachings on adultery. It has forced women to live in relationships where their husbands possess and oppress them and that, by Jesus' criterion, is adultery.

Ohio: Wartburg Press, 1956), in loc.

[27]The ground for divorce in Deuteronomy 24:1 is found in the Hebrew word that is translated *indecency,* literally translated means *nakedness*. (BDB, 788) The same word is used in the preceding chapter. Deuteronomy, 23:14 states, "Because the Lord your God walks in the midst of your camp to save you, therefore your camp must be holy, that he may not see anything indecent among you and turn away from you." It is clear from the preceding verses that *nakedness* is not meant. At issue here is Israel has gone to war and set up camp. The indecencies that the Lord must not find are *a man who has a nightly emission* (vs. 10), or *human excrement* (vss. 12–13). The intention may be something similar in 24:1. It may have meant that the woman may not have practiced cleanliness laws particularly in relationship to her menstrual period (Leviticus 15:19–33) or it simply may have meant she displayed herself or was naked (Leviticus 18:1–19). This, in oriental society, could have simply have been the fact that the wife did not use the veil, was perceived as a prostitute, and thus was an embarrassment to her husband.

No Retaliation

Matthew 5:38–42: You have heard that it was said, 'An eye for an eye, and a tooth for a tooth.' But I say to you, Do not resist one who is evil. If any one strikes you on the right cheek turn to him the other also; and if any one would sue you and take your coat, let him have your cloak as well; if any one forces you to go one mile, go with him two miles. Give to him who begs from you, and do not refuse him who would borrow from you.

Here again hermeneutics has been based not on the text but on the established order, and it should be no surprise that Luther leads the way in obfuscation of the teachings of Jesus. In an attempt to refute the Anabaptists who found great support for their pacifism in this passage, he wrote:

> This text has also given rise to many questions and errors among nearly all the theologians who have failed to distinguish properly between the secular and spiritual, between the kingdom of Christ and the kingdom of the world . . . Now he (Christ) addresses those who were charged with governmental authority and with the sword of punishment. It was a matter of obligation and necessity for them to take an eye for an eye and tooth for tooth. Thus it was as grievous a sin for them if they failed to use the sword of punishment with which they were charged as it was for the others to seize the sword and avenge themselves without authority . . .
>
> Now Christ comes along to demolish this perverted idea and false interpretation (of the Anabaptists). He is not tampering with the responsibility of government, but he is teaching His individual Christians how to live personally, apart from their official position and authority . . . (Luther's Works, Volume 21, pp. 105–6)

Luther's thinking has held sway for hundreds of years within the mainline churches and with their theologians. In his 1987 Word Commentary on Matthew Bruner gave an almost verbatim paraphrase of Luther's thought. He wrote:

> It is important first to notice (as in the murder, adultery, and even divorce legislation of Moses earlier in this sermon) how good the old commandment was that Jesus commented upon and that he now revises and puts in a new edition . . . .
>
> Justice continues to be required by law in all civilized communities today. As in Jesus' treatment of the earlier commandments against killing and adultery, this commandment against injustice is not abrogated by Jesus, it is deepened. Political society must continue to keep the old commandment of justice. The gracious and forever just Old Testament "law of tooth" is still legitimate civil legislation and will forever remind the community that God wants justice and is not pleased when the taking of the eye goes unpunished . . . (Volume 1, pp. 205–206)

Unlike the case of adultery, it does not take a great detail of exposition of the texts and historical background to expose the myths held by many Christians. The evidence discrediting the myths is readily available in the

Scriptures themselves. There is nothing in the text that stipulates that Jesus' teaching is moral teaching only for individuals in their private lives, and that there are different teachings for public and private lives (*Luther*; Albright & Mann; MacArthur; Davies & Allison). Furthermore, there is nothing in the text that would indicate that Jesus is addressing only the disciples in the Sermon on the Mount, thus implying that his teachings are just for Christians or a select group of Christians such as monks or nuns (Augustine).[28]

It cannot be underscored more that the Old Testament text to which Jesus was alluding was derived from laws ordering the public life, and not private life.[29] *An eye for eye and a tooth for tooth* would have immediately been grasped by Jesus' audience as a Law of Moses.[30] In the Old Testament there are three formulations of the law: Exodus 21:22–24 is a statement of retribution when an injury or a death occurs in a fight between two men. Deuteronomy 19:16–21 is a law that deals with slanderous witnesses who were intent on framing a person for a crime. The complete expression of the law dealing directly with the commission of a crime is found in Leviticus 24:10–23.

The issue at hand in the Leviticus text was whether a man should be put to death for blaspheming the Lord God. If the man had been a Jew, there would have been no question. He would have been stoned. However, the man was born of a Jewish mother and Egyptian father, and thus he was not a Jew. Here again is the negative attitude towards women; if the father were Jewish the man would have also been Jewish. Consequently, the Jews ask Moses to inquire of the Lord God whether or not the man should be put to death. The Lord God responds:

> He who blasphemes the Name shall be put to death; all the congregation shall stone him; the sojourner as well as the native, when he blasphemes the Name, he shall be put to death.
> He who kills a man shall be put to death. He who kills a beast shall make it good; life for life. When a man causes disfigurement

---

[28]In the text of the Sermon on the Mount, there is no attempt to seclude Jesus from the multitude as there is in other verses in Matthew, 8:23–27; 13:36; 14:23, and 15:39. It just does not make any sense that Matthew intends this audience for Jesus' most important sermon to be heard by only disciples. This would have been the smallest of audiences. At this time in Matthew, only four disciples had been selected. At the conclusion of the sermon it is very clearly stated, "And when Jesus finished these sayings, the crowds were astonished at his teachings (RSV)." It can only be concluded that the sermon was intended for the Multitudes and the teachings of Jesus were to be applied to everybody.

[29]Such things as bodily emissions (Leviticus 15) and uncovering the nakedness of various persons (Leviticus 18) may be considered individual sins atoned for through sacrifices (Leviticus 4:27 – 5:19). However, in the Judaism of the Old Testament, there could hardly be described a private life and a public life. What one did in the privacy of one's bedroom could affect the entirety of the whole people of God. As is apparent in the discussion of the holiness laws (see above), a person was defiled by menstruation, touching blood, semen, a dead corpse, etc. These individual acts would contaminate the entire people of God preventing the presence of Yahweh among his people.

[30]In reality this law held sway over much of the ancient near-east for centuries before Moses. It was the ancient *lex taliones* which was picked up from the Babylonian or pre-Babylonian culture. In humankind this was an improved attitude over indiscriminate and escalated tribal and individual retribution and retaliation. It did not demand that an eye be taken for an eye, but said that no more than an eye be taken for an eye.

to his neighbor, as he has done it shall be done to him, fracture for fracture, eye for eye, tooth for tooth; . . . You shall have one law for the sojourner and for the native; for I am the Lord your God (Lev. 24:16–22 RSV).

Seen in its entirety the law gives a proper perspective to Jesus' reference to this Law. It was obviously a law governing the corporate life of Israel. The selection of eyes and teeth from the list was not Jesus' restricting retaliation for just the loss of eyes and teeth. Jesus was employing the common rabbinical practice of quoting part of the text but implying the complete pericope.

Jesus was not just abolishing the laws of retaliation. He had broadened them to phenomenal proportions. Not only was one not to take life for life, eye for eye, hand for hand, animal for animal, but if one should be insulted by a person slapping him or her on the cheek that person should turn the other cheek; if someone should demand a person's outer garments the person should give the underclothes also; if someone should lord it over another, making a person carry a load one mile; that person should carry the load two miles. In short, retaliation is not an acceptable practice in Christianity. While the world and most Christians reject Jesus' teaching as being impractical, I believe this is another teaching of Jesus that the world needs to hear. The cost of retributive justice has long been unproductive in prevention or rehabilitation, and its cost in the destruction and repression of human lives has been immense and incalculable.

The Essence of Christianity, Love of Enemy

You have heard that it was said, 'You shall love your neighbor and hate your enemy.' But I say to you, Love your enemies, and pray for those who persecute you so that you may be children of your father who is in heaven; for he makes the sun rise on the evil and the good, and sends the rain on the just and the unjust. For if you love those who love you what reward have you? Do not even the tax collectors do the same? And if you salute only your brethren, what more are you doing than others? Do not even the gentiles do the same? You must be perfect, as your heavenly Father is perfect.

In most of the commandments of Jesus, it is obvious that Jesus is referring to the Old Testament in the statement "You have heard that it was said . . ." In Jesus' sixth commandment, however, this is not at all clear. There is no passage in the Old Testament that reads, "You shall love your neighbor and hate your enemies." While "You shall love your neighbor as yourself" plays a central role in the New Testament, in the Old Testament the command is buried among a host of miscellaneous laws in Leviticus. It follows what for modern readers may be some of the most boring reading in the Bible — laws dealing with mold, leprosy, menstruation, and prohibitions of seeing every kind of nakedness. The actual command is even a secondary part of another command that reads, "You shall not take vengeance or bear any grudges against the sons of your own people, but you shall love your neighbor as yourself" (19:18). Immediately following this verse is the admonition not to breed different kinds of cattle together, sow two different kinds of seed on one ground, or sew two different kinds of cloth into one garment. While one could hardly find a more minuscule command than that, clearly in the rest of the

Old Testament such an attitude towards the sons of Israel was prescribed by Yahweh.

While there is no specific command *to hate* one's enemy, it is an understatement of what was to be Israel's attitude towards its enemies and thus, the enemies of Yahweh. Georg Strecker, in his commentary on the Sermon on the Mount, cited a passage from the Qumran scrolls which is an excellent summary statement of the Old Testament attitude towards an enemy, "God commanded to love that he has chosen but to hate everything he has rejected."[31] Whether in the Law, the Prophets, or the Psalms, the enemies — of Israel, of individual Israelites, or of Yahweh — are not treated with love, forgiveness or even respect (See Psalms 35; 58; 63; Isaiah 10:24–27; Isaiah 13:1–21:17; etc.). There is no support for any argument that there was a difference between the way the Jews treated their enemies and the way 'barbaric' peoples treated their enemies; that somehow the Jews were more civilized. This argument would be sheer fantasy and pure myth. Instead, the argument could be sustained that the "barbarian" Greeks and Romans were much more civilized than the Jews. The Romans and the Greeks did not obliterate the nations that surrounded them unless they continually rebelled.

The Bible reveals that the Jews (Yahweh?) were quite barbaric in the treatment of an enemy. Deuteronomy 20 contains the rules for war delivered to Moses by Yahweh. For the enemies of distant lands, the Jews were to give two choices: the enemy could choose to surrender with the men to be slaves, or they could choose to die. Women and children would not be killed; they would be slaves and concubines. As is typical of other barbarians, the material resources would be booty (vss 12–14). Those persons who had the misfortune of being in adjacent territory were to be totally annihilated. Forgiveness of an enemy was not possible. No Ammonite or Moabite could enter the assembly of the Lord, even to the tenth generation, none belonging to them *forever*; because they did not meet you (the Jews) with bread and with water on the way, when you came forth out of Egypt, and because they hired against you Balaam the son of Beor . . . to curse you (Deuteronomy 23:3–4).

It is impossible to argue that Jesus supported the *iota and dot* of these laws. He *abolishes* them permanently. He nails them to the cross. Done away with is the law of hate and retaliation. The command "You shall not kill," becomes "You shall not kill (a human) for any cause or any reason." This is essential Christianity. Yet it has not been essentially acknowledged by most of Christianity. Only a few Christians – those of the first few centuries, a scattering of movements, the Anabaptists and the Quakers – have seen loving one's enemy as being the essence of Christianity. But, this is what Jesus was all about. This is the essence of the cross and the essence of Jesus' prayer on the cross, "Father, forgive them for they know not what they do (Luke 23:34)." This is the meaning of salvation and justification by faith. Paul expresses the basic idea in Romans 5:10: "If while we were enemies we were reconciled to God by the death of his son much more shall we be saved by his life." Otherwise in Christ Jesus, God loved those who were his enemies.

---

[31]Georg Strecker, *The Sermon on the Mount*, trans O. C. Dean (Nashville, TN: Abingdon Press, 1988–1976), p. 87.

The Iota or the Dot, a Dilemma

It has been obvious that Jesus did not support *the iota or a dot* of the Old Testament law regarding women, and retaliation of the enemies of Yahweh and the people of God. He totally changed the commandment on adultery so that it became a new law. In the last chapter, it was obvious that Jesus re-interpreted the fifth commandment. In the next chapter, it will even be more obvious that Jesus totally does away with the fourth commandment. With all this evidence from the Old and New Testaments, one could hardly argue that Jesus supported the *iota or the dot* or the least commandment (Matthew 5:19–20) of the Old Testament law.

Is it possible then to resolve the problem of the text? There are, I believe, two possible solutions to the dilemma faced in this interpretation. The first solution is to interpret it, as some scholars have, as part of the correction (17–20) inserted by a Matthean scribe who realized that there were contradictions between the law and Jesus' teachings and wanted to rescue the law.[32] The second solution is that while Jesus referred to the Old Testament law in verses 17 and 18, in verses 19 and 20 he was referring to the Law which he as the Messiah delivered from the Mount.

It is the second possibility that I believe to be the most logical and only provable choice. When Jesus, as God's son, ascends the Mountain as Moses did, he *gives* the law rather than receiving the law as Moses did. The Messiah's law replaces the law of Moses. In their *International Critical Commentary*, Davies and Allison assert that this is the precise motif that Matthew sets up in his gospel:

> If the opening of the sermon on the mount be linked up with Sinai . . . , then Mt 1–5 in all its parts reflects a developed exodus typology. The gospel opens with events recalling the birth and childhood of Moses. There is Jesus' baptism which parallels Israel's passing through the waters. There follows next the temptation in which Jesus re-experiences the desert temptations recounted in Deuteronomy. Finally, there is 4:23–5:2 where Jesus like Moses, sits on the mountain of revelation. In other words, every major event in Mt 1–5 apparently has its counterpart in the events surrounding Israel's exodus from Egypt . . . The typology is thus extensive and consistently thought through. So, when Jesus goes up on the mount, he is speaking as the mosaic Messiah and delivering messianic Torah (ICC, p. 427).

I would expand one item and add another item to the typology. The expansion is that for Matthew, the temptation narrative points to the failure of Israel to be faithful to Yahweh in the desert, whereas Jesus as the Son of God was faithful. The addition that I would make to the typology is that in Matthew the reporting of the genealogy is not the strictly boring recitation of the relatives of Jesus as it is in Luke. Matthew's version is, rather, a tabloid of the shocking and embarrassing history of the people of God. For instance, Matthew, as does Luke, reports that Judah was the father of Perez and Perez the father of Hezron. In verse three Matthew adds that Judah fathered Zerah. Zerah has no direct relation with Jesus except to be an ancient cousin. Matthew

---

[32]See footnote #8.

106

included him because his Mother was Tamar. Most people from their Sunday school will remember that Tamar disguised herself as a prostitute to seduce Judah (Gen. 38). The reason for this was Judah did not keep his levirate promise to give his youngest son to Tamar as a husband. When Judah discovered that Tamar was pregnant, he was going to stone her, but then Tamar revealed that the baby was his and thus revealed that he, the Patriarch, was a major hypocrite. Of course Matthew has to insert that the mother of Boas was Rahab. His purpose for this insertion must be immediately recognized by the Bible student. Matthew wants to remind the Jews that the great grandmother of King David was a harlot and a Gentile. To rub more salt into the wound, Matthew does not mention that Solomon was born of Bathsheba. He simply states that Solomon was born of Uriah's wife. Again it is readily apparent that Matthew wants to have Israel remember that their great King, David, had an adulterous affair with another man's wife and then had her husband killed.

The point of all this is to illustrate that all the history of Israel was flawed. The wilderness temptation episode reminds the Jews of their rebelliousness; the genealogy reminds them that their heroes were moral disasters; and then the anti-theses in the Sermon of the Mount ("You have heard it said . . . but I say to you . . . ") point to the deficiencies in the Law of Moses. The evidence suggests that Matthew may have had in mind a similar concept to that of the author of Hebrews. The Old Testament law and its covenant were but a shadow of the new covenant (Hebrews 10:1; 1:1–4; 3:1–19; 5:1–10; 9:1–28). They prefigured Jesus and his kingdom. They pointed in the direction of Christ Jesus.

In terms of the Sermon on the Mount he, Jesus, was the purpose of the law and the prophets. He fulfilled them; brought them to their intended purposes. He then establishes his Law as the criterion for Christian behavior. The Old law, which entrenched male dominance; which was based on retaliation for individual and corporate transgressions to human beings and to Yahweh; which placed a priority upon exterior values of circumcision and ceremonial cleanliness; and which placed the sanctity of one day over all other days; was brought to its conclusion. Even more, the Old Law established the righteous hierarchy. The Jew was the chosen of God— the gentile, cursed by God. The man was the image of God. The woman was man's possession. The priest was holy and set apart. The average man did his best to stay in touch. Jesus turned this whole judgemental system upside down and said "Judge not and you will not be judged, because with the judgement you judge, you will be judged (Matthew 7:1)."[33] The only conclusion is that Jesus could hardly be found exalting the law as the Pharisee who wrote Psalm 119 did, nor would he even have considered the ten commandments, the ten words, chiselled in stone, eternally valid for all times and places.[34]

This still leaves the problem of *the dot and iota* of the law. The solution to the problem, I believe, has been solved by Charles Carlston in a *New*

---

[33]Thanks to Paul Buller for helping me work through this thought.

[34]Terrance Donaldson, argues in *Jesus on the Mountain*, that the motif is Mount Zion, not Siani and that Jesus is the giver of the law not the receiver of the law. in *Journal for the Study of the New Testament*, Series 8 (Wilshire: Redwood Barn Ltd, 1988.), pp.3 ff.

Testament Studies article "Things that Defile (Mark VII, 14) and the Law in Matthew and Mark."[35] Like M. D. Goulder (pp. 250–289), Carlston believes that Matthew has set the Sermon on the Mount in true rabbinical fashion. Carlston asserts:

> . . . In v. 17 Jesus is said to "fulfill" which means not merely the ritual requirements of the Pentateuch but the whole Old Testament economy . . . Jesus truly reveals the will of the Father, which is given (but misunderstood) in the Scripture . . . In v. 19 we can discern the solemn oath against teachers [who detract from Jesus' teaching]: whoever sets men free from the least of these commandments (presumably the teachings of Jesus which follows in vv. 21–48) is least in the kingdom of heaven. (pp. 79–80 In footnote #7 Carlston asserts that v. 19 should be interpreted: "The least of these commandments which I am giving now:")

Carlston thought that vs. 18 was a later addition placed in the text by a Judaizing Christian. But it makes more sense that the word *my* was deleted from the law in verse 18. Jesus says as much in Matthew 24:35: "Heaven and earth will pass away but my words will not pass away." I would like to set forth a translation that displays a more proper interpretation of Matthew 5:17–21:

> Think not that I have come to destroy the law and the prophets; no not at all, I have come not to destroy them, but to bring them to their proper conclusion. For truly, I say to you, the heaven and earth will pass, but not a yohd or one stroke shall pass from my law until all is accomplished. Whoever does away with one of the least of my commands and teaches other people to do so, will be least in the kingdom of heaven, but whoever keeps and teaches these, shall be called great in the kingdom of heaven. For I tell you unless your righteousness abounds more than that of the scribes and Pharisees, you will not enter the kingdom of God.

When the Church comes to acknowledge that Jesus Christ was God incarnate; that his teachings are not just impossible ideals for which we must aim but never attain, but the very criterion around which we mold our lives — the very law of God — then pacifism will not be an impractical ideal but one of the fruits of the Spirit (Galatians 5:22), a mark and a sign of a Christian. When a Christian says Jesus is Lord, he must not advocate capital punishment or abortion. To live in luxury while there is so much suffering around us is tantamount to denying the Lordship of Jesus Christ. To treat women as objects or lesser beings, to place them in secondary status is destructive and the ultimate in making oneself a god. To return evil for evil is to deny the power of the resurrection. To participate in war on any side is to place oneself squarely on the side of the rulers and powers of this world.

---

[35]Charles Carlston, "Things that Defile (Mark VII, 14) and the Law in Matthew and Mark," *New Testament Studies* (XV: 1968–69), pp. 79–96. Henceforth Carlston.

Chapter VII

Jesus' Struggle:

Text versus Spirit

Fundamentalists and Conservatives, the Heirs to the Pharisees

Conservatives and fundamentalists have always accused biblical critics of *playing fast and loose* with the Scripture; that the critics do not honor the text, and thus denigrate the *very word of God*. The point of this chapter is that Jesus was the apotheosis of this attitude Conservatives disdain. If it were possible to go back to the events portrayed in Scripture, it would be found that the Sadducees and Pharisees hurled similar accusations at Jesus. They, indeed, would have and did accuse him of not respecting the Scriptures. The fact is that the very people that were found opposing Jesus were the Scriptural literalists and the conservatives in Judaism. It was their Scriptural literalism and dogmatism that led them to crucify Jesus.

At the center of this discussion will be the pivotal issues of Judaism: the keeping of the Sabbath and the coming of the Messiah. These two issues were the sources of the greatest conflicts between Jesus and the Jewish authorities. In these conflicts it will be apparent that the rabbis reflect a more strict, more literal understanding of Scriptures, and Jesus, a more liberal or free interpretation of Scripture.

The Issue of Sabbath

Remember the Sabbath day, to keep it holy. Six days you shall labor, and do your work; but the seventh day is a Sabbath *to the Lord your God*; in it you shall not do *any work*, you, or your son, or your daughter, your manservant, or your maidservant, or your cattle, or the sojourner who is within your gates; for six days the Lord made heaven and earth, the seas, and all that is in them, and rested the seventh day; therefore the Lord *blessed* the Sabbath day and *hallowed it*. Ex 20:8–11, RSV

While in the last chapter, it was shown that Jesus could not be found supporting *the iota or the dot* of Old Testament law, the commandments were still intact. Albeit the commandment, "You shall not commit adultery," was radically redefined to make it almost unrecognizable from the Old Testament Torah. Even though the commandment, "You shall not kill," became so all inclusive and expansive that it did away with a host of Old Testament laws. When it comes to the fourth commandment, Sabbath observance, the question will not be whether Jesus does or does not uphold the commandment, but whether Jesus abolishes the Commandment or makes a brand new commandment.

As was the case in the last chapter to find out whether or not Jesus supports the law, the first step again is to examine the Law as it is found in the Pentateuch. In doing this, the first observation to be made is that the Sabbath practice predates the giving of the Law on Sinai. God, Himself, observed it: "And on the seventh day God finished all the work which He had done, and He rested on the seventh day from all His work which was done. So God blessed the seventh day and hallowed it, because on it God rested from all His work. which He had done in creation" (Gen 2:2–3 RSV).

The second observation is that the Jews observed the Sabbath before the commandments were promulgated. After being liberated from Egypt (Ex. 16), and wandering in the desert for fifteen days, the Jews complained that it would have been better if they had perished at the hands of Pharaoh than to starve to death in the desert. In response, the Lord God provided them manna from heaven. The Jews were told to gather enough manna for one day. The remaining manna was melted in the heat of the day. If the manna was not consumed, the next morning, it would be wormy and another days supply would have to be harvested anyway. On the sixth day, however, the Jews were commanded to collect two days' worth of manna because they were not to collect it on the seventh. The reason was that the seventh day was *a solemn day of rest, a holy Sabbath to the Lord* (16:23). The manna left over from the sixth day did not become wormy or foul. As was typical of the biblical record, there were the disobedient who collected manna on the seventh day. The Lord God indignantly asked, "How long do you refuse to keep my commandments and laws? (vs. 28, RSV)" The question is perplexing. How could Israel disobey the laws (תּוֹרֹתָי) considering that the law and the commandments were not given until the twentieth chapter? One could legitimately consider directives from the Lord God to be commandments, but the inclusion of laws within the question indicates that there must have been prior laws to Sinai, and the fact that God accuses the Jews of violating them means that the Jews must have been familiar with those "commandments and laws," or they would not have been culpable. Here is not the place to speculate about all the implications of this, but simply to assert what is apparent: Sabbath observance was considered *Law* before Sinai. Therefore it would only be natural to give it the primacy that the rabbis gave it.

The third observation is that in the Pentateuch the actual formulation and interpretation of the law is expanded in different places. Of all the laws, only adultery and cleanliness laws receive more coverage than Sabbath observance in the Old Testament. In Exodus 20:8–11 (above) the reason for the sabbath is because the Lord God created "heaven and earth, etc." and rested. In Deuteronomy 5:12–15 the reason for the observance of Sabbath is that the Jews were to *remember* that they were servants in the land of Egypt and it was the Lord God who delivered them from the land of Egypt (vs. 15). Two chapters after the Exodus formulation *rest* and *refreshment* is added as being beneficial to people and work animals (23:12).

Ex 31:12–17 significantly expands the commandment.

> And the Lord said to Moses, "Say to the sons of Israel, 'You shall keep *my sabbaths*, for this is **a *sign between me and you through out your generations*,** that I the Lord, *sanctify you*. You shall keep the sabbath, ***because*** it is **holy** for you; everyone who profanes it shall be put to death; **whoever does *any* work on it, that soul shall be cut off from among his people.** Six days shall work be done, but the seventh is a

sabbath of *solemn* rest, *holy to the Lord;* **whoever does *any* work on the sabbath will be put to death**. Therefore the people of Israel shall keep the sabbath *throughout their generations* as a *perpetual covenant.* It is *a sign for ever between me and the people of Israel* that in six days the Lord made heaven and earth and on the seventh day he *rested, and was refreshed. (RSV,* **bold** and *italics* mine)

The language here could not be stronger. Keeping the Sabbath was *a sign, a covenant.* As circumcision was a sign of one's Judaism (Gen. 17:9–14) so was observing the Sabbath. The same terms used in the institution of circumcision are used here of Sabbath observance, i.e., *a sign between me and you throughout their generations, a perpetual covenant.* As in the case of circumcision, anyone who was uncircumcised was to be cut off from the people of Israel so any one who failed to keep the Sabbath was cut off from Israel, killed.

The fourth observation is that there could not be any stronger admonition against activity on the Sabbath. In Exodus 31:12–17 the repetition of phrases totally underscores the absolute and irrevocable claim that Sabbath observance had on the Jews. The command, "Keep my (the) sabbath (שַׁבְּתֹתַי תִּשְׁמֹרוּ) - (vs. 13)" occurs two more times in vss. 14 and 16. The term Holy (קדש), with its emphatic verb, sanctify (מְקַדִּשְׁכֶם, piel), is repeated three times to impress the fact that Sabbath observance was not for human beings but for God, himself (vss. 13, 14, 15). The fact that the Sabbath was to be a day of *complete rest,* as the Jerusalem Bible correctly translates it, is dramatically accentuated by the Hebrew original in verse 15. For the person who may not know Hebrew the term Sabbath (שַׁבָּת) means cease, desist, rest. In verse 15 after it is stated: "Work is to be done six days" then comes the statement in Hebrew שַׁבָּת שַׁבָּתוֹן וּבַיּוֹם הַשְּׁבִיעִי). Here the reader can see for herself or himself the origination of the word Sabbath. Literally translated it means: "But on day seven (הַשְּׁבִיעִי) rest (שַׁבָּת) rest observance (שַׁבָּתוֹן)." If the repetition was not emphatic enough the sacred name of God was then invoked "the sabbath was Holy unto Yahweh (קֹדֶשׁ לַיהוה)."

There is no record in the Old Testament of a person who was cut off (killed) from the people of Israel for not having been circumcised. There is no record of an execution of a person who dishonored his parents. There is no mention of an execution for adultery, the violation of which calls for execution more times than any command. Not even King David was put to death for adultery. In his violation he was not only guilty of adultery but he was guilty of conspiring to have an innocent man killed.

The only execution recorded for a violation of a commandment beyond the first three commandments was one involving a violation of the Sabbath Law. There may have been other executions for adultery or for dishonoring one's parents but they were not deemed important enough to make it into the text. In Numbers 15:32–36 a man is stoned for having picked up sticks on the Sabbath. The point of the text is that there was an infraction of the Sabbath law. The man may have had even good intentions for picking up the sticks but that was irrelevant. His reasons for picking up the sticks were not mentioned. The issue was plain and simple. Picking up sticks and carrying on the seventh day was a violation of the Sabbath sacred unto Yahweh. He should have done the picking up sticks on the first day or on any other day of the week, but picking them up on the seventh day of the week, meant he was to be stoned. The infraction seems minor and its penalty seems cruel and unusual in contemporary society, but in the Torah it was an affront and defiance of the most High, God. This is very important to remember when Jesus' view of the Sabbath is analyzed.

Sabbath observance was maintained uniformly throughout Judaism, from the Qumran community, the Pharisees, the Sadducees, the Hasidim, the Egyptian Jews, to the Syrian Jews and even the Samaritans. The Jewish historian Flavius Josephus, in about 93 C.E. wrote:

> And there are none of our customs that are inhuman, but all tending to piety, and devoted to preserving justice; nor do we conceal those injunctions by which we govern our lives, they being memorials and friendly conversations among men. And the seventh day we set apart from labour; it is dedicated to the learning of our customs and laws, we thinking it proper to reflect on them, as well as any [good] thing else, in order to our avoiding sin. (Antiquities: XVI, iii: 3)

In the Rabbis there is no other subject that has so much written about it. There are three major tractates written on it, Sabbath, Eru, and Beza.[1] Professor Eduard Lohse, Gottingen University, underscored the importance of the sabbath to Judaism, "The weekly Sabbath commandment is for Judaism a sign of divine election, for no people apart from Israel has sanctified God by keeping the Sabbath . . . The Sabbath commandment is the heart of the Law" (TDNT:VII, p. 8). While Judaism may have invested more power and hopes in the Sabbath than can be substantiated by the Torah, it is obvious from the biblical texts that there could not be a more important and more central teaching and law in the first five books of the Bible other than the first commandment.[2]

The following is a capsule of the teaching of the Old Testament on Sabbath observance: The very word Sabbath means to desist or rest. God himself rested on the sabbath. It is a holy day, a solemn day of rest devoted unto God. It is a perpetual sign of the covenant between Yahweh and the people of Israel for **all generations**. So important was Sabbath that God would provide extra manna on the sixth day so no one would have to collect manna on the Sabbath. So important was Sabbath observance that the severest penalty of death was administered for its violation. In short the Sabbath was a holy day dedicated to God and only secondarily was the element of rest part of the picture.

Jesus Silent on Observance

With the emphasis on Sabbath in the Old Testament and in Judaism, one has to be amazed at the silence to its practice in the teachings of Jesus. In the collection of his teachings called the Sermon on the Mount, it is not even mentioned.[3] Simply amazing is the fact that where Jesus specifically

---

[1]Beza is derived from the Hebrew word ביצה) which means egg. The tractate deals with whether or not it is permissible to eat an egg that was laid on the Sabbath.

[2]In the Old Testament circumcision is only referred to 17 times in 4 chapters, whereas the Sabbath is referred to 107 times in 17 chapters.

112

refers to the ten commandments, he totally leaves out the fourth commandment. A rich man asked Jesus what good deed must he do *to inherit eternal life* (Mt. 19:16). Jesus responded by saying, "If you would enter life, keep the commandments (vs. 17)." The man then asked Jesus to be specific and mention which commandments he meant. Certainly the man being a Jew would have thought that Jesus, a Jewish rabbi, would have included the keeping Sabbath commandment as a requirement. Not Jesus! He lists the fifth through the ninth commandments and then throws in an obscure verse, Leviticus 19:18, as requirements for the life to come (19:18–19).

Here again is astonishing proof that Jesus totally reshapes, remakes or abolishes the law. As astonishing as this is, even more astonishing is the fact that in the history of hermeneutics this evidence has been mostly overlooked. Many commentators have asserted that Jesus implied the other commandments, but this is a simplistic solution and does not hold with the struggles over sabbath observance. One can assume that Jesus does not exclude the first commandment because he does include it elsewhere (Mt. 22:28; Mk. 12:30; Lk.10:27). The second commandment would likewise be related to the first and there are no indications in all of Jesus' teaching and actions that would tend to indicate that He either reinterpreted or abolished it. But such is not the case with the fourth commandment.

The Struggle over Sabbath Observance

Matthew 12:1–8: [1]At that time Jesus went through the grain fields on the sabbath; his disciples were hungry, and they began to pluck ears of grain and to eat. [2]But when the Pharisees saw it, they said to him, "Look, your disciples are doing what is not lawful to do on the sabbath." [3]He said to them, "Have you not read what David did when he was hungry, and those who were with him: [4]how he entered the house of God and ate the bread of the Presence which was not lawful for to eat nor those who were with him, but only for the priests? [5]Or have you not read in the law how on the sabbath the priests in the temple profane the Sabbath and are guiltless? [6]I tell you something greater than the temple is here. [7]And if you had known what it means, 'I desire mercy, and not sacrifice,' you would not have condemned the guiltless. [8]For Son of man is Lord of the sabbath." (RSV)

As in the above all of Jesus' teachings on the Sabbath revolve around incidents where Jesus' or his disciples' faithfulness to the observation of Sabbath is questioned. Most of these sabbatarian controversies occur over a humanitarian event, on whether or not Jesus should heal a person on the Sabbath. The above incident is the only one that could be in any way described as self-serving. In parallel passages of Mark 2:23–28 and Luke 6:1–5, Jesus' argument contained in verses 5–7 of Matthew's portrait are missing. While missing those elements, Mark contains an additional argument, "The Sabbath was made for man, not man for the Sabbath." (2:27, RSV)

Again the question must be raised, does Jesus uphold *the iota or the dot* of Old Testament teaching on the Sabbath? Many of the commentators, who

---

[3]Neither is the other sign of the covenant, circumcision, mentioned in the sermon.

would argue that Jesus does, assert that he uses the type of argument that was common among the rabbis to put Sabbath observance in proper perspective. In the case of David eating the bread of the presence, he was supposedly using the rabbinical principle of analogy (*gezera shava*). With the priest of the temple working on the Sabbath and his being greater, he was using the rabbinical principle of kal vechomer or reasoning from the minor to the major; *a minori ad maius*.[4]

Rabbi Cohn-Sherbok in an article in the *Journal for the Study of the New Testament* destroyed such thinking. His conclusion is worth repeating:

> Assuming that Matthew, Mark and Luke accurately record Jesus' defense of his disciples for having plucked ears of corn on the Sabbath, it appears that Jesus was acquainted with rabbinical hermeneutics. Yet the arguments he utilized are not valid from a rabbinical point or view; the first, concerning David and his entourage, because it is based on a false analogy and also because it is not based on a definite precept; the second, concerning the priests eating the shew bread on the Sabbath, because their action and the action of Jesus' disciples are fundamentally dissimilar and cannot be drawn together kal vechomer. The misuse of the rabbinical reasoning should not surprise us since it bears out the truth of the Gospel in asserting that Jesus was not a skilled casuist in the style of the Pharisees and Sadducees, and helps explain why, when he argued with them, he provoked their indignation and hostility.[5]

It should not take a rabbi to expose the errors in Christian analysis of these passages or the problems that Jesus and his disciples create for Sabbath observance. When Rabbi Cohn-Sherbok says the arguments that Jesus uses are *not valid from a rabbinical point of view*, he is being kind. Jesus was playing *fast and loose* with the Scripture. Eating the bread of the presence (I Samuel 21:1–6) could hardly be used to justify Jesus' disciples picking corn on the Sabbath. The first reason is that the work of making the bread, harvesting, grinding and baking, would have happened before the Sabbath. The disciples picking the grain has to fall definitely under the category of work. Luke intentionally includes another act of work on the Sabbath, the act of *rubbing* (vs. 1). While the act is omitted in the other Gospels, it is as any farmer would know utterly essential so that the grain could be eaten. Otherwise the person eating the grain would end up with a mouth full of chaff and other debris.

If Jesus and his disciples had been good Jews they would have made preparations so that they would have been able to observe the Sabbath in its proper perspective. Certainly, he who was able to heal the blind, lame, deaf, or leprous, could have made arrangements to observe the Sabbath. Could not he who changed five loaves and two fish into enough food to feed thousands of

---

[4]Brunner, (1),447; D. Daube, *The New Testament and Rabbinic Judaism* (London: Althone Press, 1956), p. 68; Davies, Setting, p. 103–104; Green, pp. 210–211; Lohse, (TDNT, VII) pp. 21–25.

[5]D. M. Cohn-Sherbok, "Plucking Grain on the Sabbath," *The Journal for the Study of the New Testament (April, 1979)*, p.40.

people, stretch the food that his disciples had or create a source of food so that he and they would be in compliance with this central command of Yahweh? Certainly, if the Sabbath had been important to Jesus, he could have found some way to provide for his disciples' nutrition — as Yahweh provided double manna on the sixth day so that no one would have to pick up manna on the seventh.

The second reason why the act of David and his men eating the bread of the presence was a false analogy is that the bread *was* to be eaten by human beings. It was to be eaten by the priests (Lev. 24:9). This is the reason the Priest ascertains from David that the young men to whom he is about to give the bread were not defiled by having sexual relations with women (Lev. 21:1–9). The bread while technically not eaten by priests was eaten by men who had not been defiled and thus there had not been committed any grievous violation of the law.

Likewise the comparison of picking corn with the priests offering sacrifice on the Sabbath (Numbers 28:9–10) could hardly be considered *minori a maiori*. If anything the reasoning would have to be considered the other way around which would be a logical fallacy. The same reasoning could, indeed, be applied to the person who was found picking up sticks in Numbers 15:32–41 or the Jews who were attempting to pick up manna in the desert in Ex.16:27. The disciples feeding their stomachs could in no way be compared to the priests offering the sacrifice. After all, in the Old Testament, the Lord's favor on Israel is dependent on the continual offering of sacrifice. If the priests stopped sacrificing, the wrath of Yahweh would burn against Israel.[6]

There is another story of the Sabbath law being violated that needs to be examined before the subject is left. This story is found in the fifth chapter of the Gospel of John. The narrative revolves around the healing of a paralytic at the Sheep's gate in Jerusalem (5:2). This story is remarkable in the gospels for the amount of details that it contains about the person being healed. Of this fact, Raymond Brown in his *Anchor Bible Commentary* states, "The personality traits that he betrays serve no particular theological purpose and are so true-to-life that they too may have been part of the primitive tradition (AB,29, p. 209)." While the details may, indeed, be true to life, the description

---

[6]So radical is the position of Jesus in this incident that F. W. Beare concluded that the passage was the creation of the early church at least two generations removed from Jesus. He stipulated that no Jew in Jesus' day would suggest that "Man was not made for the Sabbath, but the Sabbath was made for man." Beare suggests that the seeds for the rejection of the Sabbath were in Jesus. The rejection was further developed by Paul (Gal. 4:10; Col. 1:16, and Rom. 14:5) and finally the ultimate rejection came in the acceptance of Sunday as the Lord's day by the end of the first century. Beare asserted that Palestinian Jewish Christians faced considerable persecution over their not observing the Sabbath. As a result of the struggle between Jews and Christians, he believes that the passage of picking corn into existence. F. W. Beare, "The Sabbath was Made for Man," *Journal of Biblical Literature* 79(1960), pp.130–6.

While it is evident in the church fathers that there were indeed problems over the fact that Christians chose the Lord's day over the Sabbath (Barnabus, Justin, Ignatius), there is no way to prove that these texts were the creation of the early church, and there is no way to prove that the pericopes did not originate in the life of Jesus. It seems a more logical explanation to assert that Jesus, himself, did away with the Sabbath practice as Judaism practiced it. The later Church resurrected the Sabbath and merged it with the Lord's day. The problem with Beare and many assumptions of modern scholarship has been that Judaism of the first century was a monolithic entity.

of this gentleman serves an obvious theological purpose. John included the few facts about the paralytic within his narrative because he wanted to under-score that here was a true violation of the Sabbath Law. The facts are that the man was crippled for thirty-eight years, and that he had been at the pool a long time. From these facts it would appear as if John was saying that one more day being crippled would not have mattered. The man would have been there on the first day of the week. Jesus could have healed him then.

Severino Pancaro in *The Law and the Fourth Gospel* attempts to argue that in reality there was no violation of Sabbath Law. His argument is based on the supposition that the rabbis did not believe that God totally rested on the Sabbath. They believed that both *judgment* and *creation* continued ir-respective of whether it was Sabbath or not; that is, people died and people were born on the Sabbath. The rabbis concluded that God must, therefore, do some work on the Sabbath. In his argument Pancaro is right in that the real reason for the persecution of Jesus was his statement in vs. 17, "My Father is working still and I am working." Pancaro's argument is that the Jews perceived in this statement that Jesus was usurping God's power of creation and judgment. This was the real source of the ire of the Jews. They knew that Jesus was equating himself with Yahweh. Because Jesus equated himself with God, according to Pancaro, the healing was not a violation of the Sabbath and was a manifestation of God bringing life.[7]

As plausible as Pancaro's arguments are, they miss the mark in one crucial area. It is not so much the healing to which *the Jews* object in this event, their objection is to the man's carrying his pallet (vs. 10). There is an abundance of Old Testament evidence to substantiate the prohibition against carrying anything on the sabbath. Not only is a man executed for carrying sticks on the Sabbath, but Yahweh warns the Jews through the prophet Jeremiah that they should not carry any burden on the Sabbath (Jeremiah 17:19–23). The rabbis permitted some exceptions. On the Sabbath, they did allow the carrying of such things as the Torah, ink, and some food. The reason for this was that the study of Torah was encouraged for it was to be the first and foremost love of Judaism. The carrying of one's pallet, however, was most definitely prohibited (Shabbat 73ᵃ).

The intensity of the conflict between *the Jews* and Jesus can be best be understood when it is realized that the rabbis could have pardoned the man for carrying his pallet, but Jesus' command to the man to take up his pallet was a much worse sin. In the rabbis a person who commands ("seduces") another person to violate the law is a worse offender than the person who commits the act and is to be stoned (Sanhedrin 50ᵃ; 53ᵃ; Aboth V:2). This explains why the man who was healed so quickly diverted *the Jews* attention from his *sin*, to their intense preoccupation with finding the person who commanded the violation (vss. 12 ff.). It also gives great historical authenticity to the text, and makes the whole passage highly credible.

Jesus' command to the paralytic to carry his pallet was a clear violation of the law. It could not under any circumstances be considered in the category of giving life or rendering death. Within the context of the Old Testament there is no possible way to excuse Jesus from some sort of violation of the Sabbath. If Jesus had wanted to maintain some semblance of Sabbath obser-

---

[7]Pancaro, pp. 16–18; 30–54; 160; 201–205.

vance, even if he wanted to enhance the Sabbath interpretation with acts of mercy, he could have told the man to come back and pick up his pallet on the first day of the week. It is obvious that Jesus did not support *the iota or the dot* of the fourth commandment.

Immediately following the Synoptic account of Jesus' disciples picking grain on the Sabbath there is recorded another Sabbath healing event (Matthew 12:9–14; Mark 3:1–6; Luke 6:6–11). After Jesus defends his disciples for picking grain, he goes to a synagogue. In this synagogue was a man with a withered hand and the Pharisees, knowing very well the answer, ask him whether it is lawful to heal on the Sabbath. Jesus responds, "What man of you, if he has one sheep, if it falls into a pit on the sabbath will not lay hold of it and lift it out? Of how much more value is a man than a sheep! So it is lawful to do good on the Sabbath. (Matthew 12:11–12 RSV)"

Again, the Scriptures give a one-sided response. One could possibly assume from the text that Jesus silenced the rabbis, but we know this would not be the case. It is obvious that after the man was healed "the Pharisees went and took counsel against him, how to destroy him (12:14, RSV)." They did not accept the legality of the healing. If the scriptures had recorded the Pharisees' response to Jesus it might have gone like this:

> Yes, Jesus ben Joseph, we believe it is possible to heal on the Sabbath. If the man's life or the sheep's were in danger, the Most High, blessed be He, would permit us to do acts of mercy — for the Most High, blessed be He, continues to give life irrespective of whether it is Sabbath or not. But this man, Jesus ben Joseph, was not in danger of dying, his hand had been in that shape for a long time. Waiting one day would not have made a difference. If you had reverence for the Torah of the Most High, blessed be He, you would have commanded the man to come back on the first day and then you could have healed in respect to the law of Sabbath observance.

There is no support in Jesus' teaching for Sabbath observance as it is mandated in the law of Moses. While there have been recent and commendable attempts to rescue the concept of Sabbath for the sake of ecology and human-kind's psychological and sociological needs, and while I am sure Jesus would agree with those efforts,[8] these efforts do not find direct support in Jesus' teachings. One might be able to argue that Jesus broadened the commandment, but how he broadened the commandment is not specified. Of course there is the Markan addition, "The Sabbath was made for man, not man for the Sabbath (2:27 RSV)," but who knows what that means? Does this mean that man can do anything on the Sabbath? It certainly contradicts the overwhelming Torah emphasis that the Sabbath was "holy unto the Lord." Does Jesus' statement that the "Son of man is Lord of the Sabbath" justify the early church's moving the Sabbath from the day the Lord God rested to the day that his Son was raised from the dead? One thing is for sure — none of Jesus' teachings support *the iota or the dot* of the Torah's teaching on Sabbath. It is not simply a matter of Jesus disagreeing with rabbinical teaching. Just as was the case with the adultery commandment, it must be concluded that

---

[8]*Inter-Mennonite Committee Report: First D* Drafters, Lois Barrett, Helmut Harder, Marlin Miller, et. al., 1992. raft:

117

Jesus either abolishes the commandment or he transforms it so that it is unrecognizable in its Old Testament form. However, unlike the adultery commandment, there is no positive statement establishing a new Sabbath commandment. Consequently, there is no criterion by which to determine what observation entailed.

It is obvious that for Jesus the law was neither sacrosanct nor static. But, then, for the gospel writers Jesus was no mere human. When Jesus gives the ultimate and conclusive answer to why his disciples have the right to violate the Sabbath, He says, "The Son of man is lord of the Sabbath (Matthew 12:8)." It is obvious that by "the Son of man" Jesus means much more than a mere mortal.[9] No mortal has the right to tamper with the law. Carsten Colpe in TDNT asserts that Jesus alters the Sabbath by the "Supreme authority of the Son of Man (VIII, p. 452).." Otherwise, for the gospel writers Jesus was Lord, and as God incarnate had the power to change what he felt necessary to change.

The Struggle: The Presence of God in Text or Life

John 5:39: "You search the scriptures, because in them you think that you have eternal life; and it is they that bear witness to me."

The issue in each and every confrontation over the Sabbath was not the law as the Jewish authorities assert that it was. The real issue at hand was: who was the Lord of life; the Lord God or the Law? For the Pharisees, the Sadducees, the scribes, the priests, and many other Jews, the law had become a god. It is necessary to reiterate because of the prejudice in interpretation in most Christians' circles, that the Pharisees' problem was not that they distorted the Law by adding encumbrances, but that they made the law a god. While the extent to which the idolatry of law worship had not reached the depravity displayed by the hymn worshipping the Bible in the introduction of this book (see p. xix), idolatry certainly was observable in Psalm 119. As for the Psalmist of 119, and for the Pharisees encountering Jesus, everything was dependent on the law of God. The law gives life, the law heals.

Here in their very midst was the power of Yahweh, bringing sight to the blind, mobility to the lame, health to the leper, and a message that brought hope and life to the poor and all those who could hear and accept it. This is the unanimous message of the Gospels, and the unanimous witness of the early Church. "God was in Christ Jesus reconciling the world to himself (II Cor. 5:19a)." This is how one must interpret the Gospels and this is the way one must interpret Jesus' attitude to the Law and the Scriptures. Instead of seeing the power of God and rejoicing, the Pharisees and the Sadducees could only see violations of their understanding of the law.

There is confirmation of this in the Scriptures, which has been uniformly overlooked by conservatives and fundamentalists. The confirmation is found

---

[9]This is very much against M'Niele (in Loc.) who asserts: "In Mk. 'the Son of Man' (perhaps a wrong translation of the Aramaic) clearly means 'man,' not the Messiah: the Sabbath was made on man's account; therefore ($\varpi\sigma\tau\epsilon$) that man is Lord of the Sabbath, and can do work on it if need arise." However, Carsten Colpe of the University of Gottingen in a thorough study of Ezekiel, Daniel, Pseudepigraphic works such as 4 Ezra, Ethiopian Enoch, and certain Canaanite literature, shows that by the time of the first century the concept of the Son of Man had become a Messianic figure (TDNT, VIII: pp. 400–477)

in John 5:39 which is part of the just-discussed narrative dealing with the healing of the paralytic. In his discourse on why he could work on the Sabbath Jesus states to *"the Jews* (vss. John 5:10, 15, 16, 18)," "You search the scriptures, because in them you think that you have eternal life; and it is they that bear witness to me."

The Jews, with whom Jesus was contending, were very pious people. They most likely would have had to have been people of pharisaic lineage. The Sadducees did not believe in "life in the world to come (Josephus, Antiquities, XVIII, 1:4, Sanhedrin 90b.; 90a, and commentary footnote #5, p.601)," and Essenes, who did, would not have been there. The evidence (Str, Biller., in loc.) is overwhelming that the Pharisees believed that studying Torah would produce life in "the world to come." The following are just two of many references:

> . . . The more study of Torah, the more life, the more sitting down to study (Torah), and contemplate the more wisdom, the more counsel, the more wisdom, . . . the more righteousness, the more peace . . . one has acquired unto himself words of Torah, has acquired for himself the life of the world to come. Aboth 2:7

> This is the Book of the commandments of God, the law that stands for ever; those who keep her live; those who desert her die. Baruch 4:1, J B.

As pious fundamentalists, conservatives, and Orthodox Protestants would argue that they were blessed people of the *Book*, so these pious Pharisees argued that they of all the nations were selected and blessed by Yahweh with eternal life because He knew that they would accept the Torah. (Midrash on Numbers XIV).

I have illustrated many passages of Scripture in this book where interpretation has obviously been distorted. Here again I do not hesitate to point to another obvious distortion. The reader will remember that in the first chapter I referred to a statement in defense of inerrancy drawn up in 1978 by three hundred conservative scholars. In the first article with an apparent reference to John 5:39 these scholars assert: "Holy Scripture is God's witness to himself." For these scholars the Scriptures are God's unimpeachable ("infallible," article #2) witness. They are, "without error or fault in all its teaching, no less in what it states about God's acts in creation and the events of world history, and about its own literary origin under God, than its witness to God's saving grace in individual lives (article #4, See pp. 12)." For these scholars and others who subscribe to inerrancy: if any mistakes are found within the testimony of that witness, the whole witness must be thrown out.

In the light of John 5:39 and its context, 5:19–47, this point of view is flawed from at least three aspects. First, John 5:39 does not state, "The Holy Scriptures are God's witness to himself" but, "that which witness to me (Jesus)." The statement of the function of Scripture by Jesus places a much narrower purview than that of the confession. The Bible is not to be considered a science book on how God created the world or a medical book on how to heal people. The Bible's function is *to witness to Jesus*, as the Messiah sent by God, the Father, to redeem the world.

Second, the use of the active participle verb, μαρτυρουσαι, *that which witnesses* instead of the noun, ο μαρτυς, *The Witness*, would tend to indicate that Jesus viewed the Scriptures much differently than the Chicago Conference on inerrancy. It most likely means that Jesus saw the Scriptures as dynamic and not static. The *witnessing to Jesus* of the Scriptures was an ongoing and not a fixed process. In other words, the Scriptures may have had a definitive meaning at the time of the prophesy or event recorded in the Old Testament text, but then Jesus and his disciples reinterpreted the Scriptures for their day and time. I will illustrate this practice in the next section.

Third and most important, according to John 5:19–47 the Scriptures were not God's only or primary witness. According to the text the Scripture was one of several other witnesses. Jesus states that there were five witness to him: John the Baptist (5:33–35); the miracles that Jesus himself performed (5:36); the Father (5:37–38); the Scripture (5:39); and Moses (5:44–47).[10]

Peter, Another Biblical Critic

Acts 2:22: "Men of Israel: Hear these words: Jesus of Nazareth, a man attested to by God with mighty works and wonders and signs which God did through him in your midst as you yourselves know . . . (RSV)"

While there is not one other verse or portion of Scripture that states the content of John 5:39 or 5:19–47 in the same form, there is confirmation that the attitude towards Scripture was that of Jesus and the early Church. In Acts, after the Holy Spirit falls on the disciples (Acts 2:1–11), Peter explains the event (Acts 2:14–21). Peter did not say, "Jesus, whom you crucified is the Messiah proclaimed by the Scriptures." Instead, he tells them that the signs and wonders that Jesus performed proclaimed Jesus as Messiah. Likewise, the record in Acts and the writings of the early Church were not the stories of disciples dogmatically preaching an exposition of Old Testament texts. The history of Acts and the early Church portrays a church filled with the very power of the living Lord Jesus Christ. The phrase "signs and wonders" as descriptive of the early Church is one of the most used phrases in Acts (2:43; 4:30; 5:12; 6:8; 8:13; 14:3). In Acts most incidents of preaching were evoked through the Lord performing some "sign" or "wonder" in their midst (Acts 2; 3; 4; 5:17–32; 6:8–7:53; 9:1–30; 10:1–11:18;12:1–25; 13:26–46; 14:8–18 etc.). The Scriptural texts cited in these preaching incidents are used as secondary sources, showing that what happened in the sign or wonder was the fulfillment of prophesy in the Old Testament.

Neither Jesus nor the Apostles could be accused of being literalists. Just the opposite would be the case. In fact one could use a description of Peter which fundamentalists and conservatives would abhor, and call him a biblical critic. After Peter stated that Jesus performed signs and wonders, that he was crucified, and that God raised him up, he uses as his chief text Psalm 16:8–11:[11]

---

[10]Raymond Brown in his commentary points out that Jesus does not make his case so much in terms of Old Testament law, where the violator of the law must be convicted by two or three witnesses (Dt. 19:15; 17:6; Num. 35:30), but rather by the rabbinical principle that a person cannot bear witness on his own behalf (Mishnah Kethaboth 2:9). (AB in Loc.).

[11]The text of this passage is cited not from the Hebrew text but from the Septuagint. See

^{8}I saw the Lord always before me,

for he is at my right hand that I might not be shaken;

^{9}therefore my heart was glad and my tongue rejoiced;

moreover my flesh will dwell in hope.

^{10}For thou wilt not abandon my soul to hades,

nor let thy Holy one see corruption. (RSV)

The text of the Psalm claims to have David as its author, a fact which Peter accepts. It is obvious that David has himself in mind as the one whose soul would not be abandoned in Hades (εις αδην).[12] Peter accepts the fact that David said that of himself but I will give a modern paraphrase of what he says in Acts 2:29:

> Fellow, Israelites, I know what the text says, but all the evidence — biblical, historical and physical (scientific) is that David died and was buried (I K 2:10–11; I Crons 29:28). His tomb is with us today. But we believe that David was a Prophet and therefore the text must mean something other than what it says. David did not mean himself but was referring to the Messiah who is Jesus — whom you crucified. We are here to witness that God has not allowed Jesus' soul to remain in the Pit nor his flesh to see corruption, but has raised Him up and He sits at the right hand of God. It is He who has poured out His Spirit on us and this is that which you have witness in this sign and wonder.

The rabbis, the biblical literalists — the conservatives and fundamentalists, would not have accepted Peter's argument. They would have argued that the text was very clearly applied to David who was one of seven who did not face the power of death. Baba Bathra 17^a stated: "There are seven over whom the worms had no dominion, namely Abraham, Isaac, and Jacob, Moses, Aaron and Miriam, Benjamin, son of Jacob . . . And some say David also [is included] since it is written of him, My flesh also shall dwell [in the grave] in safety."[13]

The Presence of God-Reinterpretation of Scripture

The plain truth is that most of the claims that the Church has made about Jesus and that Jesus made about himself are not based on literal understanding of Old Testament texts. They are based rather on a free or liberal approach to the Scriptures. A case in point would be the pericope in John of the healing of the paralytic on the Sabbath (John 5:1–47). John 5:16 states that after the man who was healed told the Jews who the person was who had healed him, they began to persecute Jesus. When Jesus defends himself by saying, "My father is working still and I am working (vs. 17)," it is

---

Chapter VIII this work on the use of Septuagint.

[12]While the R.S.V. properly translates the Greek, Hades, it is clear from Peter's comments that he does not have in mind the place of torment of Greek mythology, but rather the Hebrew concept of שאול [sheol, which the N. I. V. most properly translates "grave".

[13]The more predominant view may have been that David did not face corruption, because he followed the Torah, as would be the case of all true Israelites who followed the Torah (See Sanhedrin (90$^{a–b}$) XI:1–2; Jacob Neusner, *Scriptures of the Oral Torah*, pp. 230–383). Yoma 87^a Psalm 16:10. Neusner claims that the rabbis believed that the ones not facing *corruption* were the leaders of Israel who caused Israel to be obedient to the law.

stated that the Jews sought to kill him. Rudolf Schnackenburg, in his commentary on John, illuminates Jesus' statement. He observed that the Jews perceived the profanation of the Holy One, not in Jesus having called the Holy One his Father, but rather in his claim to have a special kind of sonship, by virtue of which he had the right to exercise, like his Father, the same 'constant activity.'[14]

In the discussion on Sabbath observance, it was pointed out that the rabbis *did* believe that God worked on Sabbath because He gave birth and took life. Jesus was claiming to have the same rights as God the Father to do work on the Sabbath. No human could do that! *The Jews* knew Jesus was equating Himself with God. They were outraged! They sought to kill Him!

As fundamental as Jesus' assertions about Himself are to Christian beliefs, it goes without saying that such statements were offensive not only to many and perhaps most Jews to whom Jesus was speaking, but to every generation of Jews since that time. A fact many Protestants fail to grasp must be asserted over and over again. It is the same Old Testament that they read which is the essence of the Jewish religion. Jews look at the same texts that Christians believe proclaim Jesus, and reject the Christians' arguments.[15]

Nowhere, the Jews would have said and will say, does the Old Testament say that the Messiah would be the same as Yahweh, or be Yahweh, himself. The Jews were expecting a prophet like Moses; a king like David. He would be the arm of the Lord, but he would not *be* the Lord. He would usher in the Day of the Lord, as a herald to the King. Because of the Messiah, all nations would worship Yahweh, but no nations would worship the Messiah.[16]

An examination of just a few examples of messianic passages demonstrates just how divergent is the Christian view of the texts from the literal Hebrew texts. The reader is forced to conclude that the Old Testament verses, which the New Testament and the Church have used to defend the divinity of Christ, have undergone considerable changes in meaning. The texts no longer mean what they meant when they were originally written in Hebrew. The literal meaning of the text has changed, and it changed in Jesus' and the apostles' interpretation of the text.

Isaiah 9:6: "For to us a child is born"

I have selected two messianic texts and an enthronement Psalm which allow the easiest demonstration of the differences between Christian and Jewish interpretations of the Old Testament. The first text is one that illustrates the sharp contrast between the Jewish and Christian interpretations of one Hebrew word. The text is one of the great texts which we Christians love to hear every Christmas, and when it is read we all can hear a chorus in Handel's *Messiah*. The text is Isaiah 9:6 (MT 9:5), "For to us a child is born, to us a son is given, and the government will be on his shoulders, and his

---

[14]Rudolf Schnackenburg, *The Gospel according to John* (New York: The Seabury Press, 1980), Vol. II, in Loc.

[15]See Robert P. Carroll, *The Bible as a Problem for Christianity* (Philadelphia: Trinity Press International, 1991), particularly pp. 51–52; 106–116. Henceforth, Carroll.

[16]See Sigmund Mowinkel, *He That Cometh*, trans. by G. W. Anderson (New York: Abingdon, 1954), pp. 3 ff. Henceforth, Mowinkle.

name will be called Wonderful Counselor, mighty God, Everlasting Father, Prince of Peace." While God is an acceptable understanding of אל, no Jew would understand the meaning to be God in this context. The New English translation is closer to the way the Jews would understand אל in this text. It translates the passage this way: "For a boy has been born for us, a son given to us to bear the symbol of dominion on his shoulder, and he shall be called in purpose wonderful, in battle God-like, Father for all time, Prince of peace." Sigmund Mowinkle, a founder of the Scandinavian School of Theology, and the author of *He that Cometh*, the major work dealing with Old Testament messianic passages, translates el Gibbor (אֵל גִּיבוֹר) as "Divine Hero."[17] Brown, Driver and Briggs, whose development of Gesenius' Hebrew and Chaldee Lexicon, the most authoritative lexicon to date, give Divine Hero or mighty hero as an acceptable translation of el Gibbor. They also list eight other references where אֵל "el" usually is translated as god or God, and the translation is more appropriately a human or something else like a star or a mountain.

The fact that 'mighty God' is a poor translation of אֵל גִּיבוֹר "el gibbor", as far as Jews are concerned, is borne out by rabbinic literature. Rabbi Rabbinowitz translates el gibbor in the Mishnah on Ruth (VII, 2) as "mighty strong." Furthermore the same Mishnah illustrates that the Jews would never have called the Messiah "God-incarnate." The mishnah interprets Isaiah 9:1–7 as describing Hezekiah, the righteous king of Judah c. 715–687.[18]

Isaiah 7:14: "Therefore the Lord himself will give you a sign."

Isaiah 7:14 is another verse that has been traditionally employed by the church and the New Testament to refer to Jesus. The literal understanding of the text creates major problems for that application. The text reads, "Therefore the Lord himself will give you a sign. Behold a woman shall conceive and bear a son, and you shall call his name Immanuel." The old KJV translates elimeh, עַלְמָה. as 'virgin.' The fact that the RSV translated it, "young woman," was one of the grounds for many conservatives to reject the RSV. Yet even if "virgin" were the acceptable translation of elimeh, the literal context of chapter 7 prevents the passage from being applied to Jesus. The context states that the birth of this child was to be a sign to King Ahaz that he need not worry about Samaria and Syria. They would be defeated. Verse 16 states that before this child whose name was to be Immanuel would know good from evil, the nations of Samaria and Syria would be deserted. These events all took place some time between 732 and 721 B.C.E., so it must be assumed that the child was born of the virgin or maiden in that time sequence fulfilling the literal prophesy. Otherwise, the prophesy would have been declared false. There is nothing in this passage that states that it is a prophesy for later generations. If the fundamentalists insist that the young lady of 7:14 is a virgin, then there have to be two virgin births — one with Jesus and the other in the time

---

[17]Mowinkle, p.105.

[18]It is also interesting to note that the rabbis considered Isaiah 9:6 to be descriptive of the messiah. Sanhedrin 94[a] stated that God desired the messiah to be Hezekiah, but since Hezekiah did not write hymns like David, he could not be the messiah. The identity of the messiah was not known, the person that was to fulfill the Old Testament prophesy of the messiah was to be of the stature of David or Hezekiah, but not of God, himself.

of king Ahaz. This I am sure is not acceptable even to fundamentalists, so we cannot accept the text as being literally applied to Jesus.

Psalm 2:70 "You are my son, today I have begotten you."

Mowinkle pointed out that for the Jew to identify the messiah, the king, or any other person with Yahweh was just unthinkable. This was precisely what the pagans in the land of Canaan, or for that matter, Egypt and Babylon did.[19] The pharaoh or king was the deity to be worshipped and who had life or death power over his subjects. The Roman emperor was considered a deity. Each Jew knew that no human could be god. They all knew too well that their kings were mortals and subject to the judgment of Yahweh. Mowinkle makes this point in examining Psalm 2:7. This is the verse that the synoptics record as being stated at the baptism of Jesus. The reader will remember that after Jesus is baptized the heavens opened and the voice of God (assumed, but not stated) says, "This is my beloved Son (Psalm 2:7), with Thee I am well pleased (Matthew 3:17; Mark. 1:11; Luke 3:22)

Of Psalm 2:7, Mowinkle stated:

> When in Ps. ii, 7, Yahweh says to the king at the anointing and installation, "You are my son; I have begotten you today," he is using the ordinary formula of adoption, indicating that sonship rests on Yahweh's adoption of the king. The act of adoption is identical with anointing and installation. The king is chosen as the adopted son of Yahweh (Pss. xlv, 8; lxxxix, 21). Yahweh, himself, has taken care of him like a mother and father, has educated him, teaching him among other things the art of war (Ps. xviii, 35 [34]).[20]

The king was not God and he was not entitled to do work or command somebody else to work on sabbath. The question must be asked then, if prophesies such as Psalm 2:7; Isaiah 7:14, and 9:16 were literally fulfilled shortly after they were made, and if Jesus' claims to his divinity cannot be sustained by a literal interpretation of these Old Testament scriptures, does this invalidate those claims? The answer to this question is again a most emphatic "No!" The problem Jesus was confronted with here was the same basic attitude towards the Scriptures and God He faced in the confrontations with the Pharisees and Sadducees over the law.

The Pharisees and Sadducees had basically believed that God had ceased to work powerfully with Israel. He had ceased to speak directly as He had through Moses, or indirectly (Bot kol) as He had through the prophets. All revelation had ceased with Ezra and Nehemiah. The Jews' relationship with God, as they saw it, could be best described as static. They related to him through the Scriptures, looking to the past as God's great working with their forefathers and hoping that someday Yahweh would restore his presence to Israel. Because their eyes were so fixed on Yahweh's working in the past, these Jews could not see Yahweh working dynamically in their midst, in his own son.

---

[19]Mowinkle, pp. 28–95.

[20]Mowinkle, p. 78. By permission of Abingdon Press.

Chapter VIII

II Timothy 3:16

"All Scripture is inspired by God and profitable for teaching, for reproof, for correction, and for training in righteousness."

Since there is no support in the Bible for the traditional view that the Bible is the Inerrant Word of God, the question must be asked: "Is this book, which Christians esteem so much, different from any other book that humanity has produced?" The answer to this question, biblically, and empirically speaking, is an emphatic, "Yes!" The Bible is set apart from all else which has been and will be written. In it is found the history of God choosing a people to bring forth the plan of redemption to the world. It contains the record of how God interacted mightily with those people; how God led them from slavery to a land "flowing in milk and honey;" how The Lord sent prophets to them to call them to be faithful; how when they would not listen, the Lord God used other nations to correct them, sending them into exile, and how through Cyrus, the King of Persia, God brought them back to the land.

However, the greatest story of the Bible, most emphatically, is the story of the redemption of humanity; of how God in infinite love took the form of the servant in Jesus of Nazareth. This, in itself, sets this book apart from any other book that has been or will ever be written.

But how are the Scriptures to be defined? Almost every doctrine the Church has expounded has found some clear articulation in Scripture. But, this is not the case with the doctrine of the Scriptures and their inspiration. Not only is there not a statement in the Bible that it is the word of God, but there is not a clear statement of what writings are to be considered Scripture, and how those writings *became* Scripture.

In Scripture there is only one statement that could qualify as a definition of Scripture; that is to say, there is only one statement that says, "Scripture is . . . " This is II Timothy 3:16: "All Scripture is inspired by God and profitable for teaching, for reproof, for correction, and for training in righteousness (RSV)." Not surprisingly II Timothy 3:16 has been the verse most used to defend inerrancy and it would be impossible to report all that has been written on the verse. In this chapter, however, I will show that the exegesis of II Timothy 3:16 in support of inerrancy has simply not been exegesis, but a matter of isogesis. This is to say, the verse does not support, has never supported, and should never have been used to support verbal plenary inspiration of the Bible. The concept of inerrancy was not derived from II Timothy 3:16 but was imposed on it. In the next chapter I will show that the proponents of inerrancy have derived their thinking about II Timothy 3:16 not from the Bible, but from Greek philosophy.

For much of Church history, the inspiration of II Timothy 3:16 has been viewed as being very mechanical (See pp.7 ff.). Many of the Church fathers viewed the human authors of scripture as totally incidental or non-essential to the process of inspiration. God was the author of Scripture, selecting the words, phrases, sentences, and paragraphs and writing them down. The human authors were simply God's pen. Although pen was not an expression the church fathers used. They usually stated that "God spoke Scripture" or "God wrote Scripture." (See Chapter Nine)

The first change in the predominant view, mechanical inspiration, came in the thinking of the Geneva Reformer John Calvin (1509–64).[1] In his interpretation of II Timothy 3:16 the human authors are not totally eliminated. They wrote down what they heard as secretaries would write down what they heard the boss dictate. God was still "the author."[2] Quite naturally, theologians called this the dictation theory of inspiration (Calvin's Commentaries, in loc.).

Contemporary commentators reject both the mechanical and dictation views of inspiration, basically because they do not make much sense in an intelligent view of the world or even in light of the Scriptures, themselves. However, in Chicago in 1978, three hundred of the most influential conservative scholars reaffirmed that belief in the inerrancy of the Bible was utterly essential to Christianity. At that conference the scholars reaffirmed the conservative view that the Scriptures were "wholly and verbally God given . . ." (see p. 12) While contemporary views of the way God "gave" the Scriptures may differ from those held by many in the ancient church, the result of the process conservative scholars would argue was essentially the same: *every word* of Scripture was inspired by God not just the completed text or the concepts within the text.

Most contemporary conservative scholars accept the theory of concursive inspiration set forth by Princeton theologian B.B. Warfield earlier in this century. (See p. 8) Warfield argued that it was irrelevant whether inspiration was of the whole text or individual words.[3] In more recent interpretation of II Timothy 3:16, Professor William Hendricksen called the concursive process of inspiration, organic inspiration. Hendricksen wrote:

> All scripture . . . means that which through the testimony of the Holy Spirit in the Church, is recognized as canonical, that is authoritative . . . What should be emphasized, however, is that not because the church upon a certain date, long ago, made an official decision of the Council of Hippo, 393 C.E.; of Carthage, 397 C.E., do these books constitute the inspired Bible; on the contrary, the sixty-six books, by their very contents, immediately attest themselves to the hearts of all Spirit-indwelt as being the living oracles of God . . . .All scripture is canonical

---

[1] Even Thomas Aquinas (c. 1227–1274), while he does not discuss the process of inspiration, believed that God was "the author of Holy writ" and that "Holy writ"... "was truth without fallacy." (*Summa Theologica* Part I, Article 10)

[2] In the *Institutes* Calvin asserted that the Scriptures were the result of God putting "into the minds (of patriarchs, prophets, apostles) what they then should hand down to their posterity." *Institutes of the Christian Religion*, I, VI:2. At least the Patriarchs, Prophets and Apostles had a hand on the material in some form.

[3] Warfield, *Inspiration* pp. 89–92.

because God made it so.

The word God-breathed (θεοπνευστος-inspired), occurring only here, indicates that "all scripture" owes its origin and contents to the divine breath, the Spirit of God. The Human authors were powerfully guided and directed by the Holy Spirit. As a result, what they wrote is not only without error but of supreme value for man. It is all that God wanted it to be. It constitutes the infallible rule of faith and practice for mankind.

The Spirit, however, did not suppress the personality of the human writer, but raised it to a higher level of activity (John 14:26). And because the individuality of the human author was not destroyed, we find in the Bible a wide variety of style and language. Inspiration, in other words, is organic, not mechanical. This also implies that it should never be considered apart from those many activities which served to bring the human author upon the scene in history. By causing him to be born at a certain time and place, bestowing upon him specific endowments, equipping him with a definite kind of education, causing him to undergo predetermined experiences, and bringing back to his mind certain facts and their implications, the Spirit prepared his human consciousness. Next the same Spirit moved him to write. Finally, during the process of writing, that same Primary Author, in a thoroughly organic connection with all the preceeding activity, suggested to the mind of the human author that language (the very words!) and that style, which would be the most appropriate vehicle for interpretation of the divine for people of every rank, and position, age and race. Hence, though every word is truly the word of a human, it is even more truly the word of God. [4]

It does not matter what you call it. The above description plus that of those who advocate concursive inspiration are mere fantasy, or complete speculation. There is nothing in II Timothy 3:16 or for that matter in all of scripture that would allow a person to develop such a complicated system of inspiration.

Inspired All Scripture, not Individual Words

The first ground to throw out all these theories is that the text does not state, "every *word* is inspired." It states, "All (every) *scripture* is inspired . . . " In the New Testament, when writers want to refer to words they use the terms λογοι or ρηματα. Without exception in the New Testament, γραφη refers to the Scriptures. It may refer at times to a passage or a verse of Scripture (Mt. 26:54, 56; Mk. 14:49; Lk. 4:21), but never does it just refer to words. Furthermore, to equate the inspiration of the final product, the Scriptures, with the inspiration of the *words* in Scriptures, is not only not consistent with the text, but it is a logical fallacy called *minori a majoro*. Stated simply, it is not logical to ascribe to the parts that which is ascribed to the whole.

The second ground to eliminate these theories of inspiration is that II

---

[4]William Hendricksen, *New Testament Commentary: Exposition of the Pastoral Epistles* (Grand Rapids, Michigan: Baker Publishing House Inc., 1957), in loc. By permission.

Timothy 3:16 does not define what must be considered "Scriptures" or that which is "inspired, θεοπνευστος." Put precisely, there is no definition within all of Scripture of which books are to be considered inspired, and which are not. This is one of the most critical flaws in the whole theory of inerrancy. The adherents of inerrancy have what must be considered a 'mystical', or more accurately, a magical view of the formation of the canon of Scripture. Somehow, God just handed the Church books that God asserted were on the approved list and the Church just accepted those books.

No Definition of Writings to be Considered Scripture

Contrary to Hendricksen the canonical 75 books did not "attest themselves to the hearts of all Spirit-indwelt." The Church had to struggle over what composed the "inspired" books for a great many years. The canon was not decided definitively until 419 C.E., not 397 C.E. as Hendricksen stipulates. The respected reformed theologian G. C. Berkouer rightly suggests that this late date for the closing of the Canon creates great problems for the traditional view of inspiration.[5]

Besides this very apparent fact, there were a great number of people, before and after 419 accepting Scriptures who accepted different books and rejected some of the 75 books that Protestants accept as inspired. (I certainly hope that Hendricksen would not be so arrogant as to assume that the Spirit of God did not dwell with all these folk.) The struggle over the canon is well documented in the writings of Eusebius (c. 260–c. 340), the early church historian. Eusebius documents that as late as the fourth Century, the makeup of the canon was being hotly discussed. The following is taken from Eusebius' discussion of the canon written as late as 324 C.E.:

> One epistle of Peter, that called the first, is acknowledged as genuine. And this the ancient elders used freely in their writings as undisputed work. But we have learned that his extant second Epistle does not belong to the Canon . . . The so called Acts of Peter, however, and the Gospel which bears his name and the Preaching and the Apocalypse, as they are called, we know have not been universally accepted . . . Such are the writings that bear the name of Peter, only one of which I know to be genuine and acknowledged by the ancient elders.
> Paul's fourteen epistles are well known and undisputed. It is not indeed right to overlook the fact that some have rejected the Epistle to the Hebrews, saying that it is disputed by the church of Rome, on the ground that it was not written by Paul. (Church History: III, 3:1–3, NF 2nd)

It is obvious that Eusebius did not accept II Peter. Does this make him a person upon whom the Spirit of God did not dwell? In the following portion from Eusebius it is obvious that the Shepherd of Hermas was regarded as Scripture by many in the Church:

> But the same Apostle at the end of the Epistle to the Romans, has made mention among others of Hermas, to whom the Book

---

[5] G. C. Berkouer, *Holy Scriptures,* (Grand Rapids, Eerdmanns, 1975), pp. 139 ff. Henceforth, Berkouer.

called Shepherd is ascribed, it should be observed that this too has been disputed by some, on their own account cannot be placed among the acknowledged books; while by others is considered quite indispensable, especially to those who need instruction in the faith. Hence, as we know, it has been publicly read in churches, and I have found that some of the most ancient writers use it. (Church History, III, 3:6)

Later on in the Church History, Eusebius places the Shepherd of Hermas on the list of disputed books, but he also places many of the present New Testament books on that list. It is important for today's conservatives and fundamentalists to realize that in his day Eusebius was the most knowledgeable expert on the life of the Church. It is through his eyes that we have much of our knowledge of the Church of the third and fourth centuries. These are the books that Eusebius lists as disputed in the fourth century:

Among the disputed writings which are nevertheless recognized by many, are extant epistle of James and that of Jude, also the second epistle of Peter and those that are called the second and third of John, whether they belong to the evangelist or to another person of the same name. Among the rejected writings must be reckoned also the Acts of Paul, and so called Shepherd, and the Apocalypse of Peter, and in addition to those the extant epistle of Barnabas, and the so called Teachings of the Apostle, and as I said the Apocalypse of John, which some as I said reject, but which others class with the accepted books. (Church History, III, 25:3–4, NF, 2nd)

The conclusion from Eusebius is that at the end of the third century, and throughout much of the fourth there was no consensus in the church over what was the canon. The books of James, Hebrews, II Peter, II and III John, Jude, and the Book of Revelation were definitely being debated.

Shortly after Eusebius it would appear that the Church or at least the Bishops approved the dispute over epistles. At the Council of Laodicea in 366 C.E., the bishops dealt with what texts should be used in Christian worship. Within that description they listed the acceptable books which could be read in worship and this list made up the first formal statement of the canon. This list contained all the present books of the New Testament except the Book of Revelation. In the Old Testament the list included the Wisdom of Solomon, Baruch, and the Epistle of Jeremiah. (NF, Vol. XIV, p. 159)

The Western Church did not include the Book of Revelation in the canon until 53 years later. It did so at the Synod of Carthage, or African Council, in 419 C.E. (NF, Vol. XIV, p. 419) This establishes that the Book of Revelation did not command great respect in the early church. Even a person as recent as the reformer Martin Luther felt it should have been excluded. He considered it "neither apostolic nor prophetic," and would disqualify it from the canon for the following reasons:

First and foremost, the apostles do not deal with visions, but prophesy in clear and plain words, as do Peter and Paul, and Christ in the gospel. For it befits the apostolic office to speak clearly of Christ and his deeds, without images and visions. Moreover there is no prophet in the Old Testament, to say nothing of the New, who deals so exclusively in visions and images. For myself, I think it approximates the Fourth Book of Esdras (II); I can no way detect that the Holy Spirit produced it. (*Luther's Work*, Volume 35, p. 398.)

Luther's statement that he could not detect any sign "that the Holy Spirit had produced it" was the ultimate repudiation for a canonical book. It is obvious from Eusebius that many in the early Church agreed with Luther. Does the fact that Luther could not "detect that the Holy Spirit produced" Revelation mean that the Holy Spirit did not dwell in him?

The Apocrypha, Rejected by Inerrantists

When Hendricksen and most Protestants, theologians, pastors, and lay people refer to the canon of Holy Scripture, they are referring to a canon that is much different from that which has been accepted by most of the Church for most of her history. This canon which was accepted at Synods "through the testimony of the Holy Spirit" includes the Old Testament books of the Wisdom of Solomon, Baruch, the Epistle of Jeremiah, I and II Maccabees, Judith, Tobit, Sirach, I and II Esdras, The Greek Additions to Daniel and to Esther.[6]

Historically, most Protestants and adherents to inerrancy have rejected these books, calling them apocryphal.[7] The Westminster Confession accepted by the English Parliament in 1647 as the correct understanding of Scriptures, expresses most of Protestants' attitude towards those Old or Inter-testamental books. In its classic definition of Scripture, the Confession stated:

> The books commonly called Apocrypha, not being of divine inspiration, are no part of the canon of the Scripture, and therefore are of no authority in the Church of God, nor to be otherwise approved or made use of, than other human writings. (Schaff, III)[8]

---

[6]These books were re-confirmed as part inspired Scripture by the Council of Trent in 1546.

[7]The first person in the church history to call the Intertestamental books 'Apocrypha' was Origen (c. 185–c. 254). For Origen 'apocrypha' did not have the meaning of false writing, or false writer. It meant that the book had hidden meanings but then for Origen, considering he was the father of the allegorical method of interpretation of Scripture, all scripture contained hidden meaning. Jerome (c. 340–419) is the first to refer to many of the intertestamental books as Apocrypha in the sense of the Reformed Church. In prefaces to the Vulgate, his Latin translation of the Bible, he wrote of the books of Ecclesiasticus and the Wisdom of Solomon, "As the Church reads Judith, Tobit, and the Books of Maccabees, but does not admit them among the canonical, so let it read these two volumes for the edification of the people, not to give authority to the doctrines of the Church (NF, Vol. VI, p. 492)."

In a letter written (c. 403) to Laeta, a Roman woman, Jerome advises that in reading the canonical book of Song of Songs one should "look for gold in the midst of the dirt. (*Jerome*, Vol VI, p. 194)." Even with his negative statements on the Apocrypha, Jerome, himself, mixes on an equal basis quotes from the 'orthodox' Scriptures and the 'apocryphal' Scriptures (*Jerome*, Vol. VI. pp. 4,16, 26, 30, 42, 45, 50, 60, passim). In one place, he takes the Story straight out of the 'apocryphal' book of Susanna, of young boy Daniel judging elders, and gives it the same authenticity as the Book of Daniel (*Jerome*, Vol. VI, p. 119; p. 494.; cf. pp. 2, 4.).

[8]Luther was not terribly negative on the apocrypha. The books of Sirach and I Maccabees were worthy of the Canon. The stories of Judith, Tobit, Bel and the Dragon were 'beautiful

For the Westminster Divines who believed that their lives, their government, was to be based on what they believed to be the correct interpretation of Scripture, the Westminster Confession was the ultimate denigration of religious writing. Recent Protestant scholarship would be more lenient in its interpretation of the Apocrypha. Modern conservative scholars would be more lenient. They would grant that studying the "apocryphal" literature would help in a better understanding of the period from the close of the Old Testament canon at the time of Ezra until the time of Jesus. Merill Unger in his *Bible Dictionary* best expressed modern, conservative estimation of the Apocrypha :

> The O.T. Apocrypha have an unquestioned historical and literary value but have been rejected as inspired for the following reasons:
> 1. They abound in historical and geographical inaccuracies and anachronisms.
> 2. They teach doctrines which are false and foster practices which are at variance with inspired Scripture.
> 3. They resort to literary types and display an artificiality of subject matter and styling out of keeping with inspired Scripture.
> 4. They lack distinctive elements which give genuine Scripture their divine character, such as prophetic power and poetic and religious feeling. [9]

I am aware of no conservative scholar who would argue for the inclusion of the Apocrypha among those books that II Timothy 3:16 considered "inspired (θεοπνευστος)." This attitude has some real serious historical and exegetical problems. One of the problems is very obvious: There could hardly be described as unanimous and unequivocal, a voice in either the early or the later Church endorsing the Protestant Canon as the inspired Scriptures. As far as the Church is concerned the Protestants are in the minority in their rejecting the Apocrypha.

A Variety of Canons in Early Churches

Another factor for consideration is that the canon of many of the early Churches reflect an even different Scripture than that of the Protestants. The first notable attempt to compile the New Testament Scriptures happened in Syria around 150. The Diatesseron, compiled by Tatian (c. 120–170), consisted of the Acts of the Apostles, the epistles of Paul, and the first compilation of the four Gospels overlaid in parallel fashion. Tatian (who was converted with the assistance of Justin Martyr) and much of Syriac Christianity rejected Latinate Christianity. They rejected the catholic epistles, and the epistles of John and the Book of Revelation, but they included the apocryphal Third Epistle of Paul to the Corinthians.[10]

Not long after formation of the Syrian Canon, another group of Christians in Armenia formed their own canon. Tradition has it that the Apostles Bartholomew and Thadaeus evangelized Armenia. By the year 250 C.E. Christianity was well established. Around 300 C.E. under the influence of St. Gregory the

---

religious fictions.' (*Luther's Work*, Vol. 35, 337–354).

[9]Merrill Unger, *Bible Dictionary (Chicago*: Moody Press, 1966), in loc. By permission.

[10]Bruce Metzger, *The Early Versions of the New Testament (Oxford*: Oxford University Press, 1977), pp. 10 ff. Henceforth Metzger, Early Versions.

Illuminator, Armenia's King Tiridate III converted to Christianity and established it as the state religion. This was some eighty years before the Roman Empire officially became Christian.[11] In spite of centuries of pogroms and huge persecutions, Christianity has remained strong in Armenia. Along with the same books that the predominant Church canonized, the Armenian Old Testament contained the apocryphal books of the History of Joseph and Asenath and the Testament of the Twelve Patriarchs. The New Testament contained the Epistle of the Corinthians to Paul and The Third Epistle of Paul to Corinthians.[12]

As far as the predominant Church was concerned, the works of the early Church Fathers of the second and third centuries reveal that the early Christians recognized Scriptures that are not found in the current Protestant canon. Most importantly the Church fathers of the second Century and most in the third and forth centuries quote from the Septuagint, the Greek translation of the Old Testament containing the Apocrypha, rather than the Hebrew canon which contains the scriptures recognized by the Protestants.[13]

The Myth of Jamnia and The Old Testament Canon

The argument that will be raised here by fundamentalists and conservatives, is that their Old Testament Canon predates the Canon formed at Carthage; that their canon coincides with the Hebrew Canon, and since the Old Testament was produced by Jews it would be natural to let them determine what are the Old Testament books. These scholars will argue that the Hebrew

---

[11]Constantine purportedly had a vision of conquering by the sign of Christ in 311. In 313 he declared the edict of Milan that gave Christianity equal status with all the other religions, but Constantine seemed to want to keep his feet on both sides of the fence. It was not until 337 shortly before he died that he was baptized a Christian. The religion of the empire was declared to be Christian by the Emperor Theodosius in 381.

[12]Bruce Metzger, Early Versions, p. 161.

[13]Clement of Rome (c. 96 C.E.). According to Church historian, Hans Lietzman, it is from Clement that we get the best glimpse of the early Church directly after Peter and Paul. Lietzman, I, pp. 192–200. Polycarp, Bishop of Smyrna (c. 110 C. E.) quotes Tobit as Scripture (To the Philippians 10:2). In the little epistle ascribed to Barnabus the apocryphal works of II Esdras is quoted as Scripture (12:2). The same epistle could be used to support the canonization of the pseudepigraphic Book of Enoch, (4:3; 16:6), as does the Tertullian (c. 160– c. 220 C.E.) and the little canonical epistle of Jude. The Pastor of Hermas quotes as scripture the Tobit (I Vision 1:6; V Mandate 2:3) Apocryphal Eldad and Modad (II Vision 3:4;). Wisdom (III Vision 7:3); 2 Maccabees (I Mandate 1; XI Mandate 4:2). Ireneaus, the Bishop of Lyons (c. 130–c. 202), quoted as Scripture the apocryphal works entitled Gospel to the Egyptians, (Against Heresies, II, 34:3; IV, 17:2; 20:2; 26:4) Bel and the Dragon (IV, 5:2; Susanna, (IV, 26:4), and the Book of Enoch (IV:16:2). Clement of Alexandria (c. 150– c. 215) accepted into his canon II Esdras (The Miscellanies III:16); Tobit, (The Miscellanies 2:23; 6:12); Wisdom (The Instructor 1:8 The Miscellanies 5:14 Sirach, one of his most often quoted books (Instructor 1:8; III:9, Finger-rings, III:9, The Hair, III:9, The Government; The Miscellanies I:4 etc.); Judith, II:4. Clement even quoted Philo of Alexandria as Scripture II:18. (Origen, who was Clement's student, and who was one of the Church's first scholars accepted the same books as Clement did (De Principiis I, 3:3; III, 2:4 (Hermas and Barnaas); 3:6; IV, 1:11), but his Canon was still broader. In Origen's New Testament was included the Acts of the Apostle Paul). Origin, quotes as Scripture, Wisdom, Ecclesiasticus, The Ascension of Moses, and Tobit De Principiis, I, 1:2, 5; II, 2:5; 3:6; 8:3; III, 1:14; 2:1; etc. The apocryphal book of Susannah was defended as being part of the canon in letter that he wrote Bishop Africanus ("A Letter from Origen to Africanus," Ante-Nicene Fathers, X, 370–387).

Canon was closed in the first century C.E. at the Council of Jamnia (Javneh), c. 70 C.E., long before the Council at Carthage.

Their reasoning is flawed. The closing of the Canon at the Council of Jamnia is a myth that has been almost uniformly accepted in Protestantism.[14] It is alleged that the apocryphal books were ruled out at this conference because they were written after Ezra and "there was no inspiration after Ezra."[15] Joseph Blenkinsopp of Notre Dame states that this myth originated with a British scholar, Professor H. E. Ryles (1856–1925).[16]

There is evidence that there was a great Sanhedrin (Synagogue), (Aboth 1:1), and there may be some evidence that the canonization of Sirach was discussed, but there is no evidence that it was rejected. In fact it is quoted as Scripture by later rabbis (Berakoth 48[a]). There is no evidence that the canon was established at this council.

All the evidence that is now available shows that Judaism of the first four Centuries C.E. was not a monolithic entity and the Canon of the Old Testament for most Jews was not the Hebrew Canon of thirty nine books. There were many Jews with a wide spectrum of beliefs but whose common thread was the monotheism of Moses. There were Samaritan Jews, Pharisaic Jews, Sadducean Jews, Hasidic Jews, Essene Jews — Diasporan Jews of all forms and nationalities.

Their scriptures differed remarkably. The Sadducees and Samaritans accepted only the Pentateuch. The Alexandrians accepted the Septuagint with the "apocryphal" books. The Qumran Community had many of the Hebrew and Aramaic Apocryphal books, such as Tobit, Sirach, Baruch, and Daniel.[17] Furthermore, the Qumran Scriptures contained Psalms that were not included in the Hebrew canon;[18] the book of Jubilees and the earth-shaking discovery of the book of Enoch.[19] Joseph Baumgarten in *Studies in Qumran Law* from his work with the Dead Sea Scrolls and related sources describes the situation

---

[14]Including such notable scholars as Robert Pfeiffer, *Introduction to the Old Testament* (New York: Harper Brothers Publication, Inc., 1948), p. 446(?). Henceforth Pfeiffer, O.T. and Martin Noth, *The History of Israel* (New York: Harper & Brothers Publishers, 1960), pp. 446–8; Otto Eissfeldt, *The Old Testament, an Introduction* (New York: Harper & Row Publishers, 1973), and G. W. Anderson, *Understanding the Old Testament* (Englewood Cliffs, NJ: Prentice Hall, Inc., 1957); Roger Beckwith, *The Old Testament Canon of the New Testament (Grand* Rapids: MI: Wm. B. Eerdmans, Publishing Company, 1985).

[15]According to Aage Bentzen the concept that "there was no inspiration after Ezra" was alluded to in the Apocryphal book II Ezra where Ezra dictates under the influence of the Holy Spirit 24 books of the Hebrew Canon (4:14 ff.), and was developed by Elias Levita in his book *Massoreth-ha-Massoreth* (1538) where he sets forth the three part canon with 39 books. (Bentzen, pp. 26–27). Whereas in Luther we find uncertainty of the Canon and tolerance towards the Apocrypha, by the time of the Westminster Confession Levita's thought has become established doctrine among most Protestants.

[16]Joseph Blenkinsopp in *Prophecy and Canon (Notre* Dame, Indiana: University of Notre Dame Press, 1977), pp. 3 ff. See also A. C. Sundberg, *The Old Testament of the Early Church (Cambridge*, Ma.: Harvard University Press, 1964).

[17]Martin Hengel, *Judaism and Hellenism* (Philadelphia: Fortress Press, 1974), p. 177 ff.

[18]J. A. Sanders, *The Dead Sea Psalms Scroll* (Ithaca, NY: Cornell University Press, 1967), p. 3 ff. There were five additional Psalms 151–155 and some of the Biblical Psalms had verses added to them.

of the Canon in the first century. Baumgarten wrote: "The canonical status of the Torah was, of course, fully recognized by all Jewish groups during the period of the Second Temple. There, appear significant divergence among the sects with regard to its effecting the status of subsequent religious teaching."[20]

It is beyond dispute that most of the Jewish communities in the diaspora used the Septuagint as their Scriptures. In his book, *History of New Testament Times*, Robert Pfeiffer pointed out that most of the diasporan Jews did not live as later Jews in self-contained ghettoes, but interacted freely with the gentile population. For many of the diasporan Jews, Hebrew and Aramaic had become forgotten languages.[21] While the Bible does not confirm that these Jews had forgotten or lost their Hebrew, Acts 2:6 and 2:9 confirm that the diasporan Jews spoke in the languages of the regions they came from. It is stated there that the Jews from the nations heard the uneducated Galileans speak in their native tongues. Following next is a list of fifteen different linguistic groups that people heard spoken. It could be assumed that if they all spoke Hebrew, the Holy Spirit would have had the disciples speak only in Hebrew, saving energy and confusion.

Pfeiffer stated that the crucial cultural difference between the Jews and the Gentiles was the fact that the Jews were monotheists and they followed the law of Moses, while the gentiles were polytheists. He stated that in the first century B.C.E. and the early part of the first century C.E., there was general religious toleration in the Roman Empire. Jews faced derision and persecution simply because they did not worship the god of the locality, and participate in the general religious ethos of the region. It was out of this milieu that there developed a veneration of the "apocryphal books."[22] Pfeiffer described the attachment to the apocryphal books in the Diasporan community this way:

> In the other Hellenistic-Jewish writings the accusations against the Jews were not even mentioned: the authors contented themselves with glorifying the Jews and the religion, and ridiculing paganism: these put on varying guises and different forms, are dominant themes of this literature. Even the Palestinian books written after 200 B.C.E. and translated into Greek, becoming part of the Septuagint, have in common this exaltation of the Jews over Pagans. History (I Maccabees) and fiction (Daniel, Bel and the Dragon, Judith, Esther with additions) describe the triumphs of Jews; over heathen; or presented idealized portraits of exemplary Jewish individuals (Tobit, Susanna). Ecclesiasticus extolled Judaism and deemed Hellenism unworthy

---

[19]George Nickelsburg, "I Enoch and Qumran Origin," *Society of Biblical Literature,* 25:341–356 (1986).

[20]Baumgarten, p. 27.

[21]Robert Pfeiffer, *History of New Testament Times with an Introduction to the Apocrypha.* (New York: Harper and Row, Inc., 1949) pp. 181 ff. Henceforth Pfeiffer, New Testament.

[22]Pfeiffer, NT, pp. 181 ff.

of notice. Apocalypses beginning with Daniel, announced the coming downfall of the heathen empires and the establishment of the Jewish world kingdom. And the Epistle of Jeremy caricatured sarcastically the religion of the gentiles as an extremely crass and idiotic worship of inanimate idols.[23]

It was not until late into the fourth and on into the fifth century that Rabbinic Judaism rejected the Septuagint as valid Scripture, and the only acceptable Scriptures became those written in Hebrew. The reasons for this are described by Jacob Neusner in *Judaism and Christianity in the Age of Constantine* (See also *Judaism in Society*). Neusner states that the legalization of Christianity was the single factor that made for the solidification of Rabbinical Judaism. While there may have been a good deal of derision and some persecution before that time, the pagan cultus basically left the Jews alone as far as their essential beliefs. Such was not the case with the legalization of Christianity. Now, a religion that the Jews considered a heresy became the dominant religion. It claimed the same God as the Jews. Moses and the Prophets were heralded as forefathers of the Church. Many, if not most of the Christians denigrated the Jews as being false Israel. Preachers could incite mobs into burning Synagogues and harassing Jews. It was at this time that Jews attempted to secure or reclaim their identity. This identity included establishing Hebrew as the language of Judaism. The only acceptable scriptures were those then that were written in Hebrew. Thus, most of those books of scripture, written in Greek by Diasporan Jews, were rejected from the Canon.[24]

Scriptures no Support for Protestant Bible

While G. C. Berkouer asserts that the late date of the canon creates problems for the traditional view of inspiration, he stipulates that the internal authority of the canon was "sufficiently compelling to commend itself generation after generation."[25] This assertion is consistent with the Reformed standard of Sola Scriptura. Stated simply, the doctrine of Sola Scriptura is that in all matters concerning faith and its practice, the Scriptures are the final authority. This doctrine was specifically spelled out in the Second Helvetic Confession adopted by the Swiss Reformed canton in 1566. The Confession stated:

We believe and confess the Canonical Scriptures of the holy

---

[23]Pfeiffer, NT, p. 199.

[24]Jacob Neusner, *Judaism and Christianity in the Age of Constantine* (Chicago: University of Chicago Press, 1987) p. 1 ff. See also *Judaism in Society (Chicago*: University of Chicago Press, 1983), pp. 3–26. Henceforth Neusner, *Judaism in Society*. Sid Leiman is wrong in his argument in *The Canonization of Hebrew Scripture: The Talmudic and Midrashic Evidence*, when he assumes that the canon was closed as early as the second century B.C.E. with 24 books "in most Jewish circles." But most likely he is correct that a group of Jews accepted the canon as it is found in the Hebrew canon. *The Canonization of Hebrew Scripture: The Talmudic and Midrashic Evidence (Hampden*, Connecticut: Archon Books, Inc., 1976, pp. 131–135) This group were Masorites and they lived in a couple of small ascetic communities. Neusner, *Judaism in Society*, pp. 3–26. There is no evidence that it had universal acceptance with all Jews. Therefore, it must be concluded that as far as Rabbinical Judaism is concerned, there was not a universal Hebrew Canon other than the Torah, until late into the fourth century C.E.

[25]G. C. Berkouer, Holy Scriptures, p 67 ff.; 137 ff.

prophets and apostles of both Testaments to be the true Word of God, to have sufficient authority of themselves not of men. For God himself spake to the fathers, prophets, apostles, and still speaks to us through the Holy Scriptures.

And in this Holy Scripture, the universal Church of Christ has all things fully expounded which belong to saving faith, and also framing a life acceptable to God . . . (Schaff, p. 132.)

The Scriptures derive their existence and authority not from any formulation of men or Church council, but strictly from God. John Calvin put it succinctly by stating that the Scriptures are 'self-authenticated (*Institutes*, I:VI, I–VI, 2).' Otherwise the Scriptures validate themselves. If the criterion to determine what books make up Scripture is the "internal authority" or Sola Scriptura, then the canon must of necessity be much different than the present Protestant canon. The first observation is that the New Testament authors did not consider the Hebrew Canon sacrosanct or essentially their Scripture. Many times it is obvious that the New Testament writers quote from the Greek Septuagint rather than the Hebrew text (Matthew 1:23; 4:4; 15:8–9; 22:32; 27:9–10, 43; Mark 6:6–7;9:48; 10:27; Luke 2:29; 18:20 etc.) The second observation is that the New Testament writers do not quote from nor do they mention by name the books of Judges, I and II Chronicles, Ecclesiastes, Song of Songs, Lamentations, Esther, Obadiah, Nahum, and Zephaniah. Therefore must these books be excluded from the Canon?

The third observation is that a mere reference to a fact, event, or phrase in the Old Testament books in the New Testament is used to establish the canonicity of a book, then the "apocryphal" books of Judith; Tobit; The Assumption of Moses; I and II Esdras; I, II, and IV Maccabees; Sirach; and the Wisdom of Solomon have to be given equal or stronger consideration. There are over 200 references to these "apocryphal" books in the New Testament — many more references than there are to the books of Ecclesiastes, Song of Songs, Lamentations, Ruth, and Esther, which the Protestants accept. Furthermore, the book of Esther would be totally rejected because there are no references to it in the New Testament.[26]

The fourth observation regarding which books should be included within the Old Testament canon would be the specific mention by name of the book in the New Testament. This would be irrefutable evidence of which books the New Testament writers considered to be divinely inspired, and thus good evidence of what II Timothy 3:16 meant by θεοπνευστος. This method only leads to a partial list of the books that are now within the Protestant canon. Only Isaiah (Mt. 4:14; 8:17; 12:17 etc.), Jeremiah (Mt. 2:17; 16:14; 27:35), Daniel (Mt. 24:15; Mk. 13:14), Jonah (Mt. 12:39; 16:4), Joel (Acts 2:16) and Psalms (Lk. 20:42; 24:44; Acts 1:20 etc.) are mentioned. Of course, one would have to include in this list the first five books of the Bible. It would be beyond dispute that whenever the New Testament refers to the 'Law,' the first five books of the Bible are meant.

---

[26]Nestle's text cites one reference to Esther and that is Mark 6:23. If the reference is accepted as a valid reference than it would tend to render the passage of Mark 6:14–28 spurious. This is because the words of Herod in 6:23 are similar to those of King Ahasuerus in Esther 5:3. The context does not seem to call for Herod to quote king Ahasuerus, so if it is a reference it would seem that the writer of Mark was putting those words in King Herod's mouth artificially.

By Inerrancy Standards, I Enoch is Scripture

If the mention of the name of a book is the most authoritative definition of what is considered scripture by the New Testament writers, then the canon definitely needs to be redefined. The apocryphal book of Enoch, which is not accepted by the Episcopalians or any of the branches of Catholicism, has to be given equal status with Isaiah, Jeremiah, Daniel, Joel, the Psalms, and the Law. The Epistle of Jude states, "It was of these also that Enoch in the seventh generation prophesied saying. . . . (vs. 14 RSV)" Jude then quotes Enoch 1:9, "Behold the Lord came with his holy myriads, to execute on all, and to convict all the ungodly of all their deeds of ungodliness which they have committed in such an ungodly way, and of all the harsh things which ungodly sinners have spoken against him." (vss. 14–15 RSV)

The book of Enoch would then meet two of the chief internal criteria of what is scripture. The book is mentioned by name specifically, and it is quoted in the same form that all the other prophets are quoted.

The second century church father, Tertullian, argued for the canonization of Enoch. I include Tertullian's reasoning here because I think if one accepts inerrancy, then one is forced into accepting arguments similar to Tertullian's. I am sure the most fundamentalistic scholar of today could not do this. Here is Tertullian's reasoning:

> I am aware that the Scripture of Enoch . . . is not received by some, because it is not admitted into the Jewish Canon either. I suppose they did not think that, having been published before the deluge, it could have safely survived the world-wide calamity, the abolisher of all things. If that is the reason [for rejecting it], let them recall to their memory that Noah, the survivor of the deluge, was the great-grandson of Enoch himself; and he, of course, had heard and remembered, domestic renown (account) and hereditary tradition, concerning all his great-grandfather's "grace in the sight of God," and concerning all his preachings; since Enoch had given an other charge Methuselah that he should hand on the knowledge of them to his posterity. Noah, therefore, no doubt, might have succeeded in the trusteeship of [his] preaching, or, had the case been otherwise, he would not have been silent alike concerning the disposition [of things] made by God, his Preserver, and concerning the particular glory of his own house. . . .
>
> But since Enoch in the same Scripture has preached likewise concerning the Lord, nothing at all must be rejected by us which pertains to us; we read that "every Scripture suitable for edification is divinely inspired." By the Jews it may now seem to be rejected for that [very reason just like all the [portions] nearly which tell of Christ. Nor, of course, is this fact wonderful, that they did not receive some Scriptures which spake of Him whom even in person speaking in their presence, they were not to receive. To these considerations is added the fact that Enoch possesses a testimony in the apostle Jude. (On Female Dress I:3, AN chap. 11, pp. 308–309)

Tertullian's argument seems far-fetched. But is it any more far-fetched then concursive or organic inspiration? Certainly, if God has taken all the power and energy to supervise every detail in each writer's life so that every word and every thought was exactly what God wanted, then God certainly had the power to bring Enoch's message through the deluge. If the Scriptures bear "sufficient authority of themselves," if the Scriptures are "self-authenticated," then the book of Enoch has to be accepted as canonical long before the books of Ruth, Esther, the Song of Songs, or Lamentations.

The final method of determining Scripture from apocrypha would be the "compellingness" of the content. This means that the message about God from the text must compel us to know that the writer was truly inspired. If this method is accepted then the Book of Esther truly must be excluded from the canon, for God and faith in that God are never mentioned in that book. On the other hand the "apocryphal" book of Sirach must be included within the canon, because it is filled with deep spiritual insights like this:

> The fear of the Lord brings honor and pride,
> cheerfulness and a garland of joy.
> The fear of the Lord gladdens the heart;
> It brings cheerfulness and joy and long life.
> Whoever fears the Lord will be prosperous at the last;
> blessings will be his on the day of his death. (*Sirach* 1:11–13, NEB)

Or another passage:

> Do not rely on your money
> and say, 'I am independent.'
> Do not yield to every impulse you can gratify
> or follow the desires of your heart.
> Do not say "I am my own Master;'
> you may be sure the Lord will call you to account. (*Sirach* 5:1–3, NEB)

The following passage from Baruch sounds like it has been taken straight out the Book the Psalms. Why isn't Baruch part of the canon?

> O Lord, look down from thy holy dwelling and think of us, Lord. Turn thy ear to us, Lord, and hear us; open thine eyes and see. The dead are in their graves, the breath is gone from their bodies; it is not they who can sing the Lord's praises or applaud his justice; it is living men, mourning their fall from greatness, walking the earth bent and feeble, blind and famished- it is these who will sing thy praise, O Lord and applaud thy justice. (*Baruch* 2:16–18 NEB)

The Greek Septuagint, Timothy's Scriptures

Within the Scriptures there is other strong textual evidence that the "Scriptures" of II Timothy 3:16 were Septuagint Scripture and not the Hebrew Canon. This evidence is found in the texts of II Timothy 1:5 and Acts 16:1 and it revolves around the fact that the persons who fostered Timothy's faith and his Scripture study were female — his mother and Grandmother. On that ground, alone they would have been forbidden to study Torah, the first five books of the Bible written in Hebrew. It is also stated that Timothy's mother was a Jewish Christian and his father was a Greek. Timothy's father is not mentioned, so it can be safely assumed that his father was not a believer.

In the history of Judaism, the fact that Timothy's mother, Eunice, was married to a gentile places her in the liberal Diasporan Judaism.[27] Certainly strict groups like the Masorettes would never have permitted their daughter to marry a gentile. If a daughter of a Masorette had by some circumstance married a gentile, that woman would no longer be a daughter and a Jew. As far as the Masorettes were concerned, she was dead. The reader will remember that one of the reasons that Samaritans were disliked by the Jews in Palestine is that they were Jews who had intermarried with gentiles. This meant that Eunice was an unclean person, as far as the stricter elements of Judaism were concerned. Furthermore, since Eunice married a Gentile in a male dominant society, it is highly unlikely that Eunice would have been allowed to teach her son Hebrew. Timothy's father would have spoken Greek or Latin, or maybe both. Most likely Timothy did not even know Hebrew, and as a child in his mother's house he did not have access to the Hebrew Scrolls. The best evidence from our texts would be that the Scriptures that Timothy knew and studied were the Septuagint and not the Hebrew Canon. [28]

With all the biblical and extra-biblical evidence pointing to a much different Canon than that of the current Protestant Canon, it is obvious the theory of inerrancy is flawed from the very beginning. It is not possible to determine from Scripture or, for that matter any other source, exactly what II Timothy 3:16 meant by γραφη.

If God had wanted a concept of inerrancy, God would have spelled it out in scripture at least as well as the incarnation and other doctrines of the Church. There would have been a list of the exact books to be included in the canon. Even today, no one that I am aware of imputes the authorship of the Book of Hebrews to Paul. Therefore, if Apostleship or relationship to the Apostles is the basis for acceptance in the Canon, the book of Hebrews must be rejected, as many in the early Church rejected it.

No Definition of "Inspired " - God Breathed

As it can not be determined from II Timothy 3:16, what is Scripture, so also no clear definition of "θεοπνευστος, inspired," can be constructed. Even the great Reformed scholar B.B. Warfield, considered the authority on the subject of inspiration by many conservative scholars, conceded that "inspired" was a poor translation of the word θεοπνευστος.[29] Warfield asserted that θεοπνευστος most properly translated means "God-breathed." He wrote:

> . . . From all points of approach we appear to be conducted to the conclusion that it (θεοπνευστος) is primarily expressive of origination of Scripture, not of its nature and much less its effects. What is θεοπνευστος is "God-breathed," the product of Divine spiration, the creation of that Spirit who is in all spheres of the divine activity the executive of the Godhead . . . What it affirms is that the scriptures owe their origins to an activity of God the Holy Ghost and are in the highest origin due to an

---

[27]Jacob Neusner, Judaism in Society, pp. 3–26.

[28]See Duncan M. Derrett, *Jesus' Audience* (New York: Seabury Press, 1973), pp. 31–45.

[29]Benjamin Breckinridge Warfield, Inspiration pp. 245–296.

activity of the Holy Ghost and are in the highest and truest sense His creation. It is on this foundation of Divine origin that all the attributes of Scripture are built. [30]

I must note in passing that Warfield's thinking has become so standard among conservative scholars that the prestigious *New International Version* simply translates θεοπνευστος as "God-breathed" without even a footnote. But, there is also no reason to question the translation.

The word is a combination of two Greek words θεος meaning, "God," and πνειν, meaning, "to breathe." But what is "God-breathed" Scripture? How did God breathe Scripture? As has been stated, Warfield postulated the process of the writing of Scripture as "concursive inspiration."[31] Hendrciksen called it "organic inspiration," many of the early church fathers consider that God wrote or spoke Scripture, and Calvin believed that God dictated Scripture. All these views are seriously flawed from the point of view II Timothy 3:16. The text does not say that God selected and directed all the experiences of the authors so that their vocabulary, their remembrance, their syntax, and all else would be exactly what God wanted. It does not state that God spoke Scripture or that God wrote Scripture. The text simply says "All Scripture is God-breathed . . . "

Since this is the first and only time the term is used in Scripture, it is impossible to determine its meaning from the rest of Scripture. The term is used in later writings but its usage is derived from II Timothy 3:16. Then, as it shall become apparent in chapter nine, the term becomes a blend of various Greek philosophical thoughts, with no basis in the Bible.

If II Timothy meant to imply an on-going process of inspiration such as implied in the concursive and organic theories, it would have clearly stated so. Furthermore, at the time it was written there already was a means to express the concepts of Concursive and organic inspiration. The type of thought expressed in mechanical, concursive, and organic inspiration theories was well developed by a very famous rabbi who was a contemporary of Paul's, Philo of Alexandria (c. 10 B.C.E. to c. 50 C.E.) For Philo, there are no possibilities for human efforts in the formation of Scripture and therefore no errors. Philo used the Greek θεοφορεω/θεοφερω meaning "God carried." In describing Moses' receiving the law, Philo wrote:

> ..First, he had to be clean, as in body, to have no dealings with any passion, purifying from all calls of mortal nature, food and drink and intercourse with women. The last he had disdained for many a day, almost from the time when, possessed by the spirit (θεοφορεισθαι), he entered on his work as a prophet . . . (Philo, *Moses*, I, 69)

One would assume that such modern scholars as Warfield and Hendricksen would not have deprecated such human activities as eating, drinking and "intercourse with women (their wives)," but their theories of inspiration are no less far-fetched than Philo's. The following is how Philo describes Moses at the end of his life:

---

[30]Warfield, Inspiration, p. 296.

[31]Warfield, Revelation pp. 52 ff.

Afterwards the time came when he (Moses) had to make his pilgrimage from earth to heaven, and leave this mortal life for immortality, summoned thither by the father Who resolved his (Moses') twofold nature of soul and body into a single unity, transforming his whole being into mind, pure as sunlight. Then, indeed, we find him possessed by the spirit, no longer uttering general truth to the whole nation but prophesying to each tribe in particular the things which were to be and here after to come . . . This was wonderful: but most wonderful of all is the conclusion of Holy Scriptures, . . . for when he was already being exalted . . . the divine spirit fell upon him and he prophesied with discernment while still alive the story of his death. (Moses, II, 288.)

Here is what has been for most of the last two to three centuries the standard conservative response to the biblical critics' observation that Moses could not possibly have recorded his own death and therefore could not possibly have written the last chapter of Deuteronomy. According to Philo, being "possessed by the spirit" of the all-powerful God, Moses could do anything, including describing his own death. Moses was transformed into being all "mind" or the reason of the universe. These terms are definitely not Biblical, and will be discussed in the next chapter.

For Philo this kind of inspiration was not confined only to Moses. The insignificant Gentile prophet Balaam also receives it. The story is found in Numbers, chapters 22–24 where king Balak commands Balaam to curse Moses. Philo describes Balaam's response the following way:

In solitude, he was suddenly possessed (θεοφορεῖται), and understanding nothing, his reason as it were roaming uttered these words that were put into his mouth: "Arise, O king, and listen. Lend me a ready ear. God can not be deceived as a man nor as the son of man does he repent or fail to abide by what he has once said. He will utter nothing at all which certainly will not be performed. His word is his deed . . . " (Moses I, 231)

But for Philo there was a difference between the inspiration of Moses and Balaam. Moses understood the inspiration while Balaam, the gentile, did not understand what he was prophesying. In contrast, nowhere in the biblical narration of Balaam and Balak does it state that Balaam did not understand what Yahweh said to him and what he prophesied to Balak (Numbers 22–24).

When it comes to Philo's assessment of Moses' work as a Prophet there is considerable enhancement of the Biblical narrative. In Exodus 34:29 it does state that Moses' face "shone" but nowhere does it state that his whole being was transformed into mind, nor does the text state that Moses was "possessed by the Spirit." In the narration of the "Giving of the Law" (Exodus 19:1–34:35) the scenario is one of a mortal, Moses, from the nation of Israel, standing in the presence of God. Moses' radiance was because he had been in the presence of God so long, rather than his being possessed by the Spirit of God. This is illustrated when Moses comes down from the Mountain and finds the people worshipping the golden calf, he has to plead with Yahweh not to destroy the people of Israel (32:11–14; 30–35). Moses was not simply "possessed by the spirit," and existing as the extension of Yahweh, but was his own individual and thus could represent the people.

Furthermore the law is not communicated by Moses taking it down in pen but rather by the "finger" of Yahweh writing on tablets of stones (31:18). Before the second giving of the Law, Moses does fast for forty days. Since he has already been given the law once without fasting, one could assume, although it is not stated, that he was fasting to intervene on behalf of the Israelite people, not to receive the law. There is no statement in the text that Moses would be or was possessed, transformed into mind, or that he did not have sex.

Otherwise, there is no support for Philo's theories in Scripture. It again must be underscored that if God had wanted inerrancy to be biblical doctrine God certainly would have used concepts like Philo's. It is obvious from the absence of such concepts that God did not want inerrancy to be a part of Christian doctrine. One might argue from Paul's use of θεοπνευστος "God-breathed" instead of θεοφορεω/θεοφερω, "God carried" that Paul believed the basic idea, the inspired idea, originated with God as he "breathed out or exhaled it." The writers then picked up and developed the idea as they saw fit. This would leave the origination of the thought with God and the freedom of communication to the human. Before I am accused of developing a new system of inspiration, I must state that I agree with the conservative G. C. Berkouer, when he wrote, "II Timothy 3:16 did not offer us a theory of the 'mode' of the God-breathed character of Scripture."[32] All the current theories of inspiration are sheer speculation or mere myth. I will show in the next chapter that they owe their genesis to one common source which is definitely not rooted in the Bible.

The Scriptures, Guide for Transformation

Thus far in my discussion I have dealt only with the distortion of II Timothy 3:16. While it is impossible to determine what Scriptures are θεοπνευστος and what θεοπνευστος means, it is not impossible to derive some profound light from the text. To do this, one must not isolate verse 16 from its context as is conventionally done in the defense of inerrancy. The examination of II Timothy 3:10–17 reveals that verses 16–17 give us a qualitative description of the Scriptures and their intended purposes, rather than presenting a methodology of how scriptures came into existence. The first observation to be made is that verse 16 consists of a string of eight nouns. There is not a verb in the verse. This is highly unusual. Normally, Pauline literature favored the use of verbs, particularly the participle form of the verb. The use of nouns rather than verbs underscores that what is found in II Timothy 3:16 is not a description of the process through which Scripture came into existence, but rather the description of their qualities and purpose. Literally translated II Timothy 3:16 should read: "All scripture, God-breathed, and useful for education, for admonition, for improvement, for instruction in righteousness."

The late date of the vocabulary may have led both the RSV and NEB to place the emphasis on doctrine, as if the text were meant for refutation of second and third century heresies of Gnosticism and Montanism. The context of II Timothy 3:16 leads one, however, away from such a formalistic and theological translation to a much more pragmatic, "functional"[33] translation. The whole pericope deals with real life issues and not with defining "correct

---

[32]Berkouer, p. 150(?), 180.

142

theology." The pericope reads:

> But you have followed my teaching, my way of life, my resolve, my faith, my patience, my love, my perseverance, my persecutions, my sufferings, that happened to me at Antioch, at Iconium, and at Lystra, what persecutions I endured, yet from them all the Lord delivered me. Indeed, all those wishing a pious life in Christ Jesus will be persecuted. But evil folk and swindlers will proceed to a worse state, from those who delude to those who are deluded. But as for you, continue in what you have learned, and firmly believed, knowing from whom you have learned it, and how from infancy you have known the sacred writings which are able to instruct you in salvation through faith in Christ Jesus. All God-breathed scripture is useful for education, for admonition, for improvement and for instruction in righteousness, that the person of God might be completed for every good work. (II Timothy 3:1–17)

For Paul, teaching was only one aspect of his life that Timothy followed. Paul's faith, his patience, his love, his perseverance, his persecutions, and his suffering were all part of the same package of a life that was in Christ Jesus. This is consistent with the rest of Pauline literature. While the vocabulary, style and even some of the thoughts of the epistles to Timothy seem strange in comparison with the rest of the Pauline Corpus, this passage seems to fit well within that body of work. Paul is not expounding some theory, proposition, or principle of inspiration. He is talking simply about transformed lives, lives transformed (saved) through faith in Christ Jesus, (vs. 15), *sola fides*. The Scriptures are the guide book to help (teach, admonish, improve, and train) the righteous in the life of Christ so that – and this is the heart of the matter – the righteous produce good works (vs. 17). θεοπνευστος most likely must be considered an adjectival noun modifying the main noun γραφη, or scripture. θεοπνευστος defines the type of writing that helps teach, admonish, improve and train the person in righteousness. The writings that do this are not those of Heraclitus, Plato, Aristotle, or other Greek philosophers, but the writings that find their origin in the breath of God — the writings with which Timothy was raised by his mother and grandmother (3:14–15). It is obvious from II Timothy 1:5 that Timothy's mother and grandmother were Christians before him and raised him to be a Christian. The Scriptures from which he was taught were most likely the Greek Septuagint, possibly early forms of gospels, and maybe some apostolic epistles and other writings which we do not know. There is no way to determine what they were. All indications point to a body of Scriptures that were much different from those of the Protestant Canon. Nevertheless, these writings found their origin in God and were "useful for education, for admonition, for improvement and for instruction in righteousness, that the person of God might be completed for every good work."

The Scriptures, the Witness to Jesus

As was discussed in the last chapter, John 5:39 is the clearest definition of the function of Scripture for the Christian. "You search the scriptures,

---

[33]This is the term that Rogers and McKim use to describe Berkouer's view of Scripture. Rogers and Mckim, pp.426–437.

because in them you think that you have eternal life; and it is they that bear witness to me." The Scriptures are the Witness to Jesus who is the living Word of God, the proper focus of the Church. Whenever the Church becomes the Church of the Book, the Church of the Bible, it becomes a static, rigid, and dogmatic Church that is devoid of the living and loving Lord Jesus Christ. When the Scriptures act as the witness to the Lord Jesus they will serve as a tool to help mend the Church and bring her back to her proper perspective.

Chapter IX

Inerrancy Not of God, But of Man

Fruits of the Flesh, Products of Inerrancy

Since the doctrine that the Bible is the inerrant word of God finds no support in the Bible, some hard questions have to be answered: From where does this doctrine originate? Why has it permeated so much of the Church's thought? Why has it persisted so long in Church history? Without being dogmatic or simplistic, it would be safe to assume that the reason for the existence of the doctrine, its longevity and its dominance over thought in the Church, is none other than Sin and the power of satanic forces in the World.

It does not take a theologian to inform us that the present condition of the Church is not the way that Jesus envisioned or established it. Almost every layperson will tell you the Church is in disarray. As is apparent in church history every faction vilifies the other for causing the division in the Church. In almost every case the instrument through which these divisions came was the doctrine that the Bible is the inerrant word of God. Call it what ever you like, but the end result is evil!

The results produced by inerrancy fit well into the description of the fruits of the flesh of Galatians 5:19–21: "Fornication, impurity, licentiousness, idolatry, sorcery, enmity, strife, jealousy, anger, dissension, party spirit, envy, drunkenness, debauchery and the like . . . " In the history of the Church, it is hard to find anything that produced more fruit of the flesh than the doctrine that the Bible is the inerrant word of God. Idolatry would, of course, be the first result of the doctrine. While the Torah had become a god for the Pharisees and Sadducees in Jesus' time, the Bible became a god for a great many Christians. The Bible contained the thought of God. What the Bible said was what God thought. Christians even created hymns in praise of the Bible (See p. xix). We have churches that call themselves The Bible Church, The Bible Baptist Church, and The Bible Believing Baptist Church.

In Chapter II, it was pointed out that the doctrine had not been one of the Holy Spirit, bringing about love between brothers and sisters of the faith, or unity of mission for the Lord Jesus Christ. There it was documented that the doctrine was a sword slashing the Church into slivers and a hammer smashing the Church to bits. To this day, most of the rifts the doctrine has caused have not been healed, so that the doctrine has caused "enmity, strife, . . . anger, . . . dissension, party spirit . . . "

In Paul's description, there are two fruits of the flesh which are not specifically included, but which, sadly, must be used to describe the fruits of inerrancy. These two fruits may have been excluded from Paul's list because they were so horrendous that he could not perceive any Christian ever committing such grievous sins. These two fruits of the flesh are "murder (A number of ancient manuscripts do include murder, φονοι)" and "war." As was well illustrated, the dogmatism of the Lutheran and Reformed Churches produced the massive persecution of the Anabaptists. The same dogmatism helped fuel the bloody Thirty Years' War in Europe (1609–1648); was instrumental in the practical genocide of the natives of the New World; and allowed the enslavement of Black Africans. Many wars, including the Opium war in China (1840–42); the Boer War (1899–1902) in Africa, and World I had their genesis in economic and political realities which were given impetus and support from Christianity's spreading "the Word of God." The conflagration in Northern Ireland can be laid at the feet of Protestant fundamentalists who hold on to "the Bible as the inerrant Word of God" and fear and suppress the "anti-Christ Papists." Contrary to theologians such as Carl Henry, Francis Schaeffer, and J. J. Packer, shedding the doctrine of inerrancy will not weaken the Church. The doctrine itself has weakened and practically destroyed the Church and has been instrumental in producing activities that totally deny the Lord Jesus Christ.

Development of Inerrancy

Step One, Christology, Based not on the Bible but the Logos of Philosophers

While the genesis of the doctrine is founded in Sin, the doctrine itself has traceable historical and philosophical roots which demonstrate that the doctrine is not based in a biblical faith, but a perversion of that faith. In this chapter I hope to unravel the mystery of the origins of this doctrine. In chapters 3, 4, and 5, I demonstrated that the Bible never refers to itself as the Word of God. Chapter 3 showed that the early Church fathers strictly referred to Jesus as the Word of God — but when one examines how many of them used the word, one detects that they do not have the same concept of the word of God as the biblical writers. Irenaeus (c. 130–c. 170), Bishop of Lyon in Asia Minor, is a good example of what I mean. Some time in the last half of the second century he wrote:

> But God being all mind, and all Logos both speaks exactly what he thinks and thinks exactly what he speaks. For his thought is Logos, and Logos is mind, and mind comprehending all things is the Father himself . . . But ye (the Gnostics) pretend to set forth His generation from the Father, and ye transfer the production of the word of men which takes place by means of a tongue to the Word of God, and thus are righteously exposed by your own selves as knowing neither things human nor divine. (Against Heresies: II:28, 5, AN)

In the same time frame, Athenagoras, an Athenian Philosopher wrote the following apologetics to Emperors Marcus Aurelius and Lucius Aurelius Commodus:

> That we are not atheists, therefore, that we acknowledge one God, uncreated, eternal and invisible, impassible, incomprehensible, illimitable, who is apprehended by understanding only and the reason, who is encompassed by light and beauty, and power ineffable by whom the universe has been created through his Logos and set in order . . . (I say 'His Logos'), for we acknowledge a Son of God. Nor let anyone think it ridiculous that

God should have a Son . . . the poets in their fictions, represent the gods as no better than men, our mode of thinking is not the same as theirs, concerning either God the Father or the Son. But the Son of God is the Logos [Word] of the Father, in idea and operation; for after the power of Him and by him were all things made, the Father and the Son being one. (A Plea for Understanding, X, AN III)[1]

I could go on and quote from most of the Church fathers of the second half of the second century through the first half of the fourth century, whose works survived, but they all sound pretty much the same when it comes to discussion of the Word of God. The twentieth century reader, particularly the twentieth century student of the Bible, cannot help but notice that there are some very strange sounding concepts and words within the writings of these Christian theologians. No one today would describe God as "being all mind, and all Logos" as Irenaeus did or "impassible, who is apprehended by understanding only and the reason, who is encompassed by light and beauty . . . " as Athenagoras did.

While the subject matter of this work is not Christology, it is easier to grasp how the primitive faith of the Church changed and see how these changes have brought about the present Christian beliefs. One of the transformations was the Church's attitude towards her Scriptures. The reader might be advised to here go back and review the differences between the early and later concepts of the Word of God (See Chapters 3 and 4).

The origins of change in the Christian faith can be found in the surviving works of the Church fathers who were Greek philosophers before they became Christians and who maintained their esteem for Greek philosophy after they were Christians. Consistently these Greek philosophers/Christian theologians display the connection between their Greek philosophy and their Christian faith regarding the Word of God in John 1:1. In Greek philosophy the concept of the Word logos has deep roots. The first Greek philosopher to use the term Logos/logos in the context of divinity was Heraclitus, who lived in Ephesus about 500 B.C.E. For Heraclitus, Logos was the term that described the Divine Reason which he believed permeated the universe. The following are several quotes from Heraclitus' fragmented works. They give the reader a glimpse of the formation of the Logos theology of the Church fathers, and the

---

[1]Athenagoras used many words that sound like they are straight out of the philosophers, but the word that he used that totally reflects a change in biblical theology was the word, "impassible" meaning "incapable of suffering or experiencing pain...incapable of feeling." Webster's New International. This word was reiterated in the Church fathers' thought, but proof of the control of Greek philosophical thought over the Christian fathers, is found in the fact that "impassible απαθη" is found in the Athanasian Statement of faith. This statement of faith is not to be confused with the Athanasian creed which may have been based on the statement of faith but most likely was written long after Athanasius died. This was written by Athanasius before the Nicene Creed (325 C.E.). After Jesus and Paul, there could hardly be a more important person than Athanasius in the history of the Christian Church. He was the force that moved the Church beyond the Eusebian compromise to define the Trinitarian statement of Nicaea. (Foakes Jackson, pp. 297-316),

The ultimate indication of the captivity of Christianity is found in the Westminster Confession of 1647 which states that God was "without...passion." Another term which frequently occurs in the Church fathers and which is also frequently used today is "immutable."

seeds for the doctrine that the Bible is the inerrant word of God.

> (Fragmented statement) Although this Logos is eternally valid, yet men are unable to understand it not only before hearing it but even after they have heard it for the first time. That is to say all things come to pass in accordance with this Logos, yet men seem to be quiet without the experience of it . . . We should let ourselves be guided by what is common to all, most men live as if each had a private intelligence of their own.
> 61. Human nature has no real understanding only the divine nature has it.
> (62. Man is not rational; only what encompasses him is intelligent.)
> 64. Although intimately connected with the Logos, men keep themselves against it.
> 81. Men should speak with rational awareness and there by hold on strongly to that which they share in common . . . For all human laws are nourished by one divine Law (Logos), which prevails as far as it wishes, suffices for all things, and yet is something more than they say. (Parenthesis this authors)
> 118. Listening not to me but to the Logos, it is wise to acknowledge that all things are.
> 119. Wisdom is one and unique; it is unwilling and yet willing to be called by the name Zeus.
> 120 Wisdom is one to know the intelligence by which all things are steered.[2]

One thing is sure, that as far as Greek philosophy was concerned, God had become the same as reason. While Socrates, Plato, and Aristotle do not refer to God as Logos, they were heavily influenced by Heraclitus. All three perceived God as being the rational force that permeated the universe. Plato believed that God was "the never ceasing and rational life enduring through all time;" "the divine intelligence" from which our thinking, our souls are simple matter of "recollecting" our past and future "beatific" existence (Timaeus, 36, 450^d; Phaedrus, 243–250; 124^d–126^b GB). With Aristotle the concept became the eternal mind (Nous) or the immovable Nu. The eternal Nous or immovable Nu was the rational force that gave shape and motion to the universe (*Physics*, Book VIII, chapters 1–6, 334a–346 GB). There may be some scholars who object to equating Heraclitus' Logos, Plato's Idea and Aristotle's Nous, but the Stoics and later NeoPlatonists freely blend these concepts, and it is they who are most influential on the Church fathers.

Stoicism probably had the strongest impact on the Church fathers; it was very prevalent in the first through the fourth centuries of the Common Era. Such Roman intellects as Seneca, Cicero, and Emperor Marcus Aurelius were heavily influenced by Stoicism. Stoicism was founded around 240– 250 B.C.E. in Athens by Zeno, of whom there is not a great deal of knowledge. The chief source of our early knowledge of the Stoics comes from Diogenes Laertius (3rd Century B.C.E.). The Stoics, according to Diogenes, believed that creation was composed of two principles: the active and the passive.

---

[2]Philip Wheelwright, *Heraclitus*(Princeton,NJ: Princeton University Press, 1959), p. 19 f., in loc.

Diogenes describes these principles in the following way: " . . . (The passive) then is substance without quality, the active is reason (logos) inherent in the substance, that is God. For he is everlasting and is the artificer of each several thing throughout the whole extent of matter (Diogenes, VII, Zeno, 134)."[3] The Stoics developed a full-fledged metaphysical system around the Logos thought. Diogenes reports that the Stoics believed:

> The deity, say they, is a living being, immortal, rational (λογικος, a term that was used also of God by the NeoPlatonist), perfect or intelligent in happiness, admitting nothing evil [into him] (that is not letting anything irrational into him) taking providential care for the world and all therein, but he is not in human shape. He is, however, the artificer of the universe as it were, the father of all both in general . . . (Diogenes, VII, Zeno 147.) Brackets [] editor's, Parentheses () mine

If a person did not know the source of this thinking, one might assume that they were reading the thoughts of the early Church fathers or somebody paraphrasing chapters II–V of the Westminster Confession. In reality, the Stoics and Greek philosophers are the basis of much of the thinking of Irenaeus, Justin, Athenagorus, Athanasius, other Church Fathers, or even the thinking of the framers of the Westminster Confession.[4]

Step two, Transfer the Philosopher's Logos to the Bible with combination of inspiration from Plato

From every indication that this author can determine, the identification of Jesus with the Logos of Greek philosophy did not continue to dominate theological discussion after the fifth century. The theologians did not, however, discard the philosophical concept of the word of God. Instead of Jesus being the reason of the universe, the Bible became the reason of God, God's thinking. The logos του θεου was now applied to the Bible.

The concept of mechanical inspiration had paved the way for the transfer. As early as 150 C.E. Justin Martyr (c. 100–c. 166), a Roman philosopher who had been raised in Samaria and who became a Christian and the first Christian philosopher, wrote, "However when you listen to the prophecies, spoken as in person . . . , do not think that they were spoken by the inspired [εμπεπνευσμενον (J. P. Migne), the one's breathing in; inhaling"] prophets of their own accord, but by the Word of God who prompts them (I Apology 36, CF)." In another place Justin wrote:

> For neither by nature or by human conception is it possible for men to know things so great or divine, but by gift which then descended from above upon holy men, who had no need of rhetorical art, nor of uttering anything in a contentious or quarrelsome manner, but to present themselves pure to the energy of the Divine Spirit, in order that the divine plectrum, itself, descending from heaven, using righteous men like a harp or lyre

---

[3] R. D. Hicks, trans. and ed., *Diogenes Laertius: Lives of the Eminent Philosophers*, Volume 32, *Loeb Classics* (Cambridge, MA: Harvard University Press, 1965), VII,134. Henceforth, Diogenes, Zeno.

[4] Rogers and McKim pp. 93ff.

might reveal things divine and heavenly. ("Address to the Greeks," Chapter 8, AN)

Some time around 180 C.E., Irenaeus, the famous Bishop from Lyon, expressed similar thoughts. In this passage Irenaeus refutes the Gnostic claim that they had special and mysterious revelations outside of Scripture. Irenaeus asserted, "We should leave things of that nature to God who created us, being most properly assured that the scriptures are indeed perfect since they were spoken by the Word of God and His Holy Spirit (Against Heresies II:28, 2, AN)." Clement of Alexandria (ca. 155–220 C.E..) reiterated the same concept, "God, himself, proclaimed (J. P. Migne, καρυγαντα) scripture though his son (Miscellanies, V:XIII, AN)."

It is now just a short jump to the transfer of the word of God to the Bible, and that transfer is accelerated in the works of Basil (329–379), Bishop of Caesarea and archbishop of Cappadocia, who was likewise a strong supporter of the Nicaean Creed. Basil wrote this about Jesus:

> But our Lord is also Himself the end and ultimate blessedness according to the purpose of the Word: for what does he say in the Gospel? "I will raise him up on the last day." He calls the transition from material knowledge to immaterial contemplation a resurrection, speaking of that knowledge after which there is no other, as the last day; for our intelligence is raised up and roused to a height of blessedness at the time when it contemplates the Oneness and unity of the Word. (Epistle to the Caesarian VIII, CF p.2)

In Basil's statement "the Oneness and unity of the Word," conservative Christians might think that Basil was their forefather and that Basil meant that there were no contradictions and inconstancies within Scriptures. The problem is that the context makes clear that Basil is not referring to the scripture, but rather the philosophical concept of Logos. Basil is referring to John 6:40 where Jesus states that whoever believes in the last day He will raise him up and uses this verse to discuss the resurrection. Contemporary Christians naturally would find Basil's description strange. At the time of the resurrection we are transformed from having "material knowledge" to "immaterial knowledge." At the final resurrection the ultimate experience is that "our intelligence is raised up" in contemplation of "the Oneness and Unity of the Word." Behind Basil's thought is the Heraclitean/Platonic (NeoPlatonic) concept of reason that permeates the universe. Basil, even more than the other Church fathers takes great pains to make sure that the Word of God cannot be contained in words of men. In the discussion of God speaking Creation, Basil wrote:

> . . . Let us first inquire how God speaks. Is it in our manner? Or, is the image of the objects first formed in His intellect, then after they have been pictured in His mind, does he make them known by selecting from substances and distinguishing marks of each? Finally handing over the concepts to vocal organs for their service, does he thus manifest His hidden thought by striking the air with articulate movement of the voice? Sure, it is fantastic to say that God needs such a roundabout way for the manifestation of His thoughts. Or, is it not more in conformity with true religion to say that divine will joined with the first

impulse of His intelligence is the Word of God? (*Hexameron*, Homily 2:7, CF)

While it is clear from this and the rest of his writings that Basil would never call the Scriptures the word of God, he paves the way for the transfer of the concept of the word of God to the Scriptures. He calls the scriptures "the divine Scriptures," "the divinely inspired Scriptures," and "the Word of Truth." Of these Scriptures Basil wrote: "The words of scripture are few short syllables . . . but when the meaning in the words is explained, then the great marvel of the *wisdom of God* appears (*Hexameron*, 8:8, CF)." Basil was no advocate of the principle of Sola Scriptura espoused by the later Protestants. The Scriptures had hidden meaning which the theologians with their philosophical training could reveal. This approach to interpreting Scripture was called the allegorical method. Through this allegorical method, which Origen had developed, many of the Church fathers found some of the most fantastic interpretations of Scripture and called these interpretations, "the Wisdom of God." At the same time the allegorical method allowed the Church fathers to do away with some of what they considered to be the anthropomorphic elements of Scripture and to bring the Scriptures more in line with Greek philosophy. It was certainly present in the above passage where Basil insisted that the Bible did not mean that God spoke like a human being.

Since the Logos equaled thinking and reasoning, and since the Bible was the "divine Scriptures" and "the Word of Truth," the Scriptures could contain no irrational elements, and any irrational element was a simple matter of appearance which would be explained away through allegorical method. The Scriptures in short contained divine reasoning, perfect reasoning which the philosophers (theologians) would explain. With this attitude towards the Scriptures it was a short jump from transferring the eternal logos that had been applied to Jesus, to the Bible.

That transfer takes place with St. Ambrose (340–397), the Bishop of Milan. In Church history, Ambrose has to be one of the more interesting characters and one of the most influential persons. His father was one of the most powerful prefects in the administration of the Roman Province of Gaul (France). As a young man, he was appointed to a most prestigious position. He was made Governor of Italy's Northern Province, whose capital was Milan. After Ambrose's appointment, the Christian Bishop of Milan, Auxentius, an Arian, died. This created a power struggle between the Arians who demanded a like-minded Bishop and the "orthodox" who wanted a bishop who supported the Nicene Creed. After Auxentius' funeral, a riot broke out in the most unlikely place – the Cathedral, itself. Ambrose went to the Cathedral to see if he could stop the riot. A shout went up from the crowd in the Cathedral, "Ambrose for Bishop." Ambrose considered this a call from God, gave away all his wealth, and became a priest. As a Bishop he became one of most able defenders of the Nicene Creed, and the most responsible for the Nicene Creed becoming the criterion of orthodoxy.

For Ambrose the Scriptures become the Word of God as shown in the following passage taken from *Paradise*:

> What is sin, if not the violation of divine law and the disobedience to heavenly precepts? Not by ear, but by mind do we form a judgment regarding an injunction from above. But with the word of God before us we are able to formulate opinions on

what is good and what is evil . . . In this respect we seem to be listening to the very voice of the Lord, whereby some things are forbidden and other things advised. If a person does not comply with the injunctions which are believed to have been once ordained by God, he is considered liable to punishment. The commands of God are impressed in the hearts by the Spirit of the living God. We don't read these orders as if they were recorded in ink or on tablet of stone. (Paradise, VIII, 42, CF)

While it is not specifically stated that the Scriptures are the word of God, the whole context makes it the only possibility. The Word of God is obviously not Jesus. It is not the preached word because we do not receive it "by ear, but by mind." The word is "before us," not over and around us. It is before us, so that we can hold it in our hands, so that we can read it.

For Ambrose, the Scriptures are the Word of God, but not the static, fixed, and dogmatic inerrant Word of God of the Reformers. When Ambrose says, "We do not read these orders as if they were recorded in ink or in stone," he literally means it. The Scripture are a mystical experience. One would be hard pressed to find another author who used as rich metaphors as Ambrose does to describe Scripture. In one place Ambrose describes the Scriptures as a Garden (of Eden) in which he finds God walking (Epistle XXVI). In another place he describes the Scriptures as a sea that had many streams and currents running in it (Epistle XV). The Scriptures were also a feast with many dishes (Duties of the Clergy I:32).

I include the following passages from Ambrose to show how fluid his interpretation of Scripture is, and also to illustrate the hermeneutics of allegory. The first passage is developed around Matthew 17:24–27. In this passage Jesus is asked whether he and his disciples pay the temple tax. Jesus directs his disciples to go fishing. When they go, the disciples catch a fish with a didrachma in his mouth. Jesus orders his disciples to pay the Temple tax with the coin. Ambrose makes a good deal of this didrachma:

Nevertheless, He orders a stater (a gold coin) to be given, clamping their mouths shut so they may not admit their sin. And he bids that the didrachma to be given so that they might know the Word (Jesus). They exact what was of the Law; why did they not know what was of the law? They ought not to have been ignorant of the word of God (Scripture?/Gospel?), because it was written: "The Word is near your lips and in your heart." Therefore a whole didrachma is paid to God, which is moderation in speech. "With the heart a man believes unto justice and with mouth profession of faith is made unto salvation."

Moreover a drachma can be interpreted as the Old Testament, a didrachma the price of both Testaments . . . Letters, 20, CF

In an epistle to Bishop Justus, Ambrose wrote that the ram that Abraham found in the thicket (Genesis 22:13) when he was about to sacrifice his son Isaac, was the Word of God. He then, in the following passage, assumes without any connection or any explanation that the people (possibly the Jews, but that is not clear), who don't accept Jesus will accept that the Ram was the word of God:

Therefore the Word of God is our purpose, that is then and now, fulfillment of all our questioning. This Word is infused into the wise and puts an end to doubt. Yet, even men who refuse to believe in the coming of Christ refute themselves very aptly with the result that they profess what they should not profess. They say that the 'ram' is the Word of God, yet they do not believe in the mystery of the passion, although the word of God is that mystery, the very one in whom the sacrifice has been fulfilled.

Let us first enkindle in us the fire of the mind, so that it will be at work in us. Let us seek the subject matter, which gives us that which feeds the soul, as if seeking it in darkness, for the patriarchs did not know what manna was, yet they found it, Scripture says, and they called it speech and Word of God. From this continual overflowing source all learning flows and streams.

This is heavenly food. It is signified by the person of the one speaking: 'Behold I will rain bread from heaven for you.' This is the cause, for God works, watering minds with the dew of wisdom; the subject matter is that which delights souls seeing and tasting it and asking whence comes that which is more splendid than light and sweeter than honey. They are given the answer in the Scripture narrative: 'This bread which the Lord hath given you to eat.' And this is the Word of God which God has set in orderly array. By it souls of the prudent are fed and delighted: it is clear and sweet, shining with the splendor of truth, and softening with sweetness of virtue the souls who hear it. (Letters 21, CF)

Because of the difference in time and mentality, it may be impossible to understand all the implications of Ambrose's thinking. It would appear that the Word of God is Jesus, the Bible, and the Gospel message. These most likely are not three different words of God, but manifestations of the same word of God. The Scripture is Jesus, Jesus is the Scripture, the proclamation about Jesus is Jesus, and Jesus is the proclamation. They are all indistinguishable. For Ambrose the Word of God was a mystical entity, but again the genesis for his thinking was not the Scripture. Like many of the fathers, it was in the Logos doctrine of Heraclitus, the Stoics, and NeoPlatonists. The reason that the Word can be three entities is that like Clement, Origen, Athanasius, and others, the Logos was the Reason of God and the Universe. Jesus was the pre-existent reason. Proclamation of Jesus was simply the proclamation of reason. The Bible contained God's thinking on everything including creation. Like Heraclitus and Plato, Ambrose did not believe this thinking contained in Scripture was available to the average "irrational" person. Only the theologian through the allegorical method could find God's reasoning hidden in the text.

Even though Ambrose is the first to call the Bible the word of God, the blame for the doctrine that the Bible is the inerrant word of God can not be laid at his feet. The culpability for the doctrine can, however, be placed squarely on the shoulder of one who was inspired and baptized by Ambrose,[5]

---

[5]While it was through the preaching of Ambrose that Augustine was led to study the Scriptures, it was with the assistance of a Simplicianus that he finally made the decision

Augustine. Augustine was to become the famous bishop from Hippo in Northern Africa. He had come to Milan to teach in a troubled period of his life. Being raised by a pagan father and a Christian mother created an almost unbearable conflict and inner turmoil in his early adult life. In his studies he was particularly drawn to Plato and considered himself a NeoPlatonist, having studied the works of Plotonius. He became a convert to the Manichaean religion. Manichaeism was a very ascetic form of Gnosticism, Persian Zorastrocism, Buddhism and Platonic thought. Manichaeism believed in abstaining from sexual intercourse so that one would not trap another soul in human flesh.[6] For Augustine, who had several sensual relationships this was particularly difficult. After he arrived in Milan his mother, Monica, lost no time in introducing Augustine to the brilliant Ambrose. Augustine was greatly impressed and eventually converted to Christianity.

The problem with Augustine was that while much of his thinking was consistent with the Biblical witness, much was not. When Augustine converted to Christianity he did not leave his Platonic baggage at the door, but rather brought it in and wrapped Christianity in it. Today, because of Augustine's impact on the Church, many Christians falsely assume that what they believe is based solely on the Scriptures. Such is the case with the doctrine that the Bible is the inerrant word of God.

In the analysis of the Word of God in Hebrews 4:12, I pointed out that Augustine was the first to call the Scriptures the Word of God, (See p. 39). It would be this author's estimate that Augustine uses the phrases: "Thy Truth," "His Word," "Thy Word," "Thy Books," referring to the Scripture more than any writer since his time. He likewise uses the terms "divine Book," "Word of Truth," "Thy Scriptures," and "Thy Holy Scriptures." Of course, the pronouns "His" and "Your" always refer to God. It is essential for the reader to look at other portions of Augustine's work and when one does so it is very observable just how heretical is this doctrine that the Bible is the inerrant word of God. The following portions are found in his *Confessions*:

> Now who but thee, our God, didst make for us that firmament of authority over us in thy divine Scripture? As it is said For the heaven shall be folded up like a scroll; and now it is extended over us like a skin. For thy divine Scripture is of more sublime authority since those mortals through whom you dispense it unto us underwent mortality . . .
> Other waters there be "above" this "firmament," I believe immortal, and removed from earthly corruption. Let them praise thy name—those super celestial people, thine angels, who have no need to look at this firmament or by reading to attain knowledge of thy Word — let them praise thee. For they always behold thy face and read therein without syllables in time what thy eternal will intends. They read, they choose, they love. They are always reading, and what they read never passeth away. For by choosing and by loving they read the very unchangeableness of thy counsel. Their book is not closed, nor is the scroll folded up because thou thyself art this to them, yea, and art so

---

to Convert. *Confessions*, VIII,2

[6]Leitzman, *II*,269-274. Augustine, Confessions, IV,i,1 ff.

eternally . . . The Preachers of thy Word pass away from this life into another; but thy Scripture is spread abroad over the people, even to the end of the world. Yea, both heaven and earth shall pass away, but thy words shall not pass away. (Confessions, XIII, 15 NF).

For Augustine the Scriptures are an essential part of God, as Jesus is God. Whereas in Ephesians 1:22 Paul states that God placed all things under Christ's feet, in Augustine the Scriptures are above all people, "even to the end of the World." God is even "read" by the angels. This deification of Scripture is obvious in almost every section of the XIII chapter of the Confession but the following passage is particularly revealing. This passage comes at the conclusion of a mental struggle that Augustine was going through over a time discrepancy and the number times God says his creation is good in Genesis 1. He asks how could the discrepancy be, if God is true. Augustine records God as responding:

'O man, that which My Scripture saith, I say; and yet doth that speak in time; but time has no reference to my Word, because My Word existeth in equal eternity with Myself. Thus those things which you see through My Spirit, I see, just as those things which ye speak through My Spirit, I speak. And so when ye speak them in time I speak them not in time. (Confessions, XIII, 29 NF)

At face value there is something very compelling about what Augustine had written. In the Spirit of God there is no beginning and no end, only timelessness. While this idea sounds good, it is not Christian. It is Hindu. It is Buddhist. It is Platonic. While Augustine would not admit it, the triune God has become a quartet: Father, Son, Holy Spirit, and Holy Scripture. The words written in the Old and New Testaments co-exist with God from all eternity, according to Augustine.

In fact, if Augustine is taken quite literally, John I would have to be rephrased. In Augustine's terms it would read: "In the beginning was the Word and word was with God and the Word was God . . . and the word became flesh and book and dwelt among us." He almost stated that exactly in the City of God. He wrote: "But the Scripture elevates us, as the Word came down and became flesh." In another place a slip of the pen reveals that he really did believe the Scriptures were God.

When Scriptures by the way says that God 'seeks' for himself a man; we are not supposing that God does not know the whereabouts of a man in question. He (the Scriptures) is merely speaking through a man after the manner of man because he is seeking us men (City of God, XVII, 6 CF).

There is no reason to contest Gerald Walsh's translation. The grammatical structure of the Latin supports the Scripture doing the "speaking." In another place Augustine states: "So dost Thou speak to us, our All-wise God, in Thy Book, Thy Firmament. . . (Confessions, XIII, 18 NF)"

Like the Psalmist of Psalm 119 who was healed by the Law, so Augustine believed that he was "healed" by the Scriptures (Confessions, V, 9–10; VII, 20–21). Biblically speaking — and by most standards in the Church, it is always God, Jesus, or his Holy Spirit that does the healing. But for Augustine there is no difference between the Scriptures and God. The Scriptures are what God has spoken and what He has spoken co-exists with Him in all eternity. The Scripture is God and God is the Scripture.

Here then, in Augustine, the full doctrine of inerrancy is developed. It is obvious that the doctrine is idolatrous and not based on biblical thought. What may not be clear is where the doctrine originates from. Did it originate in Augustine's thinking? Did Augustine simply take the attitude towards the Scripture expressed in other Church fathers and develop it to its fullest extent, or did it have other sources? The answer to this question, I believe, is from other sources. Those sources are found in the Greek philosophers, particularly Plato. The similarities between the Church fathers' and Augustine's thought is not due to Augustine's knowledge of many of the earlier Church fathers, but rather because the Greek philosophers shaped his thinking as well as most of the other published Church fathers.

Unlike Jerome (340–420), who will be studied in the next chapter, Augustine did not renounce his philosophical roots. While he does do a great deal of criticizing of Plato (City of God, VIII, Chapters 12–14), he believed that Plato's thinking was so close to Christianity that he must have been familiar with the writings of Moses (City of God, VIII, 11). Of Plato, Augustine wrote:

> At present, it is sufficient to mention that Plato determined that the final good to be to live according to virtue, and affirmed that he only can attain to virtue who knows and imitates God—which knowledge and imitation are the only cause of blessedness. Therefore he did not doubt that to philosophize is to love God, whose nature is incorporeal. Whence it certainly follows that the student of wisdom will then become blessed when he shall have begun to enjoy God. (The City of God, VIII, 8, CF)

Like many of the Church fathers Augustine identified the word of God of John I with that of the logos of Greek philosophy. Augustine wrote that he in his rebellious state had not seen that the Platonists even wrote about Christ. In their works translated into Latin, according to Augustine, they wrote:

> . . . not in the same words but to the selfsame effect, enforced by many and diverse reasons, that "In the beginning was the Word and the Word was God . . . And that the soul of man though "it bears witness to the Light; yet itself "is not that light, but the Word of God, being God, is the true light that lighteth every man that comes into the world." And that "He was in the world and the world was made by him and the world new him not.". . . . In like manner, I read there that God the Word was born not of flesh nor blood, nor the will of man, nor of the will of the flesh but of God . . . For I discovered in those books that it was many and divers ways said that the Son was in the Form of the Father . . . (Confessions, VII, 9, NF)

Thus, for Augustine, the revelation of the incarnation and the roots of the Trinity are even found in the Greek philosophers. The problem is that, as we saw in the third chapter of this book, the Biblical concept of the Word of God and the Greek philosopher's concepts were not the same, and the fact that many of the Church fathers equated them has done immense damage to the Church. Augustine does not credit his thinking on inspiration to the Greek philosophers, but it is not difficult to find his thinking in their work.

First, one must realize that with Heraclitus, the Stoics, and NeoPlatonists (Plotonius), Augustine accepted the depravity and irrationality of humankind — which he called "infantile imbecility," the direct result of original sin (City of God, Book XIII, Chap. 1–6,). Like Heraclitus, the Stoics, and the NeoPlatonists, Augustine believed that rationality was a gift from God. This is why he believed that Plato could "predict the incarnation." In one of his epistles Augustine uses Jethro as an example of how God used a pagan:

> Did not God talk to Moses, and yet he with great wisdom and entire absence of jealous pride, accepted the plan of his father-in-law, a man of an alien race, for ruling and administering the affairs of the great nation entrusted to him? For Moses knew that a wise plan, in whatever mind it might originate, was not to be ascribed to man who devised it, but to him who is Truth, the unchangeable God. (NF II, p. 520)

Augustine believed all good came from God, and if God did not use men (even pagan men) as his messengers, the plight of human kind would be "much more degraded."

The following quote from Plato will give the reader an idea where Augustine and other Church fathers derived their thinking on inspiration from:

> For poet is a light and winged and sacred thing, and is unable ever to indite until he has been inspired and put out of his senses, and his mind is no longer in him; every man whilst he retains possession of that, is powerless to indite a verse or chant a single oracle . . . And for this reason God takes away the; mind of these men and uses them as his ministers, just as he does soothsayers and godly seers, in order that we who hear them may know that it is not they who utter these words of great price when they are out of their wits, but that it is God himself who speaks and addresses us through them. (Ion, 534 B, D. GB)[7]

This is the type of thinking that went into Augustine and other Church fathers' thinking on inspiration. One might be correct in arguing that Augustine's inspiration is derived more from the Stoics (Diogenes VII, Zeno, 147–148) and NeoPlatonists (Plotinus III:3–16, GB). Nevertheless the philosophers are the genesis of the doctrine that the Bible is the inerrant Word of God. For Augustine, as well as many of the Church fathers, this passive reception of inspiration, this mantic inspiration was the source of Scripture. Whereas in

---

[7]Plato expresses similar thoughts in Phaedrus 245c; Republic 503 A. I must note, at the admonition of Andrew Church, that even for Plato such mantic state was a lower form of revelation. In another passage Plato states:

But the region above the heaven (the area of idea-reason-God) was never worthily sung by an earthly poet (in mantic state), nor will it ever be. It is however, as I shall tell; for I must dare to speak the truth, especially truth is my theme. For the colourless, formless and intangible truly existing essence, with which true knowledge is concerned, holds this region and is visible only to the mind (not mindless mantic), the pilot of the soul. Now divined intelligence since it is nurtured on mind and pure knowledge, and the intelligence of every soul which is cable of receiving that which befits it, rejoices in seeing reality. Plato, *Republic* VII, p. 559. Parentheses ()mine.

the early Church the authority was the power and the presence of the living Lord, for the later Church fathers authority was found in the fact that the Scriptures were spoken by the Word of God. Augustine's contribution to this scenario is that he couples mantic inspiration with the Word of God and makes the doctrine that the Bible is the inerrant Word of God.

The Disaster of the Amalgamation of Greek Philosophy and Christianity

The fact that Christianity became an amalgamation of Greek philosophy and biblical thought was hailed by the nineteenth century liberal Oxford Church Historian, Charles Bigg (1840–1908), as the reason why Christianity did not remain a small sect of Judaism but became a world religion and eclipsed in size its mother religion Judaism.[8] Likewise the German Church historian and theologian, Adolph Harnack (1851–1930), described the development of Christian (Catholic) theology :

> As Catholicism, from every point of view, is the result of the blending of ideas of antiquity, so the Catholic dogmatic, as it was developed after the second or third century on the basis of the Logos doctrine, is Christianity conceived and formulated from the standpoint of Greek philosophy of religion. This Christianity conquered the old world, and became the foundation of a new phase of history in the middle ages. The union of Christian religion with a definite phase of human knowledge and culture may be lamented in the interest of the Christian religion, which was thereby secularized, and in the interest of culture thereby retarded(?) . . . But lamentations become here ill-founded assumptions, as absolutely everything that we have and value is due to the alliance that Christianity and antiquity concluded in such a way that neither was able to prevail over the other. [9]

Professor Harnack published this work in 1886 when Germany as a united nation was in its youth and beginning to flex its muscles. Industrialism was growing by leaps and bounds, and wealth was multiplying exponentially. I can not help but wonder, if Harnack had lived to 1945 and had seen all of Europe devastated, whether he would have had such a positive assessment of the amalgamation of Greek thought and Christianity. I would like to have been able to say to Harnack that much of "everything that we have and value" has provided much devastation and pain in the world and that the "alliance of Christianity and antiquity" has allowed people like Otto von Bismarck, King Wilhelm, and German Lutherans and Catholics to live schismatic lives and inflict havoc on God's world. In essence the absorption of Greek philosophical thought into Christianity has meant the subversion of Christianity and the transformation of it from the kingdom of God to the kingdom of this world.

It has meant the church splitting apart into thousands of divisions. It

---

[8] Charles Bigg, *The Christian Platonist of Alexandria* (London: The Clarendon Press, 1913), pp. 1 ff.

[9] Adolph von Harnack, *History of Dogma*, trans. by Neil Buchanan (Gloucester, MA: Peter Smith, 1976), II, pp.13-14. Henceforth, History of Dogma.

has meant that Christians have been able to use the Bible to justify every type of behavior abhorrent to their Lord and Savior!

Chapter X

Loud Dissent to Inerrancy

It has to be acknowledged that in the history of the Church the predominant view of inspiration has been the mechanical view of Justin, Clement, Origin, Ambrose, Basil, Augustine and the Greek philosophers. Contrary to conservative theologians,[1] the early Church could not be found in unanimous support of this doctrine. There were some very strong voices in the Church which either gave no support to the doctrine or were in outright opposition to the doctrine.

The first and most persuasive voice is the Bible itself. The evidence of the Bible shows that the inspiration of the prophets and the apostles and thus, deductively, the inspiration of the authors of Scripture, was far removed from that of Plato, Heraclitus, the Stoics, and Philo. The prophets and the apostles were hardly passive automatons. In the biblical stories of the interactions between God and the prophets or the apostles, the Spirit of God does not so control the prophets or apostles as to overrule their human powers, rendering them incapable of error.

Peter, the Chief Apostle

The most decisive and destructive case against inerrancy is found in the life of none other than Peter. In Acts 10 it is reported that an angel of the Lord appeared to Cornelius, a "God fearing" Roman Centurion. The angel tells Cornelius that his prayers were answered. He should send men to Joppa, to bring back a man named Simon (Vss. 1–8). While the men were on their way, Simon Peter, was on the roof praying (vs. 9). The text states that Peter got hungry and fell into a trance. In the trance the heavens opened; a canopy, covered with living crawling things descended, and a voice said to Peter, "Rise Peter, kill and eat." Indignantly, Peter responded, "Certainly not, I have never eaten anything unclean or defiled (vs. 14 RSV)." The voice then said to him, "What God has made clean you have no right to call profane (vs. 15, RSV)." This incident happens three times in the vision. To say the least, the vision must have been unnerving ("inwardly perplexing," RSV). Peter had been taught all his life that he as a Jew had to abstain from certain animals because they were unclean (Remember Leviticus 11). In his days with Jesus, Peter saw Jesus break many of the Old Testament laws but it is not reported that Jesus violated the dietary laws and here was God telling Peter to do so. Most perplexing for Peter must have been that there was no other possible interpretation. This vision had only its literal implicit meaning. Immediately after the vision was completed, the messenger arrived to take Peter to Cornelius. When Peter arrives at Cornelius' house and the various explanations are made, Peter stated: "The truth I now grasp that God is impartial, that anybody of any ethnic background, who fears God and does what is right is acceptable

---

[1]See p. 11, footnote #25.

to God (vss. 34–35)."

When Peter says "I grasp (perceive, RSV)" he was talking about a mental activity that his mind performed. God did not do his thinking for him. Yes, God gave him the vision and sent the messenger to him, but he himself put the pieces together.[2] The reader can almost imagine the process Peter went through in his mind. Not only did he remember vividly the vision that he had on the roof, but other things may have flashed across his mind. He may have remembered how Jesus had healed a gentile servant and then proclaimed that the gentile had more faith than anyone in Israel (Mt. 8:5 ff.). Or, how Jesus used the example of the Samaritan who had helped a Jew, left dying on the side of the road, (Lk. 10:29 ff) to illustrate the love required by the second commandment. The incident may have also jogged his memory of the time when one leper of ten healed by Jesus returned to thank him, and that one was a gentile (Lk. 17:11 ff.). With these and other events, Peter concluded that Gentiles were, indeed, acceptable in God's sight and they did not have to become Jews.

There is a postscript, however, to this story of Peter and Cornelius that must remove any idea that God had given his Spirit to the Apostles so that they would not make any errors. The postscript is found in the Epistle of Paul to the Galatians. There, Paul stated, "When Peter came to Antioch, I opposed him to his face, because he was clearly in the wrong (2:11 NIV)." In Paul's narrative he reports that Peter had been associating with gentiles, which would have been consistent with the story of Cornelius. However, according to Paul, some people came from James, and Peter stopped associating with the Gentiles (v.12). In the context of Paul's argument it must be assumed that these Christians were Judaizing Christians. They assumed that before gentile men could be baptized as Christians they had to be circumcised. Consequently, when Peter withdraws from his association with the Gentiles, he was acknowledging that these Gentiles were unclean, contrary to his experience with Cornelius, and Paul was right in confronting Peter with his *error*.

This whole story makes a mockery of concursive and organic theories of inspiration. Some may even assert that it makes a mockery of the Roman Catholic papal infallibility. The point being that the apostles, indeed – here, the chief apostle, could be in error. The gravity of this particular mistake that Peter made is accentuated when we realize that the event took place after the resurrection, after Peter was filled with the Holy Spirit, and after Peter's experience with Cornelius. There are other indications in Scripture itself that the apostles were capable of human shortcomings and errors, but nothing as blatant as Paul's confrontation of Peter.[3] Since there is no indication in the New Testament that the apostles and writers of the New Testament received

---

[2]The Greek term, καταλαμβανομαι, which is translated "grasp" underscores just how human an activity this was that Peter performed. Καταλαμβανω means: "I seize," "win," "attain," "make my own," "grasp," "seize with hostile intent," "overtake," "come upon, catch," "detect." In the form that is used here (middle), it means, "find, grasp, understand."

[3]Examples of this might include Paul's inability to forgive John Mark for abandoning the cause in Pamphylia or John Mark's, for abandoning Paul and Barnabas in Pamphylia(Acts 15 36–40) or Paul's intentional or unintentional grieving of the Corinthians (II Corinthians 2:1–5). This, of course, does not include the actual mistakes which the textual critics have long pointed out exist within the text. But, of course, Conservatives have long denied those existed or they have rationalized them away.

another even more empowering experience than Pentecost; that is, an outpouring of the Holy Spirit that would prevent them from making mistakes, we must conclude that theories of concursive and organic inspiration of the Bible of do not hold up under close scrutiny of the New Testament.[4]

The Prophets

There is plenty of evidence from the Old Testament that the prophets were independent beings and were not so controlled by the Spirit of Yahweh that they did exactly what Yahweh wanted when He wanted it. The pages of the Old Testament are filled with stories of prophets' willfulness and their humanness in the reception of revelation.

Each Prophet could have told the Lord he was not interested in doing the Lord's work. Jonah did precisely that, and the Lord had to teach him by an impressive act. One would assume that a person who was endowed with the Spirit of God from birth would have been more easily convinced than Jonah (Jonah 1, 2). Furthermore, one would assume that a prophet so possessed by the Spirit of God would rejoice once the will of Yahweh was carried out, but not so with Jonah. After Jonah proclaimed the word, Ninevah turns to God, and Jonah was really angry with God (Jonah 4).

It is likewise apparent in the Bible that in any act of revelation, God does not suspend human powers of reasoning. A good example is found in Ezekiel 37. In this chapter it is reported that Yahweh placed Ezekiel in a valley filled with bones. Yahweh asked Ezekiel: "Son of Man can these bones live (vs. 3)?" It would seem logical that a person who was totally possessed and controlled by the Spirit of Yahweh would have responded: "Yes, of course, Lord, you who brought about creation can make these bones live." But, that is not the case with Ezekiel. He plays it safe and "hedges his bets." He responds: "You know, Lord God (vs.3b)." Considering all the power the Lord God had displayed to the prophet previously in the narrative, the statement shows amazing dullness on the prophet's part.

The fact that prophets are still their own persons and possess their own abilities is borne out by the Old Testament recording times when prophets actually argue with God (Exodus 4:1–17;17:4; 32:11–13; Numbers 14:10–25; Deuteronomy 9:25–29; Joshua 7:6–9; Job 31; Jeremiah 15:10–21; 20:7–18). In some of these arguments, the prophet actually prevails. That is to say, God intends one type of activity and through the Prophet's persuasive arguing, God changes His intention or the activity that was going to be carried out (Exodus 4:10–17; 32:11–14; Numbers 14:10–25; Deuteronomy 9:25–29; Joshua 7:6–15). It is clear that these arguments originate with the Prophet and not with Yahweh and therefore have to be considered the prophet's own words and not Yahweh's. Again, it must be repeated that II Timothy 3:16 states: All *Scripture* is inspired," not *all words*. Some words originate with the prophets, kings, ordinary people, apostles, and others.[5] If the reader desires a book that claims all the words are God's then she or he should read the Koran or the

---

[4]Such passages as John 14:25–31 do not speak of two different dispensations of the Holy Spirit, one at the time of Pentecost and one at the time when "the apostles sat down to write."

[5]See M. Barth, Conversation, p. 34 ff.

Book of Mormon.

Inspired Pagan Priests

There is evidence in Scripture that inspiration from God is to be found in persons whom conservatives would find totally unacceptable. This inspiration might be found in any person, including nonbelievers. Conservatives will grant that God used heathens to fill His purposes, as he used Nebuchadrezer of Babylon, or they unwittingly deliver or fulfill prophecy as Herod or Pilate or Gamiliel (Acts 5:35–42). But they have long overlooked that in the Bible God sometimes used Pagans to be the source of revelation – and not just a verse of Scripture but many verses and even chapters.

The first example is Balaam, the son of Beor. The story of Balaam (Numbers 22–24), is one of the most interesting and one of the most ignored stories in the Bible. The first noteworthy feature of the story is that Balaam is a diviner, meaning that he sought spiritual directions from natural happenings called omens, such as the entrails of animals, the lay of stones, the flight of birds, and so on. Divining was a practice strictly forbidden in the law of Moses (Exodus 22:18; Leviticus 19:26, 31; 20:6; Deuteronomy 18: 9–14). In the narrative, the elders of Moab and Midian, at the command of King Balak, took money to pay Balaam for divining a curse against the Jews (22:5–7). Balaam accepts their money and says to them, "Lodge here this night, and I will bring back word to you, as the Lord speaks to me (vs. 8, RSV)." One can assume that he is going off to do his conjuring.

The second feature of the text is that Balaam does not go off to conjure with a pagan god. It is obvious that he is going to work with the Lord God. In the Hebrew text the sacred name of the Lord is Yahweh, יהוה and the traditional usage Elohim אלהים is for God. The texts reads:

> "And God (the other Hebrew name for God, Elohim, אֱלֹהִים is used) came to Balaam and said "Who are these men with you?" And Balaam said to God (Elohim הָאֱלֹהִים), Balak the son of Sippor, king of Moab has sent to me, saying, "Behold, a people has come out of Egypt, and it covers the face of the earth; now come, curse them for me; perhaps I shall be able to fight against them and drive them out. God (Elohim אֱלֹהִים) said to Balaam, "You shall not go with them; you shall not curse the people for they are blessed." So Balaam rose early in the morning, and said to the princes of Balak, "Go to your own land; for the Lord (Yahweh יהוה) has refused to let me go with you." So the princes of Balak rose, and went to Balak and said, "Balaam refuses to come with us." (22:9–13, RSV, Hebrew from MT)

The third noteworthy feature is that Yahweh did not have to introduce himself, as he did to Moses (Exodus 3:1–6). Consequently, we must assume that this diviner had an ongoing relationship with Yahweh. Furthermore, unlike Moses, Balaam does not argue with the Lord. He does exactly what Yahweh tells him. In fact, when Balak sends more princes, Balaam responds, "Though Balak were to give me his house full of silver and gold, I could not go beyond the command of the Lord, my God (יהוה אֱלֹהָי) . . . (vs 18, RSV, English)" One could only have hoped that the Jews would have answered with such devotion and obedience.

The fourth feature is very simple. Here in the Torah, the law of Moses, are three chapters that are dedicated to the revelation of Yahweh to a gentile. While the phrase "the Word of the Lord came to the prophet" is missing, the language is very similar to that of the classical prophets. Numbers 24:15b–16 gives Balaam complete prophetic validation:

> The Oracle of Balaam the Son of Beor,
> The Oracle of him whose eye is open (perfect),
> The Oracle of him who hears words of God,
> and knows the knowledge of the most high,
> who sees the vision of the Almighty (שַׁדַּי יֶהֱזֶה) falling down, but
> having his eyes open.

Thus, Balaam stands in almost the same category as Moses, maybe not face to face, but at least "a vision of the almighty."

The fifth noteworthy feature is in Numbers 24:1: "When Balaam saw that it pleased the Lord to bless Israel, he did not go, as at other times to look for omens (RSV)." This is confirmation that Balaam was indeed a diviner who sought "omens." It must be noted that Yahweh does not tell Balaam that he must give up seeking omens (22–23). Since we must assume from 22:9 that Balaam had an on-going relationship with Yahweh, Yahweh had other times to tell Balaam to desist. Judging from the indications of Balaam's obedience in Chapter 22, if Yahweh had said that to Balaam he would have desisted right away. So, when did Balaam learn that omen seeking was wrong? It would seem as if verse 24:1 was an editorial comment by some pious Jew in later generations reading the story and not believing that here in the Torah was a diviner communicating with the Lord God, and with whom the Lord God was reciprocating. That was just not the way things were supposed to work, and he had to insert the verse to make the whole passage legitimate.

The final noteworthy feature is that Balaam does not become a Jew. He returns to his own place (24:25).

The next illustration of the dynamics of inspiration does not deal with the revelation of Yahweh, but rather how an individual, a pagan priest affected Israel and gave it direction. This illustration is found in the eighteenth chapter of Exodus. In this chapter Moses and his father-in-law, Jethro, the Midianite priest, were reunited. After observing Moses judging the people, Jethro states:

> What you are doing is not good. You and the people with you will wear yourselves out, for the thing is too heavy for you; you are not able to perform it alone. Listen now to my voice; I will give you counsel, and God be with you! You shall represent the people before God, and bring their cases to God; and you shall teach them the statutes and the decisions, and make them know the way in which they must walk and what they must do. Moreover choose able men from all the people, such as fear God, men who are trustworthy and who hate a bribe; and place such men over the people as rulers of thousands, of hundreds, of fifties and of tens. And let them judge the people at all times; every great matter they shall bring to you, but any small matter they shall decide themselves; so it will be easier for you, and they shall bear the burden with you (18:17b–22, RSV).

This is an amazing statement! Here we have a pagan priest making suggestions for the operation and administration of the life of the people of

God. The reader has to realize that these were not simply minor adjustments to the people of God. This body of elders proposed by Jethro was the forerunner of the Jewish Sanhedrin, that body which tried Jesus and regulated everyday life in Judaism. While the text states that Jethro offered a burnt sacrifice to Yahweh (vs.12), there are no indications that Jethro became a Jew and became one of the people of God. Jethro does concede that Yahweh is "greater than other gods (vs. 11)," but still the other gods exist. When Jethro departs to his home land the departure indicates that he continued on in his own way. One other feature that is not so apparent in the text is that unlike Balaam, the text does not state that Jethro derives his thoughts from his own reasoning power instead of from Yahweh.

There are other Gentiles, including Melchizedek, Rahab the Harlot, Naaman, and the widow of Zarephath, who get mentioned in the New Testament but none of these persons plays as important a role in the Old Testament as Balaam and Jethro. It would be hard to determine why these two figures did not get coverage in the New Testament. One thing is certain; their inclusion in the first five books of the Bible meant that the compilers of the Torah had not closed themselves off from learning from their Gentile neighbors.

Their inclusion in the Torah should be a lesson to fundamentalists and conservatives, to broaden their thinking on inspiration and revelation. It likewise should be a lesson to all Christians as they relate to the world of nonbelievers, whether they are missionaries to another country or live in a pluralistic country such as ours. God can and does speak through all sorts of people whether they be Christian or not.[6]

Misinterpreted Expressions:

"Spoken by the Mouth of the Prophets"

There are some statements recorded in the Bible that would appear in their translation from the Greek to contradict the obvious freedom of the prophets, apostles, and inspired persons of the Bible and would support a mechanical inspiration. The bulk of these statements are found in the Gospel of Luke and the Acts of the Apostles. These statements: "The Holy Spirit spoke before hand by the mouth of David (Acts 1:16)"; "David, thy servant, did say by the Holy Spirit (Acts 4:25)," and "God foretold by the mouth of all the prophets (Acts 3:18, 21; Luke 1:70)."

While these expressions all seem to confirm many Church fathers' conception that "God spoke" or "wrote the scriptures," that impression is dispelled when one examines the usage of the expressions in the Scripture. I believe the key to understanding all the expressions is found in the idiom "the mouth of." The expression is a Hebraism or Hebrew figure of speech that is a very earthy and concrete expression of Hebraic thought, which shines through a Hebrew writer's attempt to express himself in Greek.

In the Old Testament "mouth" has a rich variety of metaphors. In Genesis 4:11 "the mouth of the earth" receives the blood of the murdered Able (cf. Nu. 16:30, 32). Out of "the mouth of God, פי יהוה" comes the Law and the Word of Yahweh (Dt. 8:3; 32:1; Josh 9:14; II. Chrn. 36:22; Jb. 23:12; Is. 1:20, etc.). The

---

[6]Such is the point of Yale Professor Lamin Sanneh, in his superb book, *Translating the Message*, (Maryknoll, NY: Orbis Books, 1989) p. 1 ff.

difference between Aaron and Miriam and Moses was that Yahweh met Moses "Mouth to Mouth" (Numbers 12:8). The storage place of the law was not just the heart and mind, but the mouth (Joshua 1:8).

The story of Yahweh commissioning Moses to go to the people of Israel and the Pharaoh of Egypt is a good illustration of why the expression "by mouth of" cannot be considered passive inspiration. The story borders on the comical. One might expect that, if those who argue for concursive and organic inspiration would have been correct, and that God had been preparing Moses from his birth for his mission, then Moses after his confrontation with the Lord would respond, "O Yes, Lord, send me!" But this is not what takes place. What ensues is an argument between the Lord God almighty and the mortal Moses. The following is a mixture of literal translation and editorial comment and paraphrase by me:

> After Yahweh confronts Moses in the burning bush (Exodus 3:2–6), he says to Moses that he is going to send him to Pharaoh to tell him to let his people go. Without even trembling, Moses counters, "Who am I that I should go to Pharaoh and lead the sons of Israel out of Egypt? (3:11)" Yahweh assures Moses that He the Lord God would be with him. Moses responds incredulously, "If I come to the people of Israel and say to them, 'The God of your fathers has sent me to you,' and they ask me, 'What is his name?' what shall I tell them (vs.13)?" Yahweh responds irately "I am who I am!" Moses patiently listens to Yahweh tell him that he has seen the people's affliction and how mightily he would deliver them (vss. 16–22). Moses in his nonplussed way counters, "They will not believe me or listen to my voice, for they will say, 'The Lord did not appear to you (4:1 RSV).'" In the text one can almost imagine the Lord thinking to himself before responding. He then says, "(You have a point Moses.) Here's what I will do. See that rod in your hand, throw it on the ground."(4:2–3) The text records that the rod became a snake and then when Moses caught the snake it became a rod again. Then the Lord God had Moses perform what would most societies would consider two more feats of magic: He put his hand in his cloak and when he pulled it out, it was leprous. When he returned it to his cloak and pulled it out again it was healed. Then he scooped water from the Nile and poured it on the ground and it became blood (4–9). A shaman would have been amazed, but Moses was unimpressed. He complains, "Oh, my Lord, I am not eloquent, before or now since you have spoken to your servant; but I talk slow and stutter. (10)." One can feel the ire of the Lord rising. Indignantly He responds: "Now look, Moses, am I not God? Did I not make everything that is? Did I not make the mouth? Did I not make the person who speaks, or those who are deaf, those who have sight and those who are blind? Now, therefore, Moses go! I will be with your mouth and will teach you what you will say." (vs. 11–12)

The reader will have to agree that the Lord God could not have stated his case better or more compellingly. Again, Moses is unimpressed. Believing he is ending the discussion, Moses exclaims, "Oh, my Lord, send some other person. Find someone else to do that job!).” (vs. 13) Then the text states “The anger of the Lord burned against Moses . . . (vs. 14).” The Lord God was running out of patience with this prophet, but then God saw Aaron coming up the path and He gets an idea, and asks Moses:

Is that not Aaron, your brother the Levite? I know that he can speak well, and behold he is coming to meet you, and when he sees you he will be glad in his heart. And you shall speak to him and put the words in his mouth; and I will be with your mouth and his mouth, and will teach you what to do. He shall speak for you to the people; and he shall be a mouth for you, and you shall be to him as a God. (RSV 14b–16)

The scriptures do not record what Moses' response was, but the Lord must have negotiated an acceptable compromise with Moses. The next passage states that Moses went back to his father-in-law and asked to be relieved of his shepherding responsibilities so that he could return to his people. (4:18–20) While I have taken some liberties with the text I have not taken many. The literal meaning of the text remains intact. The text quite clearly shows that contrary to Philo (Irenaeus, Athenagoras, and others) Moses was not simply a lyre to be plucked by God.

This text, along with many others, should have been used to dispel not only the concept of inerrancy, but other concepts that have been derived from Greek philosophy, including immutability, omniscience, and omnipotence. Clearly the text stipulated that God had intended Moses to go to the Israelites and Pharaoh, but because Moses refused, God changed his plans and included Moses' brother Aaron. The fact that God is not immutable is likewise borne out in the other arguments that Moses has with Yahweh. In these arguments, it is clearly stated Yahweh intends to wipe out Israel or most of Israel for unfaithfulness. But, because of Moses persuasive powers, Yahweh changes His mind (Exodus 17:4; 32:11–13; Numbers 14:10–25; Deuteronomy 9:25–29).

Luke 21:15: “I will give you mouth and wisdom and none of your adversaries will be able to stand against you or contradict you.”

This statement from Jesus underscores the fact that the expression “mouth,” is not indicative of a passive receiver of inspiration. It is found in the context of a teaching of Jesus' dealing with persecution. Jesus states that his disciples will be delivered up to “synagogues, and prison . . . brought before kings and governors (vs. 12)” but they were not to worry about their defense (vs. 14). The reason for this, Jesus asserted, was that he would give them “mouth and wisdom.” It must be assumed here that Jesus was not just addressing the apostles, but all Christians in every generation and he was stating that he would be their “mouth” as he was for David, Moses, and all the Prophets. He would supply their defense in front of their detractors.

While Jesus stated that he would give his followers their mouth in time of persecution, they must not assume that they have a divine umbrella which protects them all the time. Jesus admonished his disciples, “Take care lest your hearts become weighted down in indulgence, drunkenness, and world cares . . . . Keep watch at all the time, begging to be strong so to escape what ever might come, and to stand before the son of man (vss. 34, 36 RSV).

The activities that Jesus asks of his disciples are human activities. God was not going to come down and suspend the reasoning powers of the Christians (as Plato said was the case of the poets, prophets, and soothsayers), nor would they become transformed like Buddha, nor become all light as Philo claimed of Moses. Through disciplined spiritual life, Christians were allowing themselves to be open to Christ's directions.

However, it is an inherent part of the teachings of Jesus that even if the Christian develops these spiritual disciplines, he or she does not also develop the spiritual arrogance or hubris that has so frequently accompanied dogmatic Christians who think they know exactly what God is thinking at all times. In fact, Christians who do develop good spiritual disciplines are those who are genuinely humble. One can sense that they depend on God. These are the people who agree with the apostle Paul that "now we see through a glass dimly, then we shall see face to face (I Corinthians 13:12)." Remember, as I discussed of Ephesians 6:19 in Chapter IV, even the Apostle Paul needed the prayers of the Ephesians because he did not possess *the word*.

One thing is for certain, all the indications from the Bible show that the expression "by the mouth of" does not mean passive reception of revelation. The expression may simply mean much as we in colloquial English say of a Lawyer, "He is so-and-so's mouth piece." The difference between our colloquialism and the metaphor in Hebrew is that in our practice the lawyer may derive very little of what he or she states on behalf of the client directly from the client; whereas in the Old and the New Testaments, the prophet and the Christian derive their power and their message directly from the Lord God, whom they represent to the world. The prophet does not simply echo God's words like an empty conduit but lends his mouth in thoughtful response to the inspiration received from God.

II Peter 1: 20–21: "First of all you must understand this, that no prophecy of Scripture is a matter of one's own interpretation, because no prophesy ever came by impulse of man, but men moved by the Holy Spirit spoke from God"

In the same vein as these expressions from Luke/Acts is one that is found in II Peter 1:20–21. Historically speaking the Church fathers hardly recognize the existence of these verses, but that is most likely from their not accepting the authenticity of the epistle rather than their not finding the verse useful for their interpretation (see this work p. 153).

It is not surprising that it was Martin Luther who first focused on these verses. He wrote:

> Here St. Peter attacks false doctrine. Since you know that we have God's Word, he says, cling to this knowledge, and do not be misled by other false teachers, even though they come with the allegation that they, too have the Holy Spirit. For "first of all you must understand this"–he will state the rest later– "that no prophecy of Scripture is a matter of one's own interpretation."
> Be governed by this, and do not think that you can interpret Scripture with your own reason and wisdom . . .
> Thus Peter attacks the most estimable and competent teachers. Therefore we dare not believe anyone who presents his own explanation and interpretation of Scripture. For no correct understanding can be arrived at by means of one's own interpretation. Here all teachers and fathers, as many as there are who have interpreted Scripture, have stumbled, as when they refer

to Christ's statement in Matt. 16:18–"You are Peter, and on this rock will I build My church" to the pope. Therefore one should not believe it, for they cannot prove from Scripture that Peter is ever called pope . . . (Luther's Works, 30, p.166–167).

Once again, Luther asserts that they (Lutherans) truly had God's Word, not the Roman Catholics.[7] It may be of interest to the reader that the Roman Church, while not referring to II Peter 1:21, but with it in mind, put forth the same statement as Luther in about the same words as Luther in the Fourth Session (April 8, 1546) of the Council of Trent. Concerning the interpretation of Scripture the Council declared with an air of superiority:

> . . . In order to restrain petulant spirits, it (the Council) decrees that no one, relying on his own skill shall, in matters of faith, and of morals pertaining to the edification of Christian doctrine, wresting the sacred Scripture to his own senses, presume to interpret the said Scriptures contrary to that sense which the holy mother Church, – whose it is to judge of the true sense and interpretation of the holy Scriptures (Schaff)

Noteworthy also is the fact that the modern critical scholar Bo Reicke echoes the same emphasis on the verses:

> According to vs. 20 it is important, however, to consider the danger of such arbitrary exposition of the prophecies, as was practiced by certain apocalyptical troublemakers close to the church. The guarantee against that spiritual anarchy is the recognition that the Holy Scripture must be interpreted by those who are properly qualified, who have been called by God and prompted by the Spirit, which is true of the apostles and their legitimate successors. (AB, 37, in loc.)

Of course, Zwingli, Calvin, Simon, Knox, and Wesley all thought themselves to be the legitimate successors and therefore the proper interpreters of Scripture and thought the *papists* to be impostors.

John Calvin interpreted "prophecy" as "that which is contained in Scripture."[8] Here Calvin did not mean the various prophecies that are contained in the different books but the entirety of Scripture or the content of all the Scriptures was prophecy. Most conservative and fundamentalist exegesis has followed Calvin.[9] Ray Summers in his Broadman Bible Commentary on II Peter gives a typical conservative exposition:

> Peter does not argue for inspiration of the Scriptures he assumes it. Clearly he is not defending the nature or method of inspiration.

---

[7]Most likely this sermon was preached in 1522 (as editor Pelikan suggests, Luther's Works, 30, p. ix) for if it had been preached later than 1523 he certainly would have included in this condemnation Zwingli and the Anabaptists as imposing their "own explanation and interpretation" of Scripture. Of course the Anabaptists and Zwingli made the same accusation against Luther.

[8]Calvin, *The Catholic Epistles*, in loc.

[9]See Lewis Barbieri, *First and Second Peter* (Chicago: Moody Press, 1977), in loc.; Frank Gaebelen, *The Expository Bible Commentary*, Volume XII (Grand Rapids, MI, Zondervan, Inc., 1984), in loc.; J. N. D. Kelly, *A Commentary or the Epistles of Peter and Jude* (London: Adam & Charles Black, Ltd., 1969), in loc.

And surely he is not anticipating the verbiage of any translation. The Scriptures of which he wrote were, of course, the Hebrew Scriptures (our Old Testament). The New Testament as a body of approved writings was not in existence. It was in process of being written. What the Hebrews claimed for the Old Testament, that it was written by men who *moved by the Holy Spirit spoke from God*. (BBC, Volume 12, p 179)

In examining the text the first observation to be made is that nowhere in the text does the author speak of the interpretation of Scripture. Nowhere in the text does Peter equate doctrine and dogma with prophecy. Nowhere in the Bible is prophecy equated with the Old Testament. If what II Peter had meant by "prophecy" was the entirety of Scripture, the text would have simply stated, "For no Scripture is a matter of human will, but men moved by the Holy Spirit wrote Scripture from God." This, indeed, would have cemented the case for inerrancy. But, the Greek text does not say this. It states very clearly: πασα προφητεια (all prophecy, nominative) γραφης (of Scripture, genitive). Ray Summers' interpretation is a good example of how conservative hermeneutics becomes twisted and his interpretation is one of the best ways to show how that twist came about. He is most assuredly correct in interpreting the prophetic word of verse 19 to the mountain top experience of Peter, James, and John at the transfiguration and at Jesus' baptism, and he may be right that the clause in verse 19, "a light shining in a dark place, until the day dawns, and the rising star light shines in your hearts" implies the second coming of Christ. Summers goes on to state, "To that prophetic word Peter added the prophetic **scripture** (vs. 20)." Notice now the modifier "of scripture (γραφης)" becomes the noun and the noun, "prophecy" becomes the modifier "prophetic" Then a paragraph down, Summers wrote, "The interpretation of the prophetic scripture was important to Peter. The understanding of those scriptures is *not a matter of one's own interpretation*." Now the noun "prophecy" has been completely dropped so that now the topic is the Scriptures, followed by the lengthy paragraph quoted above, where prophecy is never mentioned.[10]

While II Peter 1:21 does not state that God spoke through the mouth of the prophet, the impact of the Greek could be interpreted to mean that. In fact II Peter 1:21 could be used as even stronger evidence of mechanical inspiration of the prophets. Peter uses two genitives of agency to underscore that prophecy came about "Not by the will of people (ου γαρ (for) θελαματι του ανθροπου), but rather (αλλα) being moved (φερομενοι) by the Holy Spirit (υπο πνευματος αγιου) people (ανθροποι) spoke (ελαλησαν) from God (απο θεου)."

In the New Testament and in classical Greek, unlike θεοπνευστος of II Timothy 3:16, the term φερω, the root word for φερομενοι, which was translated

---

[10]This transference finds no support in the Bible. In the New Testament, the Scriptures are never referred to simply as "Prophecy." The term "Scripture γραφη" may be referred to as the Law or the Law of the Lord (Mt. 12:5; 22:35; 23:23; LK. 2:23, 24; Jn. 7:19, 49, 51; 8:17; 12:34 etc.), the Law of Moses (Jn. 7:23; Acts 13:38; 15:5; Hb. 9:19; 10:28), your (referring to the Jews) Law (Jn. 18:13) or the book of Moses (Jn 12:34). The Scriptures are also referred to as the Law and the Prophets (Mt. 5:17; 7:12; 22:40; Lk 16:16; Acts 13:15; 24:14) and the Law of Moses and Prophets (Acts 28:23) and to that formula in one place Luke adds "the Psalms (24:44)." In one place Matthew refers to "the writings of the prophets" as predicting the sufferings of Christ (26:56), but nowhere are the scriptures simply described as "prophecy."

"moved," was used frequently, so that its meaning is not difficult to determine. It meant, "bear," "carry," "endure," "produce," "move by bearing or force," "bring a word to bear on the subject, make a speech," or "lead some one" (A. & G.)" While the term had not been used before in the New Testament to mean inspiration, it has been used in this manner by Philo of Alexandria, as it was pointed out in the previous chapter. Clearly, Philo used it to underscore that none of Moses' human resources were used in the communication of the Law.[11] It might be that Peter meant the same thing as Philo, but there is no clear indication of that.

II Peter 1:20-21 cannot be used to support such theories of concursive or organic inspiration. It makes no reference to personality or mental power. The genesis of the prophecies was strictly from God, not from the Spirit using the personality and mind of the prophet.

The second interpretation is one that I believe is suggested by the context of II Peter 1:16-21. As I pointed out above, the verse does not speak of Scripture but rather a part of Scripture. The text is differentiating the type of "prophecy" that Peter has in mind. The reader will remember that in the New Testament there were other prophets than those recorded in the Old Testament. John the Baptist was considered a prophet (Mt. 11:7-15; 14:5; Lk 7:24-28). Zechariah, the father of John, most likely was considered a prophet, in that "he was filled with the Holy Spirit and prophesied (Lk 1:67)." Of course, it is very clear from Paul that there were many prophets in the early Church (I Cor. 12-14). Here, rather than just in the 20-21st verses, Peter is differentiating between types of prophecy and he is strictly referring to prophecy of Scripture, but what he means by "prophecy of Scripture" may not be at all what conservatives would appreciate.

The context of vss.16-21 may suggest that Peter had a very dynamic and not static view of the prophesies that were contained in the Old Testament. In verse 16 Peter states that what he and other disciples were preaching was not some "cleverly designed myths," rather they, themselves, had seen "the majesty of the Lord Jesus Christ." This majesty was confirmed to the disciples when they, standing on the mountain (cf. Mt. 17:1-13; MK. 9:2-13; Lk. 9:28-36), heard the Lord God state, "This is my Son, my beloved, in whom I am well pleased (vs. 17 RSV). It is this prophesy and many other similar messianic verses that I believe Peter has in mind in verses 20-21. In verse 19 he stated, "We have a more certain Prophetic word."[12] While the RSV translation, "more certain" is acceptable, I believe "more valid" is preferable. It is clear that Peter is contrasting two different prophecies. The more valid prophecy was that which the disciples heard on the mountain, the less valid was that written in the text. The proclamation of Yahweh over Jesus is a compilation of two verses from the Old Testament. The verses are Psalm 2:7, "You are my Son, today I have begotten you," and Isaiah 42:1, "Behold my servant, whom I uphold, my chosen, in whom my soul delights; I have put my Spirit upon him, he will bring forth justice to the nations." As I pointed out in Chapter VII in

---

[11]See pp. 219-222.

[12]The Greek word that the RSV translates, "more certain." is βεβαιοτερον and definitely is in the comparative degree. the root word in Βεβαιοτερον is βεβαιος which means "standing firm on the feet," "steadfast," "maintaining firmness," "firm," "strengthened," "established," "validated," "confirmed."(A.&G.)

the analysis of the passages of the Old Testament that were used in the prediction of Jesus as the Messiah, Yahweh is a totally free agent. The prophets were moved in their day and age to speak a message for that day and age, but Yahweh can take that message and place entirely new meaning to the verses. He can take the message found in half a verse from one place and the message found in half a verse from another place and put brand new meanings to the messages so that now the prophecy becomes new, current, and more valid than the prophecy written on the Scroll. In this passage it is clear that Yahweh is not a literalist and uses the Scriptures without restraint. This interpretation is supported in verse 20 where Peter states, "More importantly no one can interpret prophecy of Scripture on their own." He does not state in this verse who is capable of interpreting Scripture. As we saw in the earlier quote from the Council of Trent, the Roman Church has long assumed that it, as the Church, was the repository of interpretation, or the final authority in interpretation. But the text does not state that. The clue to understanding who can *interpret prophecy* is in verse 17 where, after the transfiguration, the voice of God states, "This is my beloved Son . . . "As I just stated, here God takes the messages in two different verses and puts them together. As God moved the prophets, so God is free to use the prophecy as God sees fit. God is the final arbitrator of prophecy.

There, on the hill, Yahweh spoke to the disciples. He spoke loudly and clearly. He did not speak in "visions and dreams." The disciples beheld God's face in the Lord Jesus. This was the more valid "prophetic word" than that written in the Old Testament prophets. This did not mean that the Old Testament prophets' word was invalid. God moved the prophets to speak, and they spoke the message that was valid for their day. Thus, in the day of Ahaz, a young woman bore a child and his name was Immanuel, and before that child was old enough to "eat milk and honey," the lands of Syria and Samaria would be "deserted (Isaiah 7:10–16)." Still, the Almighty could use this same passage to proclaim the birth of the Son of God, but more importantly, the apostles did not hear the voice of God through prophets; they heard the voice of God directly.

Understanding the prophecy of II Peter 1:16–21 this way shifts the meaning of "moved (φερομενοι)" from a Philonic/Platonic mechanical inspiration to a much more dynamic concept of inspiration, and it is consistent with the way Jesus interpreted Scripture. If this view is rejected then the philological evidence would support the Philonic/Platonic perspective, and this would make the only verse in the Bible that would support mechanical inspiration. Of course it still would be a logical non sequitur to apply it to the concept of the inspiration of Scriptures. One could only state that the Prophets were "moved," they were not necessarily the authors of Scripture. I do not believe, however, most conservative Theologians today would accept mechanical inspiration of the Bible.

There is a final interpretation which is a possibility and this is to assert that the actual meaning of II Peter 1:20 is lost in history. Since Peter is not around to ask what he meant, and since there is no clarification within the text what it meant, then it would be best to declare ignorance and to declare the meaning lost in history.

In concluding our discussion of the biblical concepts of inspiration there is no support for contemporary theories of inerrancy. What little support for inerrancy there is turns to favor the ancient fathers' mechanical inspiration. That early concept is so strongly overwhelmed by contrary evidence that it is also defeated. All those who defend inerrancy should be at an impasse. All their arguments from Scripture are found to be non-existent or very shallow. There could hardly be considered enough evidence in Scripture to sustain a major doctrine like inerrancy. The only argument that remains would be one which most conservative Protestants would find distasteful and that is the argument based on tradition. The only argument remaining to the inerrantists is that inerrancy is correct because it is held by the greatest number of people for the longest time.

No Support in the Earliest Fathers

There is no question that the predominant view within the Church has been that of inerrancy, and one cannot argue that inerrancy is the most ancient view of the Scriptures. Still, it is clear from the writings that are available from the end of the first century after Christ that the doctrine was not the dominant theme of the early Church. Of course, one might argue that because of the persecutions in the Church during the period between 70–180 C.E. there is not a great deal of information. But, from what is available, it is easy to determine that the type of thinking that is common in inerrantist doctrine was repugnant to some of the most influential personalities in the early church.

One of these personalities was the bishop of Antioch, Ignatius. Ignatius was reportedly martyred in the jaws of lions about 115 C.E. (Eusebius, Church History III, 36). Of the existing writings of Ignatius, the Church historian Hans Lietzmann writes:

> A very special interest attaches to these letters because they are the earliest original documents of the church which, above all others, must be regarded as the cradle of Gentile Christianity, in which also Paul had laboured for a long time, and which we have reason for calling the mother church of Rome. It is here that proselyte Christianity which was free from the law must have blossomed . . . [13]

In Ignatius, it is clear that Jesus is the Word of God, the only Word of God. Of Jesus Ignatius wrote:

> For the divinely inspired prophets lived according Jesus Christ. On this account they were persecuted, being inspired by his grace so to fully convince unbelievers that there is one God who has manifested Himself through Jesus Christ, who is His Word, not spoken, but essential. For he is the voice of an articulate utterance, but a substance begotten by divine power, who has in all things pleased Him that sent Him. ("To the Magnesians," VIII, AN, I)

Those who ardently defend inerrancy will point out that the prophets were "divinely inspired," and this, they will assert, confirms their views of II Timothy 3:16. Rather than defending inerrancy, a study of Ignatius reveals just how distorted the views of the Church became on the Scriptures. Ignatius

---

[13]Lietzman, I, 237.

goes on in the same passage quoted above to chastise the Jews for stubbornly maintaining "ancient practices" by which he means the observation of the Old Testament Sabbath and refusing to accept the resurrection and the celebration of the resurrection, the Lord's day, Sunday (To the Magnesians, IX). Then he writes that they, the Christians, will go "enduring" persecution so that they, the Christians might prove that they are "disciples of Jesus Christ, our only teacher. For even the prophets were his disciples through the Spirit and expected him as their teacher."("To the Magnesians," IX–XIII, AN, I) It is not the scriptures that are the Christians' teacher, but Jesus himself. Here is the pristine Church! Ignatius believed that the resurrected and living Jesus was present and living in and among the believers. Along with this was Ignatius' stress on unity in the Church. Ignatius knew well Jesus' prayer for unity and he knew that any division in the Church violated the very presence of the Lord Jesus ("To the Philadelphians," VII–VIII; XIII; XX; "To the Magnesians," VI; XIII; "To the Trallianes," VI; VII; XII, AN, I). Ignatius sees the Scriptures as the witness to Jesus Christ ("To the Ephesians," III–IV; "To the Philadelphians," VIII–IX). The Scriptures could not in any way be described as the essence of his religion. His religion and that of the Christians whom he led was the religion of the living Lord for whom Ignatius gave his life. The fact that Ignatius' religion was not the static religion of "the Book," but a living and powerful religion of the Spirit of the Lord Jesus is borne out in the following passage from the "Letter to the Philadelphians":

> . . . I trust to the grace of Jesus Christ, that he will free you from every bond of wickedness. I therefore exhort you that you do nothing out of strife, but according to the doctrine of Christ. For I have heard some saying, 'If I do not find the gospel in the archives (The fragmented or shorter version makes sure the reader understands that what is meant by the archives is the "ancient Scriptures.") I will not believe it.' To such persons I say that my archives are Jesus Christ to disobey whom is manifest destruction. My authentic archives are His cross and death, and resurrection, and the faith which bears on things, by which I desire, through your prayers to be justified. He who disbelieves the gospel disbelieves everything along with it. For the archives (the Scriptures) ought not be preferred to the Spirit. ("To the Philadelphians," VIII, AN)

There is no stronger statement of the thesis of this book. It is obvious that Ignatius did not share the idolatrous view of Scripture held by the rabbis of his time, the Christians of later generations, and the conservatives and fundamentalists of our day.

Clement of Rome (c. 90, 100 C.E.) likewise shows that the idolatry of Scripture had not developed in the Christian Church by the close of the first century. Clement demonstrated amazing freedom in his use of Scripture that is not found in the later Church.[14] Clement was able to discern that there are

---

[14]His use of Scripture is very similar to that of the author of Hebrews. (For an excellent discussion of freedom in the use of Scripture in Hebrews see M. Barth, *Conversation with the Bible*, "Freedom Exemplified: The Use of the Old Testament in Hebrews" (New York: Holt, Rinehart and Winston, 1964), pp. 201–235. From this and other similarities, it may be that Clement wrote Hebrews.

words that originated with men, in the Scripture. Of Psalm 51 Clement states, "This very man (referring to David) says to God (I Clement XVIII, AN, I)." Clement was saying that Psalm 51 originated with David, who was speaking to God. Later Church fathers would have said "God spoke by the mouth of David." and they would have meant it in a strictly mechanical way. In other places Clement uses a very non-definitive mode of introducing a quote from scripture, "It is said somewhere . . . (I Clement XV: XXI, ANI λεγει γαρ που, J. P. Migne, in loc)" In one place he actually changes the words of Scripture to fit his purpose. He quotes Isaiah 60:17c which literally translated from the Hebrew states, "I will appoint for you overseers in peace and rulers in righteousness." He translates it, "I will appoint their bishops in righteousness and their deacons in faith (I Clement XLII–XLV.)" Of course, in the Hebrew community there were no such persons as bishops and deacons but that did not matter to Clement. He was attempting to establish that "blameless and holy" people were appointed by the apostles to be the leaders in the Church and this was supported by the witness of the Old Testament. These "bishops" and "deacons" should be respected, listened to, and not "deposed."[15]

In one passage Clement wrote, "Look intently into the true scriptures which are through the Holy Spirit. Believe that there is nothing unrighteous or counterfeit written in them." Taken by itself that statement might lead conservatives and fundamentalists to conclude that here in Clement is support for their cause of inerrancy. But again this is not the case at all. Immediately following the above sentence Clement states:

> There you will not find righteous men rejected by holy men. Rather the lawless persecuted the righteous. They were imprisoned, but by the lawless; they were stoned by the lawless; they were killed most mercilessly by depraved, unrighteous and envious persons. Their suffering they endured gloriously. (I Clement XLV. The translation is this author's from J. P Migne, in loc.)

It is obvious that by "unrighteous or counterfeit" Clement does not mean minutiae and the details are correct, but that the "true scriptures" never report that "righteous men were rejected by holy men." Furthermore, what Clement means by the "true scriptures" is not identical with the canon that conservative and fundamentalist Protestants would claim. His canon had many books that these Protestants considered apocryphal, such as Judith (I Clement LV), Wisdom (I Clement III, XXVII), and Sirach (I Clement XXVII). Because Clement includes these it is safe to assume that other apocryphal works were acceptable to him.

When one moves on into the third and fourth centuries, the concept of mechanical inspiration is found in Clement, Origen and Irenaeus (See 269–271). But it is not found in such writers as Hippoltus (c. 170–236), Cyprian (c.200–258), and Tertullian (c. 160–220). Tertullian, in fact, would be found totally opposing the deification of Scripture. He stated that the heretics Marcion and Valentinius the Gnostic used Scripture to their own ends ("On the Prescription against Heretics," XII–XXII; AN, XV). In one place he went as far to state," . . . Arguments about scripture achieve nothing but a stomach-ache or

---

[15]It is most likely that Clement is quoting from the Septuagint which reads: και δωσω τους αρχοντας σου εν ειρηνη και τους επισκοπους σου εν δικαιοσυνη. In the New Testament επισκοπους is translated as bishop but αρχοντας is not translated as deacon.

a headache.("On the Prescription against Heretics," XVI, AN)." Tertullian would never have subscribed to the Protestant principle of Sola Scriptura. He believed that a Christian must live within the community of faith, where Jesus and his Spirit were, and where the traditions and interpretations of the apostles were maintained. The Christian then would have proper understanding of the Scriptures. The Scriptures in and of themselves were not the criterion for faith, but how the Church interpreted those Scriptures ("On the Prescription against Heretics," XX, AN).

Besides the doctrine being absent from or opposed by some very influential Church fathers, there are two very strong historical facts that would discount the possibility of inerrancy being the dominant view in the early Church. The first is very concrete. In the first four centuries, the Scriptures as we have them today did not exist. A church in any one location may have had access to only certain scrolls on which were written some of the letters of Paul. They likewise may have had some gospels or early collections of the teachings of Jesus, but most churches did not have a complete canon.

The second fact is likewise very concrete. The writers whose works supported mechanical inspiration were all Greek philosophers before their conversion. They were highly educated persons and more than likely from the wealthy classes. This would mean that they were a very elite group of people and their ideas would have been very esoteric and shared by very few people.

The Strongest Argument is that Inerrancy was Rejected by Jerome (347–420)!

There is overwhelming evidence that in the 4th century inerrancy was not a tenet of the Church. This evidence comes from Jerome, who was born of wealthy parents in Stridon, Dalmatia.[16] Of all the early Church fathers, Jerome was a true Biblical scholar and he translated the Old and New Testaments into Latin. His translation was called the Vulgate because it was translated for the common person. Its name is derived from the Latin *vulgatus*, meaning 'common' — because Latin was the language of the common person. Sadly, and ironically, the vulgate remained the only acceptable translation in the Roman Church right up until recent times, making it no longer a book for the common person, but an esoteric book for priests and scholars.[17]

Most of the reformers, including Zwingli[18] and Calvin, thought highly of Jerome. Martin Luther called him a "true Bishop and teacher (*Luther's Work*, 32, 9; 40, 284)." There was only one area in which Luther disagreed with Jerome, and that was over the issue of celibacy. Jerome ardently defended celibacy. Luther, who did marry, called Jerome's attitude "ignorance (*Luther's Work*, 33, 258)," and his adherence to "ceremonial works" of the law (*Luther's Work*, 34, 72; 177; 270–1,357). While in Church history Jerome is nowhere

---

[16]Dalmatia is in the location of present day Bosnia

[17]The reader might be interested in knowing that St. Augustine was opposed to the translation of the Vulgate on the grounds that "the people were not ready for a new translation." NF, X, pp. 286, 342.

[18]G. W. Bromily, trans. and Ed., Zwingli and Bullinger, Volume 24, *The Library of Christian Classics*, John Baillie, John T. McNeille, and Henry Van Dussen, eds.(Philadelphia, Westminster Press, 1953), pp. 136.

near as well known as Augustine, Jerome was by far the more accomplished Biblical scholar. The amazing thing about Jerome was that, unlike many of the other Church fathers, he consciously stripped himself of Greek philosophy. This was not because he was unacquainted with it. Far from it! At the early age of 12 he studied in Rome and was steeped in classical education. He would have been considered one of the most highly educated persons of the time. In 375 on a trip to the East, Jerome had a vision: Transported before the throne of God, God said to him, "Thou art a Ciceroian, and not a Christian."[19] Immediately, Jerome repented of Greek philosophy, became a hermit, and studied Hebrew ("Letters," XXII:30, NF, IV, 35).

To the benefit of the Church, one of Jerome's strengths was that he was a compulsive neurotic. He had a psychological need for exact and precise information. Because of this, he could not be content to learn Hebrew from manuscripts and other translations. He went to Israel and studied Hebrew and Aramaic from the natives. In doing this, he was not only led to reject Greek philosophy, but magical, animistic, and mechanical views of inspiration held by many of the Church fathers. ("Letters," LXXX–XCVII, NF, IV, 169–188)

When the works of this, the Church's first and foremost biblical student, are examined, one finds many of the attitudes of modern critical scholarship. In a letter he describes the problems of translation. He asserts that to translate a passage literally from one language to another may mean that one would lose the very meaning of the passage. The responsibility of the translator, he stipulated, was to get to the essence of the passage and not get lost in the minutiæ. For Jerome, to get bogged down in the details meant to lose the spiritual meaning of the texts. Then he asserted one might be accusing the apostles of "falsehood."("Letters," LVII, NF, IV, 112ff.) He then gives several examples of what he meant. The following are just two of these examples:

> . . . We read in Mark of the Lord saying *Talitha cumi* and it is immediately added "which is interpreted Damsel, I say to thee arise." The evangelist may be charged with falsehood for having added the words, "I say unto thee" for the Hebrew is only, "Damsel, arise." To emphasize this and to give the impression of one calling and commanding he added the words "I say unto thee." Again in Matthew when the thirty pieces of silver are returned by the traitor Judas and the potters' field is purchased with them, it is written, "Then was fulfilled that which was spoken of by Jeremy the prophet, saying, "And they took the thirty pieces of silver, the price of him that was valued, which they of the children of Israel did value, and gave them for the potter's field, as the Lord appointed me." This passage is not found in Jeremy at all but in Zechariah, and in quite different words, and in altogether different order.("Letters," LVII, 7, NF, IV, 115)

It is clear from the above passage that Jerome did not perceive the scriptures as being errorless. This did not make him a Godless liberal who loved to attack the Bible and pull it apart. The reader must remember that his translation was the closest that ordinary people and most priests got to

---

[19]Cicero was a Roman philosopher, politician and historian who lived from 106–46 B. C. E.

the Bible, right up until John Wycliffe translated the Bible into English (1384) (see p. 24). Then, because of the repression in the Church, few read it .

After Augustine, in the fifth century, there are very few references to the doctrine that the Bible is the inerrant word of God. Contrary to the thinking of most Protestants, this was not because the Spirit of God had departed from the Church. Far from it! Across Europe, in Northern Africa, in Asia Minor, the middle East, and even India, there were thousands and even millions of faithful Christians. The fact that there are Orthodox Christians in Syria and Lebanon, Armenian Christians in the Soviet states, Turkey and Iran, and Coptic Christians in Egypt and Ethiopia is strong evidence that there must have been a strong and vital Christianity during the Middle Ages. This is because these groups faced immense persecution from the Islamic and Oriental forces, and to survive even in their present forms meant that their ancestors must have had the Spirit of God in their midst.

While the Church faced corruption in its becoming the dominant religion in Europe, there were thousands of devoted followers of the Lord Jesus. That the Church produced such reform movements as the Benedictines (529;779); the Cistercians (1098), and the Franciscans (1207) is testimony that Christ was still very present among the Europeans. The Scriptures were held in esteem, for across Europe there were hundreds of monasteries where monks busied themselves copying Biblical manuscripts oftentimes making them beautiful works of art. But, even with this devotion to the details of the biblical manuscripts, there was not the idolatry of the Bible that came in the Reformation.[20]

Dissent after the Reformation

Even though there was uniformity between Lutheran, Reformed, Anabaptist, and Roman views of Scripture (see 12–14), not all voices of the Reformation and Post-Reformation were found endorsing the mechanical view of Scripture. In the seventeenth century some very persuasive arguments (though one could hardly say loud ones) were raised against the doctrine. The Quakers, labeled such by their detractors, rejected the view that the Bible was the inerrant Word of God. No matter what one's present view of Quakers is, it

---

[20]The first major reference to inerrancy after Augustine is found in the works of Thomas of Aquinas (c. 1227–1274) who wrote in Summa Theologica

> Even as regards those truths about God which human reason can discover, it was necessary that man should be taught by divine revelation, because the truth about God such as reason could discover would only be known by a few, and that after a long time, and with the admixture of errors. But man's whole salvation, which is in God, depends on this truth. Therefore, in order that salvation of men might be brought about more fitly and more surely, it was necessary that they should be taught divine truths by divine revelation. (Question 1, Great Books).

Thomas does not however state how this 'divine revelation' came about, so Aquinas Scholars might debate whether he subscribed to inerrancy. The concept certainly does not captivate his theology. The concept is not found in the surviving works of the martyr, John Huss (c. 1369–1415) or John Wycliffe (c.1320–1384), Theologian of Lollards and translator of the Bible (see James Henthorn Todd, ed. *An Apology for Lollard Doctrines Attributed to Wicliffe* (New York: Press, 1968). In fact Wycliffe wrote very strongly against veneration of Scripture (Lollards, p. 92 ff.).

would be hard to find a people who loved the Lord more. Because of that love, they suffered immense persecution.

One of the most literate and eloquent Friends was Samuel Fisher, a Puritan scholar at Oxford University. After converting to Quakerism in 1657, Fisher became one of the Quakers' most able defenders of the faith. In one of his polemics against Puritans, he set forth early Quaker views of scripture. He wrote:

> And because we do not with the misty ministers own the bare external text of scripture entire in every tittle, but say it hath suffered much loss of more than vowels and single lines also, yea, even of whole epistles and prophesies of men, the copies of which are not by clergy canonized nor the Bible-sellers bound up, and especially because we own not the said alterable and much outward text, but the holy truth and inward light and spirit to be the Word of God which is living [and] true touchstone, therefore they cry out against us. Yet the scriptures are owned by us in their due place, and the letter is acknowledged by us full as much as itself, to have been written by men moved of God's Spirit, and to be useful, profitable, serviceable, etc., to be read and heeded.[21]

As was observed with Jerome, here are seeds for modern textual criticism. Like Jerome, Fisher could by no means be considered to be a skeptic or a Deist who denied Christ's divinity or the miracles. Fisher believed so much in the Lord that he risked his life for him. The difference between him and his detractors, the Puritan scholastics, was that he could read the Bible better and more accurately than the scholastics. Of the belief that God had ceased to reveal himself after the close of the canon, Fisher wrote:

> Who was it that said to the Spirit of God, O Spirit, blow no more, inspire no more men, make no more prophets from Ezra's day downward till Christ, and from John's days downward forever? But cease be silent, and subject thyself as well as all evil spirits to be tried by the standard that's made up of some of the writings of some of those men thou hast moved to write already; and let such and such of them as are bound up in the Bibles now used in England be the only means of measuring all truth forever.[22]

Fisher was cynical and mocking of the reformed position, but he was right. There is nothing in the Bible that states that God would speak no more after Ezra or the Apostles. Jesus, himself, stated, "Where two or three are gathered in my name I will be there in midst of them (Matthew 12:2)." The text does not say that he would only be present in the disciples in the Bible, but he himself would be in their midst. If this were so, one could assume that he would make his presence felt, and he would speak to them in their day and age. The Word of God would not be limited to words that were recorded over 1900 years ago, or the King James Version of those words.

---

[21]Braithwaite, pp. 28–9.

[22]Braithewaite, p.290.

In another place (John 14:12), Jesus said that his disciples would do even greater miracles than he did because he was going to the Father and would give them the spirit. The text does not state here that only his closest and direct apostles and disciples would be the ones to do these miracles, but "whoever believes in me," meaning anybody who believes in Jesus. This would likewise imply that the Spirit was available to all the believers equally, as it was to the first apostles and disciples. When I was examining II Peter 1:21, I pointed out that there were prophets in the Church well into the third century C.E. This meant that in the early Church God was still dynamically speaking to the people.

Robert Barclay, who was considered the chief apologist for the early Quaker cause, wrote the accepted Quaker position on revelation and the Scriptures. I quote extensively from Barclay because his work shows how remarkably different was the Quaker position from the "orthodox" Protestant position on inspiration. Barclay's works also show just how close the Quakers' position on inspiration was to the dynamic concept of the New Testament. Barclay wrote:

> That the Spirit is inward in my opinion, needs no interpretation or commentary, He dwelleth with you, and shall be with you. This dwelling of the Spirit in the saints, as it is a thing most needful to be known; and believed, so is it as positively asserted in the scripture as anything else can be. . . .
>
> Moreover, these divine inward revelations, which we make absolutely necessary for the building up of true faith, neither do nor can outwardly contradict the outward testimony of the scriptures or right and sound reason. Yet from hence it will not follow, that these revelations are to be subjected to the test of the outward testimony of the scripture, or of natural reason of man , as to a more novel rule and touchstone; for this divine revelation, and inward illumination, is that which is evident and clear of itself, forcing, by its own evidence and clearness, as the well-disposed understanding to assent.
>
> From these revelations of the Spirit of God to the saints have proceeded the Scriptures of truth. Because they are only a declaration of the fountain not the fount itself, therefore they are not to be esteemed the principal ground of all truth, and knowledge, nor yet the adequate primary rule of faith and manners. Yet because they give a true and faithful witness to the first foundation, they are and may be esteemed a secondary rule; their excellency and certainty; for as thereby the inward testimony of the Spirit we do alone truly know them, so they testify, that the Spirit is that Guide by which the saints are led into all Truth.[23]

In other words, the Scriptures were not God. But, as in almost everything that has been stated so far in this book the Scriptures bear witness to Christ and his power within the Church. The Scriptures do not replace that power, nor are the Scriptures (and this is important for present-day Quakers) replaced

---

[23]Dean Fridlay, ed., *Barclay's Apology* (Aburtis, PA: Hemlock Press, 1967), p.46.

180

by present day inspiration.

While Quaker thought could hardly be described as universally accepted, there is an area where Quaker thought has had a universal impact. This is in the area of slavery. It has now been accepted within almost all branches and churches within Christendom, that slavery is a violation of God's purpose for people. Yet, there is not one verse in the Bible that abolishes slavery. In fact, there were many Southern preachers who justified the practice of slavery by using several texts from the Scriptures. Most Quakers saw that slavery was an abomination in God's sight, by virtue of the "divine inward revelations, which we make absolutely necessary for the building up of true faith, neither do we nor can we outwardly contradict the outward testimony of the scriptures or right and sound reason."

The reader must be amazed by how similar the views of Robert Barclay were to the twentieth century theologian Karl Barth — only 400 years before Barth (see pp. 15–16). The issue was not that Karl Barth copied Robert Barclay. It was that both men were anchored in the Bible, and their detractors — orthodox Protestants, conservatives, and fundamentalists were not.

The Scholar, William Law

The Quakers were not alone in dissenting from the doctrine of inerrancy. They were aptly joined in dissent from the doctrine by the English Cambridge University Scholar and High Church Man, William Law (1686–1761). Law wrote:

> Would you then have me to say, that the written word of God is that Word of God which liveth and abideth for ever, that Word which is the wisdom and power of God, . . . the Word which in Christ Jesus is become wisdom, and righteousness and sanctifi- cation in us, would you have me say that this is to be understood of the written word of God? But, if this cannot possibly be, then all that I have said is granted, namely that Jesus is alone that Word of God, that can be Light, Life, and Salvation of fallen man. Or how is it possible to exalt the letter of Scripture owning it to be a true outward, verbal direction to the one, only true Light and Salvation of man?[24]

One could not get a more Scriptural statement than that, and Law's statement is a fitting conclusion to this book. There is biblically speaking only one Word of God and he is Jesus, the Christ. He is the living and abiding One. It is around him and in him that we must mold our lives. The fact that the voices of Ignatius, Clement of Rome, Chrysostom, Jerome, the Quakers, and William Law were minority voices in church history should not distract from the correctness of their position. All the evidence, as I have abundantly pointed out, supports them.

On the other hand, the church has used the doctrine that the Bible is the inerrant word of God to deviously undermine almost every teaching of Jesus. It has used the doctrine to justify every war in which it or various nations were involved; to justify slavery, to crush and oppress the poor. The use of this doctrine has kept women in a subservient position: depriving them of the

---

[24]Stephen Hobhouse, William Law (London: George Allen & Unwin, LTD.,1927)

vote in nations and in the Church and oppressing them in many circumstances to the advantage of men. The doctrine has been used to license the conquering, subjugating and colonizing of primitive or weaker peoples. The doctrine has been used to validate the amassing of fortunes at the expense of most of God's children and God's creation. The doctrine that the Bible is the inerrant word of God is an evil and idolatrous doctrine which must be eliminated from the thinking of the Church. It has no part in the thought of Jesus and to own the doctrine is to deny the Lord Jesus. The Church must reclaim Jesus as the *only* Word of God, the hope for humankind, and the salvation of the world. May God be Glorified forever. Amen.

A

Aaron, 81,121, 166, 167
abandon, 121
abandoned, 121
Abbey, 4
Abhidh, 2
abhor, 120
abhorrent, 159
Abina, 72
abolish, 77, 87, 88
abolished, 100, 113
abolisher, 137
abolishes, 105, 109, 113, 118, 181
abolishing, 104
abomination, 181
abortion, 108
Aboth, 78, 91, 92, 116, 119, 133
Abraham, 31, 57, 58, 121, 152
Abram, 31, 32, 59
abrogated, 102
abrogates, 92
abrogating, 101
absolute, 3, 7, 11, 28, 33, 79, 111
absolve, 17, 25
abstract, 56
abstraction, 32, 42, 56
abuse, 94, 100
acceptance, 5, 9, 17, 81, 139
accepted, 4, 6, 10, 11, 20, 28, 36,
    47, 51, 60, 74, 79, 80, 87, 88,
    121, 128, 129, 130, 133, 137,
    138, 157, 180, 181
accuracy, 8, 84, 86
accurate, 7, 41, 54, 83, 85, 89, 90
accurately, 33, 77, 87, 96, 114,
    128, 179
accusation, 9, 81, 84, 85, 93
accusations, 93, 109, 134
accuse, 6, 109
accused, 9, 14, 109, 120, 142
accusing, 86, 177
acrostic, 72
Adam, 98
adherents, 128, 130
adjectival, 143
administration, 151, 164
adoption, 124
Adrian, 11
adulterer, 98
adulteress, 98, 100, 101
adulterous, 107
adultery, 33, 92, 93, 94, 96, 98,
    99, 100, 101, 102, 106, 109,
    110, 111, 117, 118
Adventists, 27
adversaries, 51, 71, 167
advocate, 54, 90, 108, 127, 151
Africa, 39, 52, 146, 154, 178
African, 129
Africans, 146
Ahab, 34
Ahaz, 123, 124, 172
Albright, 103
Alexander, 75
Alexandria, 140, 150, 171
Alexandrians, 133
alien, 75, 157

Allah, 2, 52
allegation, 168
allegiance, 22, 75
allegorical, 151, 153
allegory, 152
Allison's, 90
Allison, 89, 103, 106
Almighty, 164, 166, 172
alphabet, 69
alphabetical, 72
altar, 32
ambiguity, 50
Ambrose, 38, 39, 151, 152, 153,
    154, 160
America, 7, 27
American, 3, 6, 12, 13
Americans, 13
Ammonite, 105
Anabaptist, 21, 22, 25, 178
Anabaptists, 20, 21, 22, 23, 24,
    25, 26, 50, 54, 88, 102, 105,
    146
anachronisms, 131
analogy, 114, 115
analysis, 8, 89, 114, 154, 172
analyzed, 14, 112
anarchist, 22
anarchy, 169
ancestors, 178
ancient, 1, 4, 5, 13, 40, 74, 83,
    106, 126, 128, 129, 145, 173,
    174
ancients, 5
angel, 3, 32, 160
angels, 37, 154, 155
anger, 18, 37, 51, 92, 145, 167
angry, 73, 162
animal, 56, 98, 104
animals, 30, 110, 160, 163
animistic, 177
annihilated, 105
anointing, 124
antagonism, antagonisms,
    antagonists 9, 71, 74
anthropomorphic, 151
Antioch, 143, 161, 173
Antiochus, 75
Antiquities, 112, 119
Apocalypse, 55, 128, 129
Apocalypses, 135
apocalyptic, 37, 52
apocalyptical, 169
Apocrypha, 60, 130, 131, 132, 138
apocryphal, 130, 131, 132, 133,
    134, 136, 137, 138, 175
apologetics, 146
apologist, 180
Apology, 149
apostle, 38, 48, 67, 128, 129, 137,
    160, 161, 168
apostles, 4, 6, 7, 8, 53, 56, 120,
    122, 129, 131, 136, 139, 160,
    161, 162, 165, 167, 169, 172,
    175, 176, 177, 179, 180
apostleship, 139
apostolic, 6, 129, 143
apotheosis, 109

Aramaic, 133, 134, 177
archaic, 6
archbishop, 150
archer, 34
argue, 17, 105, 106, 114, 116, 117,
    119, 126, 131, 132, 142, 162,
    163, 166, 169, 173
argued, 24, 78, 114, 119, 121, 126,
    137
argument, 40, 45, 58, 66, 81, 84,
    99, 105, 113, 114, 116, 121,
    132, 137, 161, 166, 173, 176
arguments, 18, 78, 92, 114, 116,
    122, 137, 162, 167, 173, 175,
    178
Arian, Arians, 151
aristocrats, 25
Aristotle, 143, 148
arm, 85, 122
armament, armaments, 43, 51, 55
armed, 51
Armenia, 131, 132
Armenian, 132, 178
armies, 45
armor, 52, 55, 57
arrogance, 33, 73, 168
arrogant, 128
arrogant, arrogantly, 25, 57, 70,
    71, 73
arrow, 34
art, 15, 177, 178, 124, 149, 154
articulate, 29, 150, 173
articulation, 125
artificer, 149
artificial, 69, 72
ascension, 3
ascetic, 2, 154
Asenath, 132
ashes, 32, 34, 76
Asia, 52, 146, 178
assimilates, 82
assumption, 7, 40, 54, 61, 136
Assyria, Assyrians, 43 45
Athanasius, 149, 153
atheists, 146
Athenagoras, 146, 147, 149, 167
Athenian, 146
Athens, 148
athlete, athletic, 71
atrocities, 23, 24
attack, 6, 7, 12, 13, 34, 44, 54, 56,
    177
attire, 34, 55
attitude, 1, 18, 48, 67, 71, 72, 73,
    78, 83, 87, 93, 96, 98, 99, 100,
    103, 105, 109, 118, 120, 124,
    130, 131, 147, 151, 156, 176
Augsburg, 26
Augustine's, 88, 92, 154, 155, 156,
    157, 158
Augustine, 39, 40, 88, 103, 154,
    155, 156, 157, 160, 177, 178
Aurelius, 146, 148
authenticity, 116, 168
authorities, 22, 25, 35, 53, 55, 87,
    109, 118
authority, 3, 5, 7, 10, 11, 12, 17,

115, 125, 132

contemporary, 12, 14, 20, 29, 30, 35, 36, 48, 49, 88, 90, 112, 126, 140, 150, 172

contempt, 78

content, contents, 54, 120, 126, 127, 138, 169, 177

context, 11, 31, 40, 57, 67, 98, 101, 116, 119, 123, 142, 147, 150, 152, 161, 167, 171

contexts, 83

continuity, 83

contradiction, 4

contradictions, 7, 9, 88, 89, 106, 150

contrast, 14, 33, 46, 72, 76, 87, 122, 141

contrasted, 52, 90

controversies, controversy, 10, 71, 113

convention, 11

conversations, 112

conversion, conversions, 52, 176

convert, 1, 15, 154

converted, 1, 63, 131, 132, 154

converting, 14, 68, 179

convict, 137

convicted, 7, 85

conviction, 53, 54

cooking, 56

Copernicus, 6, 24

Coptic, 178

copulation, copulations, 96

copyist, 11

Corban, 81

Corinth, 8

Corinthians, 19, 48, 55, 67, 131, 132, 168

corn, 114, 115

Cornelius, 9, 17, 160, 161

corollaries, 37

corporate, 104, 107

Corpus, 143

corrections, 11, 79

corrupted, 88

corruption, 4, 121, 154, 178

cosmic, 52

council, 4, 6, 17, 24, 126, 129, 133, 136, 169, 172

councils, 4, 51

counsel, 117, 119, 164, 154

Counselor, 123

counterfeit, 175

cousin, 106

covenant, 17, 19, 22, 58, 107, 111, 112

covet, 99

coveting, 93

cradle, 173

craftsmen, 75

crazy, 38

create, 60, 79, 114, 115

created, 17, 30, 34, 36, 37, 63, 64, 76, 110, 119, 145, 146, 150, 151, 154

creates, 30, 37, 46, 62, 86, 123, 128, 135

creating, 54, 73, 83

creation, 4, 30, 31, 34, 35, 45, 69, 72, 110, 116, 119, 139, 140, 148, 150, 153, 155, 162, 182

Creator, 31

credendum, 5

creed, 4, 150, 151

creedal, 4, 5

creeds, 4, 15, 29

crime, 33, 103

crippled, 116

crisis, 83

criteria, 83, 137

criterion, 4, 51, 101, 107, 108, 118, 136, 151, 176

cross, 66, 105, 174

crucified, 48, 56, 120, 121

crucify, 60, 109

cruel, cruelty, 54, 112

crumbs, 34

crusades, 1

cultural, 9, 134

culture, 100, 158

cultus, 135

curse, 59, 105, 141, 163

cursed, 107

cursing, 85

curtain, 35

custom, 23

customs, 25, 112

cynics, 74

cypress, 35

Cyprian, 175

Cyrus, 125

D

Dahood, 73

Dakota, 77

Dalmatia, 176

damaged, 19, 96, 97

Damascus, 31, 48, 56

Dame, 133

damnation, 24, 25, 55

Damsel, 177

danger, 117, 169

Daniel, 75, 130, 133, 134, 135, 136, 137

darkness, 35, 52, 55, 57, 153

Darwin, 6

daughter, 85, 96, 109, 139

David, 27, 72, 81, 99, 107, 111, 113, 114, 115, 121, 122, 165, 167, 175

Davies, 89, 90, 103, 106

deacons, 175

dead, 38, 42, 56, 85, 117, 133, 138, 139

deaf, 114, 166

death, 1, 2, 5, 18, 35, 41, 55, 66, 67, 75, 85, 96, 98, 99, 100, 101, 110, 111, 112, 116, 121, 124, 138, 141, 174, 103, 105

debate, 19, 77, 101

debated, 129

debauchery, 145

deceit, 51

deceive, 21

deceiver, 18

decree, decrees, 4, 36, 101, 169

defenders, 7, 151, 179

Defile, defiled, 108, 115, 160

definition, 38, 43, 98, 125, 128, 128, 130, 137, 139, 143

deification, 155, 175

Deism, 7

Deist, 6, 7, 34, 179

deity, 124, 149

deluge, 137, 138

delusions, 33

demagogues, 54

demonic, demons, 19, 43, 50

demonstration, 48, 122

denial, 19

denigration, 86, 131

denomination, 10

denominational, 12

denominations, 11, 20

deportation, deported, 35, 75

depravity, 118, 157

deprecated, 140

derision, 55, 134, 135

derivative, 84

derive, 86, 136, 142, 168

derived, 42, 56, 58, 93, 103, 125, 140, 157, 167, 176

Derrett, 83

describe, 23, 42, 66, 89, 98, 134, 145, 147, 152, 100

described, 1, 7, 8, 11, 18, 19, 20, 21, 26, 42, 46, 47, 48, 55, 60, 61, 62, 68, 75, 76, 87, 92, 113, 124, 131, 134, 135, 147, 158, 174, 181

describes, 33, 40, 46, 55, 65, 100, 133, 140, 141, 149, 152, 177

describing, 53, 55, 61, 98, 100, 123, 140, 141

description, 14, 32, 37, 40, 41, 52, 75, 98, 115, 120, 127, 129, 142, 145, 150

desire, 2, 28, 113, 174

destroy, 33, 34, 51, 77, 108, 117, 141

destroyed 21, 45, 55, 67, 70, 97, 114, 127, 146

destruction, 1, 16, 17, 33, 34, 43, 55, 63, 104, 174

destructive, 93, 108, 160

detractors, 167, 178, 179, 181

detractors, 86

Deuteronomic, 98

Deuteronomy, 43, 61, 76, 82, 96, 97, 98, 99, 100, 101, 103, 105, 106, 110, 141, 162, 163, 167

Deux, 8

devil, 22, 23, 25, 46, 51, 54

diabolical, 23

diaspora, 134

diasporan, 133, 134, 135, 139

Diatesseron, 131

dictate, 126

dictated, 88, 140

dictating, 6

dictation, 126

diction, 56

Galileans, 134
Galilee, 78
Galileo's, 24
Galileo, 6
gall, 4, 56
Gamaliel, 26, 163
Gandhi, 87
Garden, 152
garland, 138
garment, garments, 80, 104
Gaul, 151
genealogy, 106, 107
generation, 77, 78, 80, 105, 122, 135, 137, 146, 167
generative, 46
genesis or Genesis, 30, 31, 35, 37, 57, 59, 61, 84, 91, 98, 99, 142, 146, 152, 153, 155, 157, 165, 171
Geneva, 38, 126
genitive, 170
genius, 70, 94, 97
genocide, 146
Gensichen, 20
gentile, 50, 63, 107, 134, 139, 141, 161, 164, 165, 173
gentiles, 40, 48, 60, 62, 64, 66, 68, 71, 104, 134, 135, 139, 161, 165
Georg, 105
Gerald, 155
Gerhard, 30, 56, 89
germ, 71
German, 4, 19, 27, 158
Germany, 19, 23, 24, 89, 158
germs, 81
Gesenius, 123
gestures, 93
gezera, 114
ghettoes, 134
Ghost, 6, 21, 139, 140
giant, 35
gibbor, 123
girded, 55, 80
girl, 94, 96, 97
Gittin, 101
glass, 168
glittering, 43
glory, 15, 45, 52, 59, 62, 63, 64, 66, 67, 100, 137
Gnostic, 150, 175
Gnosticism, 142, 154
Gnostics, 146
Godhead, 139
Godless, 13, 33, 50, 177
godly, 4, 157
gods, 30, 31, 99, 147, 165
gold, 55, 70, 152, 163
golden, 2, 141
goods, 97
Gordis, 83
Gordon, 45
Gottingen, 77, 112
Goulder, 91, 108
governing, 83, 97, 104
government, 22, 23, 102, 122, 131
governmental, 102

governments, 22, 45
Governor, 151
grain, 41, 113, 114, 117
grammatical, 62, 64, 155
grandmother, 107, 138, 143
grass, 45, 60
grave, 35, 121
graves, 138
Grebel, 25
Greeks, 105, 150
Gregory, 131
groom, 97, 98
grudges, 104
guard, 69
guardian, 97
Guelich, 100
guilt, 100
guilty, 97, 100, 111
Gunkel, 30

H
Hades, 121
halachah, 79
hallmarks, 72
hammer, 33, 44, 145
Handel's, 122
handwashing, 86
Hans, 20, 76, 173
harlot, 107, 165
Harnack, 158
Harold, 5, 12
harp, 149
harvest, 33, 94
Hasidic, Hasidim, 61, 112, 133
hate, 57, 104, 105, 164
hatred, 71
havoc, 52, 158
head, 10, 50
heal, 113, 114, 117, 119
healed, 19, 115, 116, 117, 121, 145, 155, 161, 166
healing, 115, 116, 117, 119, 121
healing, 3, 34, 38, 71, 155
heals, 37, 71, 118
health, 1, 3, 95, 118
hear, 30, 34, 36, 38, 44, 46, 68, 94, 104, 118, 120, 122, 138, 153, 157, 172
heard, 33, 40, 50, 64, 92, 99, 100, 102, 104, 107, 126, 134, 137, 148, 171, 172, 174
hearing, 30, 46, 148
heart, 112, 121, 138, 143, 152, 166, 167
heart, 5, 14, 17, 33, 35, 37, 38, 44, 45, 46, 47, 53, 59, 70, 71, 80, 92, 93, 99, 100
hearth, 76
hearts, 33, 46, 71, 78, 126, 128, 152, 167, 170
heathen, 33, 62, 134, 135
heathens, 163
heaven, 9, 18, 19, 24, 35, 41, 46, 63, 70, 76, 85, 91, 104, 108, 109, 110, 111, 141, 149, 153, 154, 155
heavenly, 55, 104, 150, 151, 153
heavens, 31, 35, 124, 160

Hebraic, Hebraism, 165
Hegelian, 7
Heidelberg, 89
Heinrich, 4, 7, 21, 67
heir, heirs, 31, 79, 99, 109
hell, 24, 25, 46, 55
Hellenic, 75
Hellenism, 134
Hellenist, 75
Hellenization, 75
Hellenized, 75
helmet, 50, 55
Helvetic, 4, 6, 12, 22, 26, 135
Hendricksen, 126, 128, 130, 140
Henry, 12, 146
Heppe, 7, 8
Heraclitean, 150
Heraclitus, 143, 147, 148, 153, 157, 160
herald, 122
Herbert, 36
hereditary, 137
heresies, 142, 146, 150
heresy, 7, 15, 135
heretical, 154
heretics, 51, 53, 175, 176
Herman, 30
Hermas, 128, 129
hermeneutics, 26, 41, 54, 57, 102, 113, 114, 152, 170
hermit, 177
Herod, 163
Heroditus, 86
heroes, 38, 107
Hesse, 19
Hexameron, 151
Hezekiah, 123
Hezron, 106
hierarchy, 17, 24, 107
Hillel, 76, 101
hills, 35
Himalayan, 2
Hindu, 1, 2, 87, 155
Hinduism, 2, 3
Hindus, 1
Hippo, 39, 88, 126, 154
Hippoltus, 175
historian, 18, 112, 128, 158, 173
historians, 86
historical, 2, 8, 11, 47, 86, 88, 89, 102, 116, 121, 131, 146, 176
historically, 47, 60, 78, 90, 130, 168
history, 1, 4, 5, 6, 7, 11, 13, 14, 31, 35, 50, 57, 60, 63, 74, 76, 83, 86, 87, 93, 99, 106, 107, 113, 119, 120, 125, 127, 128, 129, 130, 132, 134, 139, 145, 151, 158, 160, 172, 173, 176, 181
Hiyya, 79
hoarfrost, 34
Hoen, 17
holiness, 28, 96
homeland, 71
Homer, 40
Homily, 151
homosexuals, 11

Lordship, 20, 28, 108
Louis, 10
love, 3, 4, 5, 23, 54, 57, 60, 83, 91,
    93, 104, 105, 116, 122, 125,
    143, 145, 154, 156, 161, 179
loved, 105, 177, 179
loving, 17, 20, 90, 105, 144, 154
Lucius, 146
Luke, 22, 35, 62, 68, 85, 101, 105,
    106, 113, 114, 117, 124, 136,
    165, 167, 168
lust, 99, 100
lustful, 93
lustfully, 92, 93, 99
lusts, 93
Luther, 5, 16, 17, 18, 19, 20, 21,
    23, 24, 25, 26, 27, 30, 36, 41,
    46, 47, 48, 49, 50, 73, 88, 93,
    102, 103, 129, 130, 168, 169,
    176
Lutheran, 4, 5, 10, 20, 22, 24, 25,
    26, 27, 100, 146, 178
Lutherans, 5, 10, 22, 26, 27, 41,
    48, 51, 158, 169
lying, 33, 34, 51, 59
Lyon, 146, 150
lyre, 149, 167
Lystra, 143
M
M'Nielle, 101
MacArthur, 103
Maccabees, 74, 130, 134, 136
Maccabeus, 75
magic, 30, 31, 166
magical, 31, 44, 177, 128
magistrates, 4
Magnesians, 173, 174
Mahatma, 87
maiden, 123
maidservant, 109
Maimonides, 83, 84
maiori, 115
maius, 114
male, 90, 92, 94, 95, 96, 97, 107,
    139
malice, 4
Mamre, 31
mandated, 117
Manichaean, 154
Manichaeism, 154
manifestation, 116, 150
manifestations, 153
mankind, 127
Mann, 103
manna, 110, 112, 115, 153
manservant, 109
mantic, 157, 158
manuscript, 11
manuscripts, 11, 74, 145, 177, 178
Manz, 22, 23
Marburg, 19
Marcion, 175
Marduk, 31
Mark, 73, 74, 101, 108, 113, 114,
    117, 124, 136, 177
Markan, 81, 117
marriage, 93, 96, 98

married, 96, 97, 99, 101, 139
marries, 100, 101
marrow, 38, 43, 53
marry, 96, 97, 139, 176
marrying, 101
Martyr, 131, 149
martyrdom, 22
martyred, 173
Martyrs, 23
Mary, 3, 19
Masorette, 139
Masorettes, 139
Mass, 24
Matthean, 106
Matthew, 35, 37, 41, 49, 69, 73,
    74, 78, 80, 81, 84, 85, 86, 87,
    88, 89, 90, 91, 92, 100, 101,
    102, 106, 107, 108, 113, 114,
    117, 118, 124, 136, 152, 177,
    179
Mays, 73
Mckenzie, 35, 36
meal, meals, 18, 74, 81, 101
mechanical, 7, 126, 127, 140, 149,
    160, 165, 170, 172, 173, 175,
    176, 177, 178
Megillah, 79, 82, 85
Melancthon, 19
Melchizedek, 165
Memamsa, 1
Menno, Mennonites, 21
menstruation, 104
merchants, 75
mercy, 9, 34, 42, 70, 73, 113, 117
Merill, 131
merit, 82
message, 3, 14, 15, 18, 25, 38, 41,
    45, 46, 47, 48, 50, 54, 55, 56,
    57, 58, 59, 60, 65, 67, 68, 86,
    118, 138, 153, 168, 172
messages, 48, 172
messenger, 36, 160, 161
messengers, 157
Messiah, 44, 55, 62, 89, 90, 106,
    109, 119, 120, 121, 122, 123,
    124, 172
messianic, 106, 122, 123, 171
metaphor, 34, 35, 42, 43, 44, 79,
    168
metaphoric, 30
metaphorical, 32, 100
metaphors, 43, 152, 165
metaphysical, 149
method, 7, 11, 13, 136, 138, 151,
    153, 169
Methodist, 15, 27, 28
Methuselah, 137
Micaiah, 34
Midian, 163
Midianite, 164
Midrash, 63, 76, 77, 91, 119
Migne, 149, 150, 175
Milan, 38, 151, 154
military, 43, 52, 55
mindless, 9
minds, 9, 45, 69, 153
ministry, 38

minori, 114, 115, 127
Minutia, 79
miracle, 9
miracles, 49, 120, 179, 180
Miriam, 121, 166
misfortune, 105
mishnah, 77, 78, 123
Mishnahs, 83, 84
misinterpreted, 50, 165
mission, 12, 14, 145, 166
missionary, 14
missions, 14
Missouri, 10, 27
misspelled, 72
misstyled, 54
mistake, 35, 63, 100, 161
mistakenly, 84, 92
mistakes, 8, 11, 76, 119, 162
mistresses, 99
misunderstood, 108
misuse, 114
Mitchell, 73
Moab, 163
Moabite, 105
mobs, 135
moderates, 11
modern, 10, 15, 30, 39, 40, 46, 54,
    62, 68, 71, 72, 81, 85, 89, 93,
    95, 104, 121, 131, 140, 169,
    177, 179
modernizing, 1
Mohammed, 2, 52
monasteries, 178
money, 17, 138, 163
Monica, 154
monks, 103, 178
monographs, 89
monolithic, 17, 133
monotheism, monotheists, 133,
    134
Montanism, 142
Moore, 76
moral, 6, 13, 53, 103, 107
morals, 169
Mormon, Mormons, 2, 3, 28, 163
Mormonism, Moroni, 3
mortal, 67, 118, 140, 141, 166
mortals, 54, 124, 154
Mosaic, 78, 106
Moses, 7, 51, 59, 60, 61, 63, 69,
    74, 76, 77, 78, 79, 80, 83, 86,
    88, 90, 94, 96, 98, 101, 102,
    103, 105, 106, 107, 110, 117,
    120, 121, 122, 124, 133, 134,
    135, 136, 140, 141, 142, 156,
    157, 163, 164, 166, 167, 168,
    171
Moshe, 86
Moslems, 1
mosques, 1
mother, 73, 74, 82, 84, 85, 94, 103,
    107, 124, 138, 139, 143, 154,
    158, 169, 173
mothers, 43, 82, 85
motives, 80
mountain, 106, 123, 141, 170, 171
Mountains, 2, 35

Persian, Persians, 75, 154
personality, 8, 115, 127, 171
perspective, 20, 22, 24, 27, 35, 68, 78, 83, 104, 114, 144, 172
perversion, perversions, 20, 146
Pesahim, 80, 81, 92
Peter, 26, 36, 42, 45, 46, 48, 49, 60, 64, 120, 121, 128, 129, 160, 161, 168, 169, 170, 171, 172, 180
Pfeiffer, 134
Phaedrus, 148
Pharaoh, 51, 60, 110, 124, 166, 167
pharisaic, 77, 84, 119, 133
Pharisee, 107
Pharisees, 71, 72, 73, 74, 75, 76, 77, 78, 79, 81, 84, 85, 86, 88, 93, 101, 108, 109, 112, 113, 114, 117, 118, 119, 124, 145
phenomena, 60, 95
phenomenal, 104
Philadelphians, 174
Philip, 19
Philistines, 33
Philo, 140, 141, 160, 167, 168, 171
philological, 172
Philonic, 172
philosopher, 1, 2, 146, 147, 149
philosophers, 56, 143, 146, 147, 149, 151, 156, 157, 160, 176
philosophical, 10, 140, 146, 149, 150, 151, 156, 158
philosophize, 156
philosophy, 7, 125, 147, 148, 149, 151, 156, 158, 167, 177
phrase, 31, 32, 40, 50, 11, 120, 136, 164
phrases, 8, 111, 120, 126, 154
Physics, 148
piel, 111
piety, 6, 22, 72, 112
Pilate, 163
pilgrimage, 141
pious, 5, 23, 24, 52, 61, 75, 78, 86, 93, 119, 143, 164
Pirke, 78
pity, 73
Plato, 143, 148, 149, 153, 154, 156, 157, 160, 168
Platonic, 150, 154, 155, 172
Platonists, 156
pleasures, 2
plectrum, 149
plenary, 53, 125
plenary
Pliny, 86
Plotonius, 154, 157
poem, 72
poet, 157
poetic, 131
poets, 147, 168
pogroms, 1, 132
polemics, 179
political, 8, 13, 20, 25, 102, 146
polygamy, 99
polytheists, 134

poor, 44, 65, 85, 118, 123, 139, 181
Pope, 17, 24, 25, 26, 169
population, 134
pornographer, 99
possess, 70, 78, 100, 101, 162, 168
possession, 2, 56, 70, 98, 100, 107, 157
possessions, 94, 98, 100
potters, 177
poverty, 39, 84
Prabhupada, 2
Prague, 24
praise, 21, 39, 52, 69, 72, 138, 145, 154
pray, 15, 19, 21, 56, 104
prayed, 16, 62
prayer, 15, 16, 62, 105, 174
Prayerbook, 27
prayers, 57, 160, 168, 174
praying, 160
preach, 22
preached, 6, 25, 38, 39, 45, 46, 79, 137, 152
preacher, preachers, 12, 13, 25, 38, 39, 49, 50, 51, 53, 135, 155, 181
preaching, 17, 20, 24, 25, 48, 53, 67, 120, 128, 137, 171
preachings, 137
Predestinarian, 27
prefigured, 3, 107
prefix, 84
pregnant, 107
prejudice, 118
prejudices, 53
preparation, 56, 71
preposition, 42
Presbyterian, 10, 11, 15
Presbyterians, 10, 11, 27
Preuss, 10
pride, 33, 138, 157
priest, 17, 24, 61, 75, 107, 114, 115, 151, 164
priestly, 7, 31, 76
priests, 24, 75, 113, 114, 115, 118, 163, 176, 177
primacy, 110
primitive, 27, 115, 147, 182
Princeton, 5, 8, 126
prison, 167
probation, 25
proclaim, 28, 48, 56, 59, 67, 69, 90, 122, 172
proclaimed, 14, 34, 38, 39, 45, 46, 47, 48, 49, 50, 54, 55, 56, 64, 89, 120, 150, 161, 162
proclamation, 33, 45, 46, 48, 49, 56, 67, 68, 153, 171
profanation, 122
profane, 113, 160
profanes, 110
progeny, 75
prohibited, 116
prohibition, 93, 116
prohibitions, 104
Prolegama, 7

promiscuous, 99
promise, 9, 30, 48, 49, 58, 59, 69, 107
promised, 6, 47
promises, 40, 57, 58, 59, 60, 63
pronouncement, 56, 92
pronunciation, 69
proof, 55, 59, 97, 100, 113
prophecies, 33, 149, 169, 171
prophecy, 89, 163, 168, 169, 170, 171, 172
prophesied, 3, 137, 141, 171
prophesies, 62, 90, 124, 171, 179
prophesy, 90, 91, 120, 123, 129, 168, 171
prophesying, 33, 141
prophet, 3, 17, 32, 33, 34, 43, 44, 52, 70, 116, 121, 122, 129, 140, 141, 162, 164, 167, 168, 170, 171, 177
prophetic, 33, 56, 91, 129, 131, 164, 170, 171, 172
prophets, 3, 4, 6, 7, 8, 32, 33, 34, 37, 39, 44, 53, 56, 61, 70, 78, 80, 86, 87, 88, 89, 90, 91, 105, 107, 108, 124, 125, 135, 136, 137, 149, 160, 162, 164, 165, 167, 168, 170, 171, 172, 173, 174, 179, 180
proselyte, 173
prostitute, 96, 99, 107
prostitutes, 99
Protestant, 4, 5, 6, 7, 11, 17, 19, 20, 22-23, 26, 27, 35, 131, 132, 135, 136, 139, 143, 146, 176, 180
Protestantism, 17, 20, 133
Protestants, 20, 41, 119, 122, 128, 130, 131, 132, 136, 151, 173, 175, 178, 181
protesting, 10
Proverbs, 76, 82
Psalm, 34, 37, 39, 40, 69, 70, 71, 72, 73, 76, 84, 87, 107, 118, 120, 121, 122, 124, 155, 171, 175
Psalmist, 69, 70, 71, 72, 73, 78, 87, 118, 155
Psalmists, 69, 70
Psalms, 51, 69, 70, 73, 105, 133, 136, 137, 138
psychological, 1, 117, 177
Ptolemies, 75
punishment, 39, 41, 102, 108, 152
purge, 11, 96
purging, 54
purified, 31, 94
Puritan, 179
Puritans, 179
Purva, 1
Q
qots, 91
Quaker, 179, 180, 181
Quakerism, 179
Quakers, 105, 178, 179, 180, 181
Qumran, 52, 55, 86, 105, 112, 133
R